How To Make $100,000 a Year
# Gambling for a Living

*By*
David Sklansky and Mason Malmuth

## A product of Two Plus Two Publishing

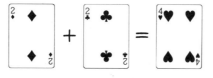

SECOND EDITION

FIRST PRINTING
SEPTEMBER 1998

*Printing and Binding*
Creel Printing Co.
Las Vegas, Nevada

*Printed in the United States of America*

# Gambling for a Living
## COPYRIGHT © 1997, 1998 DAVID SKLANSKY
## and MASON MALMUTH

For information contact: **Two Plus Two Publishing**
**226 Garfield Dr.**
**Henderson NV 89014**
**(702) 896-1326**

ISBN: 1-880685-16-7

*Dedicated to the memory of Dan Langfur*

# Table of Contents

i

# iv Table of Contents

# About David Sklansky

David Sklansky is generally considered the number one authority on gambling in the world today. Besides his eight books on the subject, David also has produced two videos and numerous writings for various gaming publications. His occasional poker seminars always receive an enthusiastic reception including those given at the Taj Mahal in Atlantic City and the World Series of Poker in Las Vegas.

More recently David has been doing consulting work for casinos, Internet gaming sites, and gaming device companies.

David attributes his standing in the gambling community to three things:

1.  The fact that he presents his ideas as simply as possible (sometimes with Mason Malmuth) even though these ideas frequently involve concepts that are deep, subtle, and not to be found elsewhere.
2.  The fact that the things he says and writes can be counted on to be accurate.
3.  The fact that to this day a large portion of his income is still derived from gambling (usually poker but occasionally blackjack, sports betting, horses, video games, casino promotions, or casino tournaments).

Thus, those who depend on David's advice know that he still depends on it himself.

## Other Books by David Sklansky

*Hold 'em Poker*
*The Theory of Poker*
*Getting The Best of It*
*Sklansky on Poker*
*Poker, Gaming, and Life*

*Hold 'em Poker For Advanced Players* by David Sklansky and Mason Malmuth

*Seven-Card Stud for Advanced Players* by David Sklansky, Mason Malmuth, and Ray Zee

# About Mason Malmuth

Mason Malmuth was born and raised in Coral Gables, Florida. In 1973 he received his BS in Mathematics from Virginia Tech, and completed their Masters' program in 1975. While working for the United States Census Bureau in 1978, Mason stopped overnight in Las Vegas while driving to his new assignment in California. He was immediately fascinated by the games, and gambling became his major interest.

After arriving in California he discovered that poker was legal and began playing in some of the public cardrooms as well as taking periodic trips to Las Vegas where he would play both poker and blackjack. In 1981 he went to work for the Northrop Corporation as a mathematician and moved to Los Angeles where he could conviently pursue his interest in poker in the large public cardrooms in Gardena, Bell Gardens, and Commerce.

In 1983 his first article "Card Domination — The Ultimate Blackjack Weapon" was published in *Gambling Times* magazine. In 1987 he left his job with the Northrop Corporation to begin a career as both a full-time gambler and a gambling writer. He has had over 500 articles published in various magazines and is the author or co-author of 12 books. These include *Gambling Theory and Other Topics,* where he tries to demonstrate why only a small number of people are highly successful at gambling. In this book he introduces the reader to the concept of "non-self weighting strategies" and explains why successful gambling is actually a balance of luck and skill. Other books he has co-authored are *Hold 'em Poker For Advanced Players,* written with David Sklansky, and *Seven-Card Stud For Advanced Players* written with David Sklansky and Ray Zee. These two "advanced" books are considered the definitive works on these games.

His company Two Plus Two Publishing has sold over 300,000 books and currently has 20 titles to its credit. These books are

# x About Mason Malmuth

recognized as the best in their field and are thoroughly studied by those individuals who take gambling seriously.

## Other Books by Mason Malmth

*Gambling Theory and Other Topics*
*Poker Essays*
*Poker Essays, Volume II*
*Blackjack Essays*
*Winning Concepts in Draw and Lowball*
*Hold 'em Poker For Advanced Players* by David Sklansky and Mason Malmuth
*Seven-Card Stud for Advanced Players* by David Sklansky, Mason Malmuth, and Ray Zee

## Booklets with Mason Malmuth

*Fundamentals of Craps* by Mason Malmuth and Lynne Loomis
*Fundamentals of Poker* by Mason Malmuth and Lynne Loomis
*Fundamentals of "21"* by Mason Malmuth and Lynne Loomis
*Fundamentals of Video Poker* by Mason Malmuth and Lynne Loomis

# Introduction

Gambling is fun! That's one reason why so many people do it. But there is another facet to gambling: It can be profitable, and you can make a good living from it. *We know because we've done it.* For those of you who are unfamiliar with us, we are not only writers on many aspects of gambling, we are also professional gamblers. Now, the term *professional gambler* is frequently thrown around lightly. However, we're *not* throwing it around lightly. When we say "professional gambler" we mean somebody who makes his or her living from gambling. It's not that we usually win, it's that we *always* win significant money at the end of the year. We have done it for over twenty years in the case of David and over fifteen years in the case of Mason.[1]

This book is called *Gambling for a Living.* There is no hype in that title. We will show you how you can make a living gambling in the legal casinos and cardrooms in this country and around the world (without cheating). Furthermore, if you follow the guidelines in this book and have a little bit of talent, drive, and initiative, there is no reason why you cannot "earn" in excess of $100,000 a year by gambling.[2]

Now let's look at this a bit more closely. What are we saying here? What are we trying to accomplish with this book? And how are we going to do it? Well, we are going to show you how to take advantage of the extensive opportunities to gamble profitably that are now available in the United States and around the world. Put

---

[1] Yes, we also make good money from our books, but that's only been for the last five years or so.

[2] Don't however expect to give this book a quick read and then start making this type of money. As we just said, it takes talent, drive, and initiative.

1

another way, we are going to show you how you can turn the odds in your favor. This may seem a bit amazing or preposterous to some of you who have likely been told that the edge is always with the house and that gamblers are doomed to lose if they play long enough. That statement *is* true for some games. However, the statement is *not* true for many other games. We will show you where it's true and where it's not. We will show you which games are *beatable* — and how to beat them — plus we'll show you which games are truly *unbeatable*.

Why have we chosen now to write this text? Because many things have happened in the last few years that have made the idea of gambling for a living a lot less farfetched for many people. In other words, the time is right.

Basically five major events have recently occurred. First there has been a giant increase in the number of casinos in the United States. When we first started gambling for a living you had to play in Las Vegas, in the cardrooms of Gardena, California, or possibly one of the racetracks around the United States to have any hope of being a successful professional gambler. Now it's much different. Numerous states have casinos. Some states such as Mississippi and New Jersey have a giant casino industry. Poker rooms (or cardrooms) are also far more widespread, particularly those offering bigger games. By that we mean games that are high enough to beat for significant money. California is still the poker capital of the world, but poker is no longer confined to just Gardena. Big games can now be found throughout the state, notably in San Diego, Oceanside, some of the neighboring cities of Los Angeles (including Gardena), San Jose, San Pablo, and some of the neighboring cities of San Francisco. These places are now offering games big enough to allow the best players to win serious money by the end of the year. Other states that have recently opened cardrooms offering higher stakes games include Arizona, Connecticut, Mississippi, Louisiana, New Jersey, Washington and Illinois.

The second event involves horse racing. There are now many places that will book tracks from around the country, giving you the opportunity to pick and choose from many races. Instead of the nine or ten betting opportunities that you would have if you went to a track, these horse books give you as many as two hundred races on a given day from which to select your bets.

Third is the recent introduction and phenomenal growth of progressive slot machines and ultraliberal poker machines. When we first started gambling, these machines did not exist.

Number four is the proliferation of tournaments. These not only consist of poker tournaments, but competitions for virtually all casino games, including those games that usually are not beatable. But they *are* beatable in the tournament format, as we will show later in this book.

Last but not least is a change in the attitude of the population itself. Gambling has become an accepted pastime for many people. Plus it has become more and more apparent that to be an expert gambler you ought to be well educated, intelligent, and dedicated. As these attributes are shown to be more and more necessary for success, the stigma of gambling has eroded. We now see many people becoming professional gamblers who could be successful in a lot of other fields. Previously it was only con men, hustlers, pool players, and the like who gravitated to gambling. Now it is common to find college graduates and even people with more advanced degrees. Thus, you can retain your respectability when you enter the gambling field.

So, for all these reasons, we thought it was time to write a guidebook of sorts for those of you who want to make your living gambling. In the following chapters we will give you a thorough introduction to the key points necessary for all the games that are theoretically beatable. In many cases we'll give you far more than an introduction. We will delve rather deeply into some subtle, expert concepts. We will discuss how to gamble for a living at poker, blackjack, horse racing, sports betting, video poker, progressive slot machines, casino promotions, and casino tournaments.

We also will show you why professional gambling must normally involve *only* these venues. There is no hope for making a

## 4 Introduction

living if you are going to be playing dice, roulette, baccarat, keno, or some of the newer casino games like Let It Ride (unless you are playing a tournament or taking advantage of some promotion where the casinos have miscalculated). But those first games mentioned, if played well enough, can truly offer you the opportunity to win in the long run. And we are talking about serious money. Making $100,000 a year is definitely an obtainable goal for those who have the talent and the drive to learn the games well.

We want to make one other point. Besides money, the main reason we gamble is simply because we love it. After all these years the games are still fun to play. We can set our own hours, live in many different locations, and take a vacation whenever we want. Yet the challenge is always there. Gambling for a living can be a great way to spend your life.

Finally, we would like to express our appreciation to Paula Cizmar for editing this work. Thanks to her, our ideas are now more clearly stated and thus should be more easily understood. In addition, we wish to thank Dave Clint for his cover design and art work throughout the book. And we need to thank Donna Harris for her comments — especially in the poker section — and proof reading.

# A Quick Note

We assume the reader has some experience with the games we will be talking about. If you are totally new to a particular game and do not understand all the rules governing play we recommend *The New Gambler's Bible* by Arthur Reber, and the *Fundamentals* series (which includes booklets on poker, video poker, craps, and blackjack) by Mason Malmuth and Lynne Loomis.

Each one of the beatable games involves so much knowledge that we obviously cannot tell you everything that needs to be said about them all in one book. We are going to give you a serious overview of the type of skills needed to beat them. However, once you decide a particular game fits your style or your preferred place of living, then you must go even further to become a true expert. Part of going further is of course, just gaining experience. The fact is, there is no substitute for experience, and it is a crucial part of becoming successful.

The other part is further reading and studying. That's why this book is liberally sprinkled with references to other books. In some cases they are *our* other books. We do not apologize for this. To go into the details of every game would make this a two-thousand page work. Nevertheless, you will learn plenty about each game from this text. But to put the finishing touches on any game you choose to play, you should read and study those books we recommend. That being said, let us now start our journey. When done, you should be well on your way to "Gambling for a Living."

# Part One

# Blackjack

# Blackjack

# Introduction

In 1962, an incredible event occurred in the world of gambling. A young MIT physics professor by the name of Edward O. Thorp showed that blackjack was a beatable casino game. Six years earlier, an article had appeared in the *Journal of the American Statistical Association* written by Roger Baldwin, Wilbert Cantey, Herbert Maisel, and James McDermont that had given a reasonably correct "basic strategy" — an accurate method of play based on a player's cards and the dealer's upcard. As groundbreaking as this was, Thorp wanted to improve upon it.

Using a "newfangled" computer to investigate blackjack, Thorp was able to produce a highly accurate basic strategy, show that blackjack without keeping track of the cards was virtually a dead-even game when his basic strategy was employed, and most importantly, produce a counting method that would give the player an edge over the casino.

At the time of this writing it has been more than thirty-five years since Thorp showed that the player can have the best of it. This wasn't thought to be true when the game came into being. Even now, many old-time casino executives find it hard to believe that Thorp was right. But the fact is, today blackjack is a highly beatable game. There are probably more professional blackjack players than there are any other form of professional gambler. Yet as we shall see, beating blackjack is not all that easy. It takes a lot of work and dedication — plus the ability to live with some frustration.

# The Game Itself

Before we get into how to get an edge at blackjack, let's take a quick look at the game itself. First, we will assume that you know the rules and that you understand that a dealer hits a total of 16 and stands on 17.[3] All casinos play blackjack this way — except some casinos will hit soft 17 while others won't.[4] In addition, unlike home games where the dealer may take ties, the casino considers these to be ties, or pushes as they are more commonly called, and all bets are returned to the player. That is, no money is won or lost.

So that immediately brings up the question of how does the casino get its edge. Suppose you played exactly the same way as the dealer, namely hitting 16 and standing on 17. Why wouldn't you beat the dealer since you have the extra payoff of 3-to-2 on blackjack and the dealer doesn't? (Before you read the answer you may want to think about this to see if you can figure it out yourself.) The answer lies in the fact that when we say the dealer doesn't take ties, this is not completely true. The dealer does take a certain type of tie. Namely when both you and he bust. This will happen about 9 percent of the time if your playing strategy mimics the dealer. Thus, if you played the same way as the dealer your disadvantage would be that 9 percent except for the fact that you get 3-to-2 on blackjack. Even with the blackjack bonus, a mimic-the-dealer strategy is giving the house about a 6 percent edge.

But decent players do much better than this, and there is a simple reason for it. They do not play exactly the same as the dealer. They stand on busting hands when the dealer shows a small card, and they will double down or split in obvious situations. If you just

---

[3] If you are new to blackjack or perhaps have only played it a small amount we recommend the *Fundamentals of "21"* by Mason Malmuth and Lynne Loomis.

[4] Soft hands are covered later in the text.

# 10 Part One: Blackjack

use common sense, your disadvantage ought to be in the 1 or 2 percent area. But that, of course, is not good enough.

# Why Basic Strategy?

There is no reason to just use common sense when it comes to blackjack strategy. Thanks to Thorp, others, and the computers they used, the perfect basic strategy has been determined. And this strategy is *not* a matter of opinion. Blackjack is purely mathematical, at least as far as what the right play is. (Later on, you will see that there are nonmathematical facets to the game, but those facets have to do with fooling the casino into believing that you are not a good player. But from the pure stand point of playing properly, it is 100 percent mathematical.)

So why is basic strategy so important? The answer is that even if you are not keeping track of the cards in any way, if you play the proper "basic strategy," that is, the strategy that has been calculated or simulated by Thorp, Julian Braun, Peter Griffin, Stanford Wong, Arnold Snyder, and others, you will be playing very close to an even game. In fact, if you are playing basic strategy against a one deck game with reasonably good rules, you *are* playing an even game. (Against a multiple deck shoe you will be at a disadvantage. But your disadvantage will still be as small as 5- or 6- 10ths of 1 percent and sometimes even less at a casino that offers very favorable rules.)

# Basic Strategy

The following is a very good approximation of the perfect basic strategy.[5] If you never bother to learn the absolutely perfect basic strategy the mistakes you will be making by using this strategy would cost you only a few hundredths of a percent.[6]

The first category involves what are known as *hard hands*, where any ace you may hold would have to count as a "1." (A soft hand is where your hand contains an ace and your total is not over 21 even if you count the ace as 11.) Since you will never stand on hard 11 or less and you will always stand on hard 17 or more the only problem hands are hard 12 through 16. (These hands are called "stiffs.")

When you have a 12 through 16 you do not always hit it like the dealer does. But you do hit if the dealer is showing a seven, eight, nine, ten, or an ace. The reason you do is because the computer says so. However, it might be a helpful memory aid if you imagine that the dealer has a ten in the hole. If he did, you would of course hit. Since this also happens to be the correct basic strategy, "putting him" on a ten works in these cases.

Against a deuce through six you stand with your stiffs with two exceptions. That is, if you have precisely a 12 you should hit against a deuce or a trey. Again to help you memorize this strategy you might assume that the dealer had a ten in the hole. Common sense would tell you that if you have a stiff and the dealer also has a stiff you are better off standing and hoping he busts. But in this case

---

[5] Basic strategy will differ slightly depending on the number of decks used and/or the rules that a particular casino offers.

[6] See one of the good blackjack books for perfect basic strategy in all situations. Some of them are listed in Appendix B: Recommended Reading at the end of this book.

putting the dealer on a ten doesn't point you to the exceptions since it would be right to stand on 12 if you *knew* the dealer had 12 or 13.

(At this point we must again emphasize that we are talking about the "basic strategy," which is the strategy that you use if you are not keeping track of the cards. If you keep track of the cards you sometimes deviate that strategy.)

The next category is called "hard doubling hands." In the case of hard hands totaling 11 or under you clearly do not stand, but you do frequently double down. Always double down when you have a total of 11,[7] double down with a 10 against deuce through nine, and double down with a 9 against trey through six. Notice that when you double down you will sometimes reduce your chances of winning the hand because you only get one card. If you double with a total of 10 versus a dealer's upcard of five this isn't true, but if you double with a total of 10 versus an eight you will sometimes wish you could hit again. Nevertheless the right play is to double because of the extra money you put into action.

Now lets look at soft hands. Obviously any soft hand below 17 should never be stood on. Not as obvious is the fact that a soft 17 should also never be a standing hand. It will either be a hitting hand or sometimes a doubling down hand (if the casino allows it). When you do hit soft 17, what you do next depends on what you caught and what the dealer has showing. Even soft 18, believe it or not, should sometimes be hit. This is the correct play if the dealer has a nine or a ten showing. Soft 18 should also sometimes be doubled down on as we will explain shortly. Notice that if you do hit a soft 18 and catch a six for instance, you would hit it again because you now have a hard 14 against a nine or ten showing. Similarly if you hit a soft 17 and then caught a card above a four you would hit against a seven through ten. (You would also hit again if you caught an ace against a nine or ten.)

---

[7] If you are playing in a four- or six-deck game, or in a two-deck game where the dealer stands on soft 17, do not double down with a total of 11 against an ace.

In *Beat the Dealer,* Thorp showed that you can double down with some of these soft hands. It was a big surprise to many people because on the surface it seemed that a hand like

is not a doubling down hand. After all it will usually catch a bad card. Furthermore, even when the dealer has a five showing he will usually not bust. But, what Thorp discovered was that the *combination* of the two possibly good things that can happen to you — the dealer *busting* or you catching a small card — meant that your soft 16 was worth doubling down when the dealer had a weak card showing. In fact, you should double down with an ace-deuce through an ace-seven when the dealer has a four, five, or six showing. (We are simplifying slightly.)

The last category is splitting. First, you should never split tens, fives, or fours. This is common sense. Two tens is too good a hand to break up although you will occasionally see people doing it, especially against a five or a six. Unless you are counting cards, this is a terrible play. As for fives, no one but a maniac would even think of splitting them because you can just as easily get twice as much money out there by doubling down. Why would you split a good hand that totals 10 to two terrible hands that each total 5. The situation with two fours is almost as obvious although there are some situations where the expert might split them.[8]

Deuces, treys, sixes, and sevens are all basically in the same category. Without being totally precise we can say that you should split deuces, treys, sixes, and sevens when the dealer has a trey through seven showing.

---

[8] If double after split is allowed, split fours against a dealer's five or six.

Now that leaves us with a pair of nines, which are probably the ·
cutest plays. If you meet someone who claims to be an excellent
blackjack player, or a professional blackjack player, ask this person
against which upcards he or she would split nines. The way this
player responds will, better than any other answer, tell you
immediately whether or not he knows what he is doing. So what's
the answer? It is that you should split nines against deuce through
six, eight, and nine. But that you stand against a seven. Yes that's
right. You stand against the seven, but split against the eight and
nine.

The reason you play nines like this is again simply *because the
computer says to*. However, if you are trying to see the rationale
behind what the computer says, notice, then, that there are different
rationales depending on the dealer's upcard. First, you should split
the nines against small cards simply because you are trying to "press
your edge." Generally, the dealer is in bad shape with a small card
up and you would like to get twice as much money out there on two
different nines rather than sticking with a mere 18.

Second, against an eight the nines should be split because there
is a high probability that you will push with the dealer if you stand
and an 18 isn't that great of a total to have in case the dealer doesn't
have an 18 with you. He might have an ace underneath or might
draw out on you. On the other hand, if you split you are more likely
to win both of those hands than lose both of them, and whenever
you win one and lose one you frequently will be doing exactly what
you would have done if you hadn't split them. So splitting against
an eight changes a possible tie to at least one likely winner and
frequently will give you two likely winners. Statisticians would say
that your overall expectation has increased.

Third, splitting against a dealer's upcard of nine should also be
done because 18 is not in very good shape in this situation. You
simply turn out better (in the long run) if you split them. If the
dealer does have a ten underneath, you will now have a chance of ·
getting a push out of these two nines rather than losing the bet.

And finally, the reason you don't split them against a seven is
because of the "bird in hand is worth more than two in a bush"

concept. Your 18 against a seven wins well over 60 percent of the time. It is not worth risking that rather high chance of a win in order to speculate on two nines. (It goes without saying that the reason you don't split versus a dealer's upcard of ten or ace is that there is too good a chance that you will lose both hands.) There are two more options for which we need to give the correct basic strategy. One is surrender and one is insurance. If you can find a casino that has surrender, and more casinos than ever are now offering this option, it is helpful to the tune of a few hundredths of a percent.[9] The correct strategy (again assuming that you are not keeping track of the cards) is that you should surrender a total of 16 against a dealer's nine, ten, or ace and surrender a total of 15 against a ten.

By the way, for those of you who want to do a little thinking, what percentage of the time would you have to lose your bet in order to make a surrender correct instead? (This assumes that there were no pushes but if you are going to stand a push cannot occur.) So assuming that you are going to stand on a stiff, how often would you have to lose to make surrendering better? (Again, why not take a minute to think before we tell you.)

For those who didn't have the patience to think about it or were unable to figure it out, look at it this way. If you play four hands for $10 each and surrendered every hand you would be down $20, $5 per hand. If you didn't surrender but won only one of those four hands you would also be down $20, losing $30 and winning $10. So you need to lose at least 75 percent of the time before you should surrender.

Now we come to insurance. Again we are not talking about cases where you are counting, because insurance is occasionally a strong play for a counter. But for those who are not counting, you should understand that insurance is a very bad bet. Now some of you may say, "But what if I have a blackjack?" Shame on you. It is just as bad when you have a blackjack as any other time. The fact

---

[9] If you are counting cards and increasing your bet at the appropriate times it is worth much more.

is that your own ten makes the insurance bet even a little worse than normal. Insuring a 20 (two tens) would on average be even worse yet.

Please realize that insurance is simply a side bet where you are betting that the dealer has a ten in the hole, and the casino is giving you 2-to-1 odds on that bet. Off the top of the deck the true odds are 2¼-to-1 (36-to-16). The fact that you might have a good hand or a bad hand for that matter has nothing to do with whether you buy insurance. You only would consider buying insurance if you were counting the cards and you knew that the side bet had become a good bet.

Just to prove our point, let's look at the case where you have blackjack a little bit closer. If you have a total of 21 on your first two cards and you do buy insurance, yes, you do get a guaranteed payoff of one unit. But it's not the right strategy to follow because giving up half a bet is giving up too much simply to turn your hand into a guaranteed winner rather than a possible push. In the long run you do better by taking your one and a half bets when they come and accept your pushes when they come.

To be a winning blackjack player you must press all your edges. You cannot refrain from gambles, whether those gambles be doubling down on an 11 against a ten, doubling down on soft 15 against a five, splitting two eights against a ten, or not insuring your blackjacks. These are all plays that are gambling plays with only a small degree of an edge. But if you don't take every edge that is available you might discover that you don't have the best of it.[10]

We again want to remind you that our basic strategy is not quite perfect. We are simplifying it somewhat for the sake of ease of retention. Also, there are slight differences in basic strategy depending on the number of decks that you are up against and the rules of the game. For instance you should split a few more pairs if

---

[10] We will see later that when you are counting cards there are times when you should violate this advice. That is, you should not take every edge. You do this in an effort to convince the casino that you are not a highly skilled player.

doubling after split is allowed. But for almost all purposes, the basic strategy that we have just given will get the job done.

Keep in mind that if you want to become a professional blackjack player, you must have the basic strategy *down cold* so that you don't have to try to remember it when you are playing your hand. You are going to be using up all of your brain power counting and possibly coming up with basic strategy alterations. The basic strategy itself had better be completely second nature, something that you don't have to think about. To be a serious player you must practice playing basic strategy for at least fifty to a hundred hours until it is automatic. Then having done that, you can start delving into counting.

# How Did Basic Strategy Come About?

We would like to digress for a moment and talk about how proper strategy was developed. This should help convince you that these strategies are correct and that you need to follow them faithfully when in action.

The way these strategies were arrived at usually didn't involve pure calculation, although many of the plays have been double-checked with calculations. What was utilized was massive computer simulation — millions of hands were "dealt" by the computer until it became perfectly clear as to what the correct play was.

For example, let's take the case of a total of 16 versus the dealer's upcard of ten. What Thorp and others originally did was tell the computer to hit the 16 and then, if necessary, give a hit or hits to the dealer. This they did millions of times. Next, they repeated the process, except that now the computer stood with that same 16, millions of times.

The proper play was the one that did better. It didn't have to be a play that would make money. It might very well be a play that would simply lose less in the long run. In fact, that is the case when you have a 16 against a ten. You lose money either way but you lose less in the long run by hitting instead of standing (unless you are counting and the "count" strategy tells you otherwise). To give a second example, take the case of 14 versus four. Once again you lose money either way. But if you stand you win about 40 percent of the time. If you hit you win less. So this time it is better to stand.

These two hit versus stand examples were fairly straightforward. Doubling down is a little more complicated. When you double down, your chances of winning are never increased, and sometimes your chances are decreased. If you have an 11 against a five, doubling down will add twice as much money to your bet. But it won't help your chances of winning the bet. However, whenever

19

you have 11 against a five you will only take one card anyway. So if 11 against a five is a profitable situation, doubling it is twice as profitable. But what about a hand like 11 against an eight? If you don't double down you will win more often than if you do because when you have an 11 against an eight you will sometimes catch a small card, in which case you would have done better to have hit it again. With an 11 against an eight, according to the computer, you win if you don't double down approximately 61 percent of the time. On the other hand, you win only 59 percent of the time if you do double down. But winning a double bet 59 percent of the time is better than winning a single bet 61 percent of the time. (Fifty-nine percent is an 18 percent edge while 61 percent is a 22 percent edge — but it's 22 percent of half as much.)

Splitting decisions can be even more complex. Sometimes splitting turns a losing hand into a winning hand. The best example would be two eights against a seven, where if you don't split you rate to lose money, but if you split you rate to win money. But that isn't the only possible reason to split. For instance, if you don't split two nines against a six you rate to win money, but if you do split you rate to win even more.

What about the case of two eights against a ten? If you don't split you rate to lose money and if you do split you still rate to lose, just not as much. Two eights against a ten rates to lose about 52 cents for every dollar bet. Splitting gives you two hands that rates to lose approximately 22 cents each for every dollar bet for a total loss of 44 cents. However, that's still better than not splitting.

For a final example let's look at two tens against a six. If you split the tens, you will win money. Yes, that's absolutely correct even though this play violates basic strategy. The thing is, in the long run it will not win as much as if you had stood. Standing you win an average of 70 cents per dollar bet, whereas if you split you have two hands that each win you an average of 27 cents per dollar bet for a total of 54 cents. So you have cost yourself about 16 cents per dollar bet if you split.

Hopefully you now have a better idea of how basic strategy was originally developed. You can be sure it was done very thoroughly, and there is no question that its recommendations are absolutely correct.

# Introduction to Counting

When Thorp discovered that there was a method that figures to win by playing blackjack honestly he started an uproar. His book, *Beat the Dealer*, became a national best seller right along with major novels because it was so unheard of that a casino game could actually be advantageous to the player. Today the enthusiasm has waned somewhat because people have discovered that beating blackjack is not always that easy.

The first problem with getting the best of it at "21" is that it takes a fair amount of practice and study. This makes it a little more difficult to beat than most people think. However, this is actually a good thing, because if blackjack was that easy to beat everyone would be doing it — and there would be no blackjack as we know it.

The second problem, which is probably the greater problem, is that even when you do play well your edge is small, and therefore your short-term results are very volatile. Most professional blackjack players refer to the game as a "roller coaster ride" and at times find playing blackjack to be rather frustrating.

There is also a third problem: If you, in fact, are good enough to win and have the bankroll to sustain temporary losses, you now have to deal with the casinos. If they determine that you are a winning player they will either stop you from playing or change the game to one that has almost no edge for you. For example, some casinos have been known to reshuffle a six-deck shoe after every hand against a suspected card counter.

However, with all that being said, there are many hundreds if not thousands of people who are still making good money, and in some cases very good money, playing blackjack. You can too, but you must do your homework, be well capitalized, and learn how to handle the casinos. But first, you must learn to count.

Before we have you simply memorize a bunch of rules let's first see if we can get a handle on why counting works. There are actually two reasons why it makes money. The more important of the two is that it identifies situations where the player has an edge. The second reason is that counting will show you cases where the basic strategy is no longer the proper play and will tell you what strategy changes you should make.

# The Theory Behind Counting

Thorp realized two things when he did his original research on blackjack. First, he understood that if somebody was keeping track of the cards there would be times when the cards in the deck were better for the player than normal. Second, since he had developed a strategy where the disadvantage was tiny even when you weren't keeping track of the cards, it stood to reason that only a small alteration in the deck to the player's favor would be enough to give the player an actual edge. This second idea was actually not new with Thorp.[11] Many people, for instance, understood that if the deck had an extremely high proportion of aces remaining there could be an advantage to the player. What they didn't know was that things didn't have to be so extreme and that advantages would occur fairly frequently. Thorp also realized that as the deck changed there was not only the possibility of having an edge, there was also the possibility that the basic strategy would no longer be the proper strategy to use. Thus, card counters were born.

The basic theory behind counting cards has to do with the fact that when there is a higher than normal proportion of high cards, especially aces and tens, (and to a much smaller degree nines) remaining in the deck, the player — even playing basic strategy — will often have an edge. Why is this?

One reason is *not* because there are going to be more 20s dealt. Yes, you will get more 20s when there is a high proportion of high cards. (Counters say the deck is rich.) But the dealer also gets more 20s, which makes up for it. However, the fact that *blackjacks* are more common *is* relevant. Yes, the dealer will also get more blackjacks. But the dealer is not being paid 3-to-2 and you are. If

---

[11] In *Beat the Dealer* Thorp even describes some of the original successful blackjack players. These people were winning on a consistent basis before the results of his research was published.

you continually swapped blackjacks with him, you would come out way ahead.

Normally, making a blackjack is about a 5 percent shot. If this goes up to even 6 or 7 percent that's very helpful to you in spite of the fact that the dealer will also catch more blackjacks. Remember, the dealer doesn't get paid 3-to-2. Furthermore, if you are keeping track of the cards there are times when insurance is the proper play. We will get to that in more detail shortly, but for now understand that you can "save" yourself some money some of the time the dealer has a blackjack.

The second big reason why the player has an advantage when the deck is heavy in high cards has to do with the fact that his option not to hit his stiffs — an option that the dealer doesn't have — becomes far more advantageous. For instance, in a normal situation if you were dealt a 15 and the dealer had a five showing you are still an underdog to win even though you make the correct play of standing. But when the deck gets highly positive, that is, very rich in high cards, you may actually be a favorite to win the hand. You are certainly not as much of an underdog as you were.

So what do we do with this counting information? We do a few things. Number one: When the deck becomes rich we consider betting more, especially when the deck gets quite rich. Depending on the number of decks and the rules, you will start to have an advantage if the deck becomes somewhere between slightly and moderately rich. You will have a significant advantage, maybe 2 or 3 percent if the deck becomes very rich.

So the idea is that you would like to bet three, four, or five times as much as your typical bet — perhaps even more if you can get away with it — when the deck gets rich. This means that even though you will be playing against a non-rich deck more than half the time, if you bet properly you will have more than half your *money* bet when the deck is rich.[12] This ought to give you an overall advantage.

(We also need to mention that the reason we say you should bet as little as possible when you have a disadvantage is because you can't simply drop all the way down to the minimum bet without alerting the pit boss that you are a counter. Most pit bosses don't understand counting in detail, but they do know somebody who swings his bets wildly is very possibly a counter. Thus, there is a limit as to how much you can *spread* your bets. There will be more discussion on this later.)

The second aspect of counting that helps you with your advantage is that not only do you bet according to the count, but you play your hand according to the count. For instance, a very negative deck could have as much as a 10 percent disadvantage if you stuck with basic strategy, but if you deviate from basic strategy in very negative decks the disadvantage rarely gets to more than about 3 percent.[13] You will also make strategy changes when the deck is positive. In fact, they are more important than those that occur when the deck is bad since this is when your big bets will be made. In all cases proper strategy changes have the effect of increasing your edge.

Deviations from basic strategy will occur more often in single- or double-deck games than in shoe games. This is because there are less extreme swings in the composition of the deck in the shoes and therefore opportunities to deviate from basic strategy won't come up as often. However, if you are playing for a living you should know the appropriate strategy changes no matter how many decks

---

[12] You actually don't have to have the majority of your money bet when you have an advantage to have an overall edge. For instance, if you could have 40 percent of your money bet with a 2 percent edge and 60 percent of your money bet with ½ percent disadvantage, you would still have an edge.

[13] Specifically you hit more but double down and split less. There will be more discussion on this shortly.

you choose to play against. In fact, if you are using a large bet spread in a shoe game, then the appropriate strategy changes, even though they won't occur as often, may have a larger impact on your overall results than if you were playing in a single-deck game and were using a small bet spread.

The third reason to count could have been put into the category of strategy changes but it really deserves its own category: It is knowing when to take insurance.

Insurance is simply a side bet as to whether the dealer has a ten in the hole. It is a bad bet unless the remaining cards contain *at least one-third tens.* However, when the deck becomes rich in tens it will contain a higher proportion than this and now the correct play is to buy insurance. This is true regardless of the hand you hold (except that you are going to count your own cards when you make your determination).

A fourth but somewhat less important reason to count, which is also a type of strategy change, involves the surrender option. When there is a high proportion of big cards in the deck there are more opportunities to surrender correctly and they gain you a lot more than normal. For example, 16 against a ten normally wins 23 percent of the time giving you a slight edge when you surrender. But when the deck is positive you may only win as little as 15 or 20 percent if you have to play the hand (stand). Thus, surrender becomes a very profitable play in the sense that your long-run profit comes from money saved as well as from money won. Furthermore, hands like 14 versus ten or 15 versus nine become proper surrenders in the right spots. And, of course, on the other side of the coin, if you are counting you will know those times when you should stop surrendering altogether.

# How to Count

When Thorp first came up with the concept of counting, his method to keep track of the cards was to form a ratio between the number of non-tens and tens left in the deck. Off the top of a single deck you have 36 non-tens to 16 tens, which gives you a ratio of 2.25.

$$\frac{36}{16} = 2.25$$

If a high proportion of small cards came out, that ratio would go down; Thorp realized that your edge started to become significant when the ratio was 2.0 or less. *Beat the Dealer* was written using this criteria.

Thorp had strategy tables that showed at which particular ten count you would deviate from basic strategy. For instance, if the ratio dropped to 2.1 and you held a total of 12 against a dealer's deuce you would now stand instead of hit.

However, it was soon obvious that most people could not handle the "Ten Count." This was even more true as multiple decks started to come into use. So what some others did was to come up with a method that was far easier. This method is called the "Point Count."

There are many variations of the Point Count. For those who want to delve into them in detail we recommend the books by Peter Griffin, Arnold Snyder, Ken Uston, and Stanford Wong. We will discuss only one of these counts. However, it is the one used by most pros and is at least 90 percent as accurate as far more complex counts. It is also relatively easy to implement. It is known as the High-Low Count.[14] In the High-Low Count the player simply adds 1 whenever he sees a deuce, trey, four, five, or six, and subtracts 1 whenever he sees a ten or an ace. Sevens, eights, and nines count as zero and can be ignored. For those of you who think that this is difficult to do, the fact is it really isn't with some practice. The idea is to use some tricks.

For instance, when you see a ten and a four your eye should learn to just cancel it and call it nothing. Once you have a little more experience, three card combinations become sort of automatic. If you see a jack, a five, and a trey, just think plus one.

You start your count off at 0, and if the count becomes positive it becomes helpful to the player because it most likely indicates that there is a higher proportion of tens and aces in the deck than normal.[15, 16]

The point at which the player has an advantage depends on two things, namely the number of decks and, to a lesser extent, the rules. For a single deck a count of +3 will virtually always indicate an edge, usually over 1 percent. But this is not necessarily the case in a shoe game (where many decks may be in use). For instance, if the first three cards out of a six-deck shoe were small this would not have much effect on the overall proportion of big cards to small

---

[14] An excellent detailed discussion of the High-Low Count appears in *Professional Blackjack* by Stanford Wong.

[15] We say most likely because there are the occasional times when the sevens, eights, and nines that are not counted have a spurious effect on the count.

[16] You can sometimes have an edge even when the deck is not especially rich in tens and aces. This usually occurs when extra fives have shown. If the first three cards out of a single deck are one ten and two fives, this is a favorable deck even though the ten count ratio is 2.27-to-1.

cards. But professional players have a way of handling this problem. They form what is called the "true count," which is the actual (or running) count divided by the number of decks remaining.[17]

For instance, if the cards out give you a +4 that is the true count if it is right at the beginning of one deck remaining. If it's at the beginning of four decks remaining it's +1. And if it's at the beginning of two decks remaining it's +2. (If it's in the middle of the last deck in the shoe then it is +8.)

---

[17] Some experts will divide by the number of half decks remaining to form what are known as half-deck true counts. They serve the same purpose as regular full-deck true counts.

# Betting Strategy

The basic idea as we have already stated is to bet more when the count is good if you can get away with it. But how much more is correct? Exactly how much you should bet depends on your edge and your bankroll. If you can easily afford the fluctuations, which means having more than two hundred big bets, you should bet as much as you can when you have a reasonable edge.

If there is some possibility of going broke, then your bet should be in proportion to your count. For example, if you bet $100 when you have a true count of +3 in a six-deck shoe, then you should bet approximately twice as much or $200 when the true count is +6. When the count is smaller, close to zero, or well below it, you of course would be betting less.

To help get you started we recommend the following. In a single-deck game bet only one unit if the true count is +1 or less; if the true count is +2, +3, or +4 bet two units; if the true count is greater than +4, bet either three or four units. Your decision — whether to bet three or four units — should be based on how much bet variation you think a particular casino will tolerate.[18] In a shoe game, bet only one unit if the true count is +2 or less; if the true count is +3, +4, or +5 bet two units; if the true count is greater than +5, bet either three or four units. Sometimes when playing against a shoe, you may want to bet even more when the count is higher than +5.[19]

---

[18] You should be more apt to bet four units on a good count if you have won the previous hand betting two units. Now it just seems like you are letting your winnings ride. Another time it is easy to bet four units is of course when your previous bet was four.

[19] Again, see the books that we recommend for more discussion on how to bet and on how much to bet.

# Strategy Changes

Now we will look at some of the more important strategy changes. If you varied your bet appropriately, used only these changes, and played in a good game you would have a nice edge. In other words, the vast majority of your edge will come from what you are learning right here. However, we need to point out that there is a specific true count strategy for almost every situation. When you are playing professionally you ought to know these exact true counts. (See the books we recommend.)

So what are some of the important strategy changes? First, let's look at those changes that will occur when the deck is rich. Probably the most important one is that 16 should no longer be hit against a ten. Hitting 16 against a ten is a close play, and once the deck becomes somewhat positive, you should no longer do it. The correct play now is to stand. Of course, if you can surrender, that play is even better.

Other hands that it is proper to stand on as the deck becomes better are 15 against a ten and 16 against a nine. However, the deck needs to be more "positive" than it does for the 16 versus a ten where it only needs to be slightly on the plus side for standing to be correct. Once again if it is proper to stand it is even more proper to surrender, if you can find a place that allows it.

With a good deck 10 against a ten and 10 against an ace become double downs. The dealer has already looked to see if he has blackjack and doesn't . You, however, can still catch 21. Thus, you double down. Another strategy change at a moderately high count, believe it or not, is to split two tens against a five or a six. The only drawback to this play is that some pit bosses might mark you as a counter when you make it. You have to decide whether the risk is worth the reward.

Other strategy changes with a good count include doubling down with 11 against an ace and 9 against a deuce. These are two plays that you don't normally make against six decks. In addition you should double down with a soft 18 or soft 17 against all small cards, split two deuces against a deuce, and split two nines against a seven. You should also stand with 12 versus a dealer's deuce or trey.

You will also be making strategy changes when the deck is bad. Obviously as the count gets negative you start hitting more. You would certainly hit your 12s against a four, five, or six, and hit a 13 against a deuce.[20] Doubling down should be done less often. Clearly an 11 against a ten, a 10 against a nine, or a 9 against a trey or four become bad double downs as the deck gets bad. In addition, you shouldn't double down with soft hands any more.

Splitting is not as clearcut since the small cards that are left can be helpful as well as hurtful in some cases. Consequently we won't recommend any splitting changes from basic strategy for poor decks.

---

[20] Plays like hitting a 15 against a five require such a terrible deck — and come up so rarely — that they are not worth discussing unless you are trying to beat a one-deck game with a flat bet.

# Turning the Theory
# into Money

There are two big downfalls for blackjack players. One: They are under bankrolled. And two: They are barred or are shuffled upon. We'll discuss the bankroll requirements in the next section. But first, let's talk about playing conditions.

Blackjack, besides being a game of mathematical skill, is also a game of "cat and mouse." The casinos don't want you to beat them out of their money, and they have instructed their pit personnel in this regard. Thus, the biggest reason why there aren't hordes of blackjack players making good money is because the casinos are aware of the possibilities of getting beat, and even though they are not expert at it, they do make cursory attempts to stop it. Fortunately, if you are smart, you can overcome these attempts.

To be successful you must get a good game, and a good game means that they will deal deeply into the deck or the shoe before they shuffle. Arnold Snyder and others have shown how much various penetrations are worth.[21] If you read this material you can see how obvious it is that a few extra cards penetration is worth more than the gains that you might make from any obscure strategy change. Penetration is the name of the game. Favorable rules are nice and you should also strive to find them. But good rules and poor penetration is still a mediocre game while modest rules and good penetration can be a great game.

Thus, once you, the professional blackjack player, have achieved a certain level of competence you must strive not only to have a good game dealt to you, but to maintain it as well. We laugh when we see advertisements from so-called blackjack experts who claimed to have been barred from lots of casinos. This sure doesn't

---

[21] See the books, *Beat the One-, Two-, Four-, Six-, and Eight-Deck Game,* all by Arnold Snyder.

sound like an expert to us. If you can't get a good game, all the counting skill in the world won't do you any good.

So is it possible to maintain a good game? And is it possible to play unharrassed for a long enough time so that you can make a good living? The answer to both of these questions is, "Yes." But for most players, it is not easy.

First, you must act in a way that will not raise the suspicions of the casino. This, of course, involves many different aspects and attitudes. One would be mere physical appearance. The idea is to look more like a tourist than either a gambler or a mathematician. Probably the worst way you can look would be to come in with slightly disheveled hair and jeans. This is precisely the way a typical graduate student would appear. You must dress the part. For example, if you are betting a lot of money you need to wear appropriate clothes. If your bankroll is more modest, dress modestly. Possibly the best way you could look would be to have a 38-23-36 figure and be about 29 years old with lots of diamonds and a little tattoo on your shoulder.[22]

In other words, when playing blackjack you should dress nicely, appear natural, and appear to be enjoying yourself. A spouse by your side can help, and there is nothing wrong with ordering a drink or two — you don't have to drink them.

But one thing is certain. If you have the demeanor of someone who is paying too much attention to each card, you may tip off the pit that you need to be watched. So if you miss a card, don't worry about it. (And of course you don't count it. Just pretend it's not there.) All in all it's important not to look like somebody who knows his stuff or who is trying hard to win at the game.

This brings up an important point. The manner in which you play your hands as far as which hands you think about and which ones you don't can impact how the pit views you. If you are a

---

[22] On the other hand women, especially young women, who are betting very big money are often suspect at the blackjack tables. This is because most of the big money in a casino is bet by men and any women betting large amounts will draw extra scrutiny.

professional player you should never have to think about any hand. If you do, you need more practice. Your plays should be automatic. But that doesn't mean it isn't valuable to *pretend* to think about some hands. Just don't pretend to think about the hands that a card counter would think about. You should only think about those hands that a tourist might struggle with. This might be a 14 against a deuce or a 15 against an eight. But if you hold a total of 16 against a dealer's ten you need to make your decision instantly. An amateur counter might pause in this spot and that delay could give him away.

# The Most Successful Player We Know

We want to take a moment and tell you about the most successful blackjack player we know. Since he is still active we won't mention his name, but this is a real person who has won a great deal of money. Many of the best blackjack players are aware of him. Yet, in general, he has shied away from publicity.

What makes this man so successful is that he has "got it down pretty good." His play is smooth, he appears to be a tourist, he plays within his bankroll, and he only pauses on those hands on which a traveler who is visiting a gambling center would pause.

But there is also another interesting characteristic about him. He is definitely not the best blackjack player we know. He uses a simple count. Many of the unusual strategy changes, (which only rarely occur), he doesn't even know. His long-run overall results by his own admission have been about ⅔ of 1 percent of his total bet. This falls far short of what an expert can theoretically do, which is to make between 1 and 1½ percent of their total action. However, this particular fellow has been playing blackjack pretty much without any heat for 30 years and has made millions. What he loses on accuracy he has made up on longevity and the ability to play. This should be your goal also.

# Bankroll Management

In the introduction to this chapter we warned that blackjack can be very frustrating. Why? Because even though you have an advantage, you are far from guaranteed to win each time you play. In fact, you may go for long periods of time without winning. Thus it is extremely important that you have the bankroll to sustain you through these inevitable losing streaks.

Many blackjack players overbet their bankroll, and this has been known to destroy some of them, including those who otherwise played very well. Since you are expecting to win on average a mere one bet an hour, you require a bankroll in the neighborhood of two hundred such bets (and sometimes more) in order to be 95 percent certain that you won't go broke. The precise amount of money you need is dependent on your edge and how you are varying your bets. But for all but the most advantageous games, you are living dangerously if you don't start with at least two hundred big bets.

Here is where much of the frustration comes in. Suppose you drop a hundred and fifty bets. If you play regularly — even if you play well — this will occasionally happen.[23] Now, you don't rate to win it back for one hundred and fifty hours, which means that you will go for a very long time without showing a profit. Of course you may get it back quicker, but it might be even longer than your expected one hundred and fifty hours before you get into the "black."

---

[23] That doesn't necessarily mean that you are now within 50 bets of going broke. When we say that you are probably safe with 200 bets to start we assume that this bankroll will increase so that even a 200+ bets losing streak will usually not bust you. If you start with a 200-bet bankroll we don't recommend increasing the size of your bets until that 200 has become at least 400.

This brings up a related idea. You have to learn that when you are a blackjack player, you will not usually be at your peak. Griffin has shown that at most 1.6 percent of the time your present hand will put you at a new peak. This means that since you usually won't be at your all-time high, you will feel like you are losing most of the time. For those readers who are mathematically inclined, you might want to review Griffin's rigorous proof, but here's an easy way to show that this idea is correct. Suppose that you have a 1 percent edge and that you are flat betting. What percentage of the time will you be at a new peak? Specifically, lets say that you are betting $100 per hand, have a 1 percent advantage, and you plan to play 10,000 hands. Since you are "earning" $1 per hand at the end of 10,000 hands you expect to be ahead $10,000.

$$\$10,000 = (\$100)(.01)(10,000)$$

Now to win the $10,000 in 10,000 hands there will be a time when you are up $100 for the first time, there will be a time when you are up $200 for the first time, there will be a time when you are up $300 for the first time, and so on. Altogether how many peaks will you have reached? Well, in this example since you are betting $100 per hand you will have reached 100 peaks over a period of 10,000 hands. Therefore 1 percent of your hands are at new high.[24]

So in this example, you will be at or below your peak 99 percent of the time — and that's assuming a 1 percent edge. In fact, as we have already stated a 1 percent edge may be a little too high for most players. (They may make a few mistakes, or have to camouflage their play, or not be able to vary their bets as much as they would like. Thus an edge of ⅔ of 1 percent is probably more

---

[24] This is of course slightly inaccurate because of blackjacks, double downs, splits, insurance, and surrender bets.

realistic.) This means that in reality you will be at your peak less than 1 percent of the time, and this can be extremely frustrating.

By the same token however if you are betting an average of $100 per hand and you are playing 100 hands per hour you can expect to make approximately $67 per hour or over $100,000 per year. And if you could afford $1,000 per hand and could find good games at these stakes you should make $1 million per year. (But you would need a bankroll of at least $200,000 to start.)

Now this brings us to another question related to your bankroll: How much should you bet per hand? There is a precise formula for this and it's called the Kelly Criterion. Basically, you should bet in proportion to your edge when you have the advantage, and you make as small a bet as possible when you have a disadvantage. For example, if you have a 1 percent advantage you should bet 1 percent of your bankroll. If you have a 3 percent advantage you should bet 3 percent of your bankroll. And if you are at a disadvantage, you should bet as little as possible, and perhaps nothing if you can get away with it. By following the Kelly Criterion you can expect your bankroll to grow at an "optimum rate" and your "risk of ruin" will be minimized.[25] However, this assumes that your actions do not affect the game you are being dealt. Going out of your way to be precise regarding how much you bet could easily be something that is picked up on by the house. The real truth is that you don't want to be anywhere near this precise. You want to appear to be betting like a tourist — and tourists frequently bet in a haphazard manner.[26]

---

[25] Actually the mathematically optimum bet for blackjack is slightly below these figures. There are two reasons for this. One involves the fact that you sometimes split or double down. The other involves the fact that you are frequently betting with a disadvantage.

[26] See *Blackjack Essays* by Mason Malmuth for more discussion on this topic.

# At the Tables

So now you are a blackjack player. All you have to do is go to a casino, sit down at a blackjack table, start counting cards, and bet away as the count goes up. At the end of the day, you can cash your chips in, go home a big winner, and then return the next day to collect some more. Well, it's not that easy. To be successful at blackjack there are several things you must do in addition to being highly skilled at card counting and playing.

First, you must scout the games and only play at those casinos where the games are favorable. This usually means good deck penetration with decent rules. We have already mentioned this but we want to emphasize it again: Penetration is the name of the game. This is true whether you are playing in a hand-held game or in a six-deck shoe. There are casinos in Las Vegas that offer six-deck shoe games where you can double down on any two cards, double after split, surrender, split and resplit all pairs including aces, and they stand on soft 17. But if the dealer cuts off three decks, you should find another table. On the other hand, a six-deck shoe with much more modest rules is well worth playing if only one deck is removed from play.

The same is true in the hand held games. For example, a single-deck game where your doubling is restricted to only a total of 10 or 11 and the house hits soft 17 can still be a great game if the majority of the cards are dealt.[27] On the other hand, if the casino chooses to deal out only one round, as some do, you wouldn't want to play in their single-deck game even if the rules were good.

You must also limit your time at any one casino. If you "camp out" as some amateur counters are known to do, it won't be long before the casino either asks you to leave or alters the game —

---

[27] Games like this were once quite common in Northern Nevada and can still be found there at times.

usually by shuffling much earlier than normal. When this happens, you will discover that your casino time is nonproductive. We recommend that you usually spend no more than an hour in one casino. But this should be a very flexible number. At some small "joints," fifteen minutes or a few large bets may be more appropriate. At some of the large Las Vegas Strip casinos where they have some tolerance of card counters, you may go past an hour especially if you walk from pit to pit. However, always keep in mind the size of your bets. If you are playing a shoe where you are using a large bet spread and have just made a series of large bets you probably want to cut your play short. These large bets will be a tipoff to the pit that your game may need some scrutiny. But if you are gone, they will frequently forget about your play and you will be welcomed back the next time you pay them a visit. One last thing to keep in mind when deciding whether to quit is whether you are winning or losing for that session. Since winners tend to get more scrutiny you should leave a little earlier if you are winning big, and you can extend your stay when losing.

How often should you visit a casino? Opinions vary. Ours is on the conservative side. At a large casino that is used to big action, you might be able to visit it several times in a week before you give it a rest. But at a small casino, once every couple of months should be plenty. (We could give some specific examples, except that casino conditions are always changing. Just remember that it is better to be safe than sorry.)

Another good point is that it is important not to play when the shift is changing in the pit. In a sense, each casino is really three casinos in one. Communication between shifts is not always that good. Thus, it is important that only one shift gets a look at you at a time. This will help to maximize your time at the tables.

As you can see, our view of blackjack requires a lot of leg work. Stay on the move. Go from casino to casino. Limit your time and be aware if you have made some big bets. Thus, if you are in a location where only a small number of casinos are available it would be more difficult for you to play blackjack for a living. However, it still would be worth doing as a supplement to your income. (Whether that be other gambling games or a "straight" job.) Then as little as one casino will do.

The best blackjack players that we know are well aware of these constraints. Thus many of them do a great deal of traveling. They spend some time in Las Vegas, then go to Atlantic City, and perhaps take a quick trip to Connecticut. Then they go to Mississippi and travel up the river. Next they return to Nevada where they make quick stops in Reno and Tahoe. Then they take a break. And then they begin the cycle again. This way they spread their action out and generally play unharrassed for many years.

Blackjack is very similar to the old fable of "the goose that layed the golden egg." If you try to squeeze too many eggs out of it, you will discover that your profitability is limited. But if you are willing to hit a lot of casinos for short time periods, making sure that you never get overexposed, you will be able to get a reasonable amount of time in at the tables. Just keep in mind that there is a cap as to how much you will be able to play. So again, if you are trying to gamble where there is only one place to play you wouldn't be able to do it as a full-time job. You could only supplement playing poker or poker machines, or whatever you are doing.

To finish this section, we want to say a few words about the subjects of getting barred and getting comps. If you play a lot of blackjack, it is inevitable that you will at some time be asked to leave by a casino. In fact, this will happen to you more than once. Our advice is to comply with what casino management wishes quickly. By staying and arguing, you will only imprint yourself on their memory. If you don't argue, you will probably be able to play again at that casino and even on that shift. (But you should probably stay out of there for at least a few months and frequently longer.) So just grab your chips and go.

As for comps, most high-rolling (and many low-rolling) tourists like to have their play "rated" so that they will be able to have a meal or see a show at no charge. Both authors have spent their share of time as a guest of a casino and can vouch that many of these comps are very enjoyable. On the other hand, "hustling" for comps will make the casino watch your play more closely. We are convinced that constantly getting yourself rated and then squeezing as much as possible out of a casino will only lead to more frequent barrings or a poorer game. If a host introduces himself and offers a meal or a show, you should, of course, accept if you like the invitation. But asking for a host and then demanding that he treat you right because you just played for thirty or forty minutes could prove to be very costly to you in the long run.

# Camouflage Plays

Suppose you think that you are being watched by the casino. You have a large bet out and are dealt a blackjack. Rather than your 3-to-2 payment you instead double down! Whether you win or lose you have just made a play that should convince the pit that you are not a threat. But, even if you are counting cards, if you make many plays like this often you can expect to go broke. So in general we do not like these types of "wild camouflage" plays. But there are a few plays that you can make which may alleviate fears that the pit may have and yet cost you very little.

For instance, it hardly costs anything to insure a blackjack. It does cost you something those times when you do it. But if it's part of your overall strategy and it get's the "heat" off you, it can be well worth it because it should only reduce your overall edge by a couple hundredths of a percent.[28] Other examples would be to always stand on soft 18 against a ten and to hit on a total of 12 against a dealer's four.

Another reason why these are good camouflage plays is that the opposite plays are the hallmark of a basic strategy player. They don't buy insurance, hit soft 18 against a ten, and stand with a 12 against a four. If you do the opposite, you won't cost yourself much, and you will more than offset your loss with increased longevity.

There are also a few mathematically correct plays that you should be reluctant to make, even when you have a large bet out. Splitting tens against a dealer's five or six would be the best example. Even though the count will sometimes call for it, a big bet followed by a split of tens versus five or six can, to an astute pit

---

[28] Part of the reason why this reduction is so low is that when counting cards there will be times when you have made a large bet and it will be correct to insure a blackjack. The main reason however is that the situation comes up so rarely.

boss, be a giveaway that you might be counting cards. To make this play, you must consider your risk versus the reward. Not doubling on a soft 20 against these same upcards would be another play that you should probably skip, even if the count says that it is correct to do so.

# One or Six Decks

One question that blackjack players constantly debate is whether you should be playing against hand-held games (which include single-deck) or against shoes. We feel that there is no reason why you have to stick to one or the other although the principles behind beating a one-deck game are a bit different than what you need to beat the shoes. When we say principles we are not referring to the underlying mathematics of the game, but more of the way that you approach the games on a day to day basis.

Many people will tell you that single-deck games are better. They point out that with the same rules the basic strategy player is at less of a disadvantage, and if you are counting, the deck will go favorable more often. Of course, this is true. But the shoes are actually very beatable also, because the casinos are not nearly as paranoid about them as they are about their single-deck games. (If this attitude ever changed and the casinos did become much more paranoid about their shoes, then they would no longer be worth playing.) They are beatable because the casinos will tolerate much larger bet spreads than they will in the hand-held games. And the fact is, if you are going to play shoes, you must use a large bet spread. Furthermore, if you do plan to beat shoes you should use some other techniques besides plain counting. These include joining a team and/or "backcounting" — standing behind the table and counting down the shoe while others play, entering the game only if the shoe becomes rich.[29]

Remember that against shoes you probably want to use a simplified count. (There are several reasons for this. First, it is a little harder to count down a shoe, and if you make a mistake you have that whole shoe to worry about. [If you do make a small

---

[29] Backcounting is also known as Wonging since it was Stanford Wong who first pointed out the value in playing this way. See his book *Blackjack Secrets* for more discussion.

mistake just pretend you didn't make it and keep on going.] With one deck if you do make a mistake they will soon be shuffling so you can afford a few more errors. Second, you must consider how important your strategy changes are. In a shoe, your main source of increasing your expectation above basic strategy comes from your bet spread. In a one-deck game it can be more advantageous to use a more complicated count because strategy changes can now add a lot. For instance, you can easily beat a deeply dealt one-deck game with no bet variation at all, and, in fact, if the rules are very good, the penetration doesn't need to be that great.[30] You would never be able to do this against a shoe.)

If you do play against one deck, you can definitely confine your bets to either one chip or two chips and still have a nice edge, as long as they deal halfway down. Against one deck you might want to use a more complicated count, or you may want to track some additional cards.

For instance, you may want to stick with the simple High-Low Count but also keep track of sevens, eights, and nines, either separately or all in a clump, because there will be situations that come up in single-deck games that are not handled well by the regular counts. For example, suppose you have a total of fifteen against a dealer's upcard of eight. Normally you would hit this hand. But the fact is that it can be very advantageous to stand if you know that there is a high proportion of sevens and eights in the deck because sevens and eights are much more important than nines and tens in this situation. (Notice that if there are an excess of sevens and eights left in the deck, then that is a reason to stand because they will bust you. It is also a reason to stand because the dealer might have one of them in the hole, which will give him a stiff that a seven or eight will now bust. So you can see that it is much more important to know the proportion of sevens and eights remaining

---

[30] At the time of this writing there is a casino just outside of Las Vegas that offers a single-deck game with double after split and surrender. A counter can easily beat this without ever changing his bet.

than it is to know high cards to low cards in this situation. Therefore, if you are going to play against the single deck you might want to get into ideas like this.[31] On the other hand, we need to warn you that keeping additional side counts is not easy, and it will take a lot of practice. But it can be done, and there is great benefit to mastering this technique.)

In spite of these advantages for one deck, the fact is, if you are going to be betting very large amounts of money, you will almost have to play the shoes. Most casinos are just too paranoid about their hand-held games to let you win a lot at one time. Against the shoes they will tolerate bigger bets and large bet spreads. If you do get lucky and win a lot quickly, it is much less likely to arouse suspicion or bring on serious scrutiny. The same cannot be said if you are playing against a single deck.

---

[31] See the chapter on "The Key Card Concept" in *Getting the Best of It* by David Sklansky.

# Preferential Shuffling

Preferential shuffling is a reverse card-counting procedure that an unethical casino can employ against unsuspecting players. The casino instructs their dealers to be aware of the cards that have been dealt and to shuffle accordingly. Specifically, they are told that if a lot of high cards appear early, (meaning that the deck is unfavorable to the player), they should deal an extra round. This forces the player to play against a deck where his expectation is more negative than it should be. On the other hand, if many small cards have appeared, meaning that the deck is now rich in high cards, the dealer would shuffle and a favorable situation would be lost.

There was a time when many casinos regularly practiced preferential shuffling. Hopefully, those times are now over. The casinos have learned that it is in their long-run best interests to shuffle fairly and deal an honest game. But unfortunately, preferential shuffling can also occur *unintentionally*.

How does this happen? One way is that a casino that offers a single-deck game frequently will instruct its dealers to deal out half a deck and then to shuffle. The typical dealer will now try to do this. However, she cannot deal out exactly twenty-six cards each time. Usually what happens is that after about half a deck is dealt, the dealer will decide whether another round should be played before it is necessary to shuffle. Consequently, the same number of rounds will not always be dealt between shuffles. If the first couple of rounds are made up of mostly high cards, which means that not as many cards as usual are needed, the dealer will be more inclined to deal an extra round, and this extra round will occur in a deck comprised of mainly small cards where your expectation is negative. But if a lot of small cards come out early, the dealer will then decide that there are probably not enough cards left to deal an extra round, and she will now proceed to shuffle away a favorable deck.

Notice that something awful has happened to anyone playing blackjack in this situation. Even though the casino is being honest and ethical, it may be preferentially shuffling and not even aware of it. Even more important is that this unintentional preferential shuffling might turn you into a long-run loser.

So what should you do? In a single-deck game where only about half the cards are being dealt, be conscious of the number of rounds that the dealer deals. If the same number of rounds are achieved between shuffles, there is probably no problem.[32] On the other hand, if the dealer deals to roughly the same point between shuffles but the number of rounds varies, then it may be best to find another game.

---

[32] The number of rounds is also dependent on the number of players at the table. If this number changes then the number of rounds will change as well. The only time this problem ought to go away completely is if you are playing head up.

# Team Play

Blackjack players will frequently band together to form what is known as a " team." A team is simply a group of players who pool their money together and play out of a joint bank. There are many aspects to team play, and we will discuss the ones that we consider to be most important.

Probably the most meaningful aspect of team play is that you can safely bet bigger. For example, suppose you have a playing bankroll of $20,000. Then using our 200-bet criteria your maximum bet should be in the neighborhood of $100.

$$\$100 = \frac{\$20,000}{200}$$

Now suppose you and four others each put up $20,000 for a total of $100,000. Now your maximum bet should be in the neighborhood of $500.[33]

$$\$500 = \frac{\$100,000}{200}$$

And this larger maximum bet applies to each of you. That is, you and all of your team mates will not only be able to bet fives times as much, but you will expect to earn five times as much. This is the main value of a team. For not that much money, you will be able to

---

[33] This is actually a slightly high number because two or more team members may be playing simultaneously.

bet as if you were a high roller and even with a positive expectation of less than 1 percent you will expect to do quite well.

There are several other advantages of team play. You will have other players to practice with and to plot strategy. There will be psychological support whenever you find yourself in the middle of a bad run. You may be able to coordinate your travel plans (with other team members). Your "paydays" can be more consistent since with many players, negative short-term results by any individual are usually erased by someone else. And, you may make some new friends.

But teams aren't necessarily quite as good as they sound. Most teams have personnel problems at one time or another. When the inevitable bad run occurs some members become suspicious that the losing team member is stealing. This can cause hard feelings and a great deal of stress. Teams tend to be only as strong as their weakest psychological link, and if you don't have confidence in your team members or they don't have confidence in you, don't expect the team to last.

Some teams have used polygraph tests in an effort to reassure everyone that all players on the team are reporting their results honestly. But it is our experience that these tests are not that reliable and we are aware of situations where lie detection results were inaccurate and caused teams to come apart. False positives do occur, and the skill levels of those individuals who administer these tests can vary widely. A polygraph test can only be as good as the person giving it.

In other words, for a team to be successful, you need to get to know your teammates well. Sometimes this takes some effort but it is well worth it. Try to work with knowledgeable people who have a legitimate bankroll. "Brokes" who claim to be expert players usually do not make good teammates. They frequently are that weak psychological link we just talked about.

Despite our criticisms, unless you have a great deal of money, team play is frequently the way to go. It allows you to bet much larger amounts without increasing your risk, and many of the best blackjack players on today's scene are involved with team play.

Finally, we want to mention one aspect of team play which has at one time or another received a great deal of publicity in the world of blackjack. It is what is known as the "big player" concept. A big player is someone who "wanders" around a casino and appears to occasionally stop at a table where he proceeds to make a few large bets. In reality, he is being called into the game by a teammate who is already playing at that table and counting cards. There was a time when this idea took down a lot of money, but today casinos are usually aware of it and closely scrutinize anyone who plays in this manner. A good discussion of the big player concept appears in Ken Uston's book *Million Dollar Blackjack.*

# Other Ways to Beat Blackjack

So far we have talked about basic strategy and card counting, but there are other ways to beat blackjack. Some of these methods are extensions of card counting, whereas others are unique unto themselves. What follows is a brief discussion of each one.

**Technique No. 1: Dealer tells.** After the dealer looks under his hole card when he has an ace or a ten up (in those casinos which still look under their hole cards), he now has knowledge of his hand. By getting the dealer involved in your play, either positively (he likes you) or negatively (he hates you), you can get additional information based on his mannerisms which will help you play your hand. Specifically, the dealer may "tell" you if it is correct to hit or stand.

Now, dealer tells are not easy to master. But a few years ago, a book called *Read the Dealer* written by gambling expert Steve Forte appeared, and it is the definitive work on this subject. We need to give you one caution however. Even though the techniques in this text are quite powerful, they are probably not for everyone, since it is quite easy to "see" tells because you want to rather than because they are really there.

**Technique No. 2: Ace tracking.** This technique will help you predict when the aces will appear. The idea is to memorize the exact order of a few cards that are placed in the discard pile before an ace. For example, suppose that an 8♦, 4♣, and 6♠ are placed in the discard pile before an A♥. If the shuffle is simple enough, and you see the first couple of cards in this sequence during a round of play, but the A♥ does not appear, then it will probably come out on the next round. Knowing this can give you a significant edge over the house, and an expert ace tracker, under ideal conditions, can actually do better than an expert card counter. However, notice that we said under ideal conditions. Not only is this technique very difficult to master, there are not many casinos that use a shuffle simple enough for ace tracking to be applied.

**Technique No. 3: Shuffle tracking.** Again, if a casino uses a simple shuffle it is sometimes possible to follow a clump of high or low cards through the shuffle. When that is the case, you cut this clump to either the top or bottom — whichever is appropriate, and adjust your count accordingly. A terrific discussion of shuffle tracking appeared in the September and December 1994, and March 1995 issues of Arnold Snyder's *Blackjack Forum* magazine.

**Technique No. 4: Playing the warps.** In a casino that still checks under aces and tens to see if the dealer has made blackjack, the big cards will sometimes become slightly bent if the casino leaves the decks in play for a long time. This will have the effect of bending the aces and tens the opposite way from which the small cards will be bent. A skillful player can then use this information to his advantage, especially in insurance situations. However, most casinos have learned not to leave their cards in play for too long, and there are not many opportunities left to make this play.

**Note:** The next three techniques all come under the general heading of hole card play. That is, you are trying to read the dealer's hole card either before or at the same time that the dealer gets to see it. Needless to say, this information is very powerful, and your edge over the casino is quite large.

**Technique No. 5: Spooking.** Spooking is reading the dealer's hole card from the rear as the dealer checks to see if he has blackjack. The "spook" is usually situated at a table (and playing blackjack himself) behind the dealer whose hole cards he is looking at. The spook then gets to see the hole card at the same time the dealer does. (Remember, the dealer who is being spooked is not the dealer at the spook's table.) After the information is obtained, the spook then signals his partner what the hole card is, and his partner now plays his hand appropriately.

It may seem to some of you that spooking is a form of cheating, and in some localities it may be considered to be just that. We advise that if spooking is something that you want to pursue, make sure that you know precisely what the law is in the area in which you plan to play.

**Technique No. 6: First basing.** First basing is the art of seeing the dealer's hole card at the same time the dealer sees it. Sometimes, if the dealer does not employ good (dealing) procedures, you can see his hole card if you are standing far to the right when the dealer checks to see if he has made a blackjack. The advantage of first basing, as opposed to spooking, is that a second person is not needed to read what the dealer has. On the other hand, more dealers are spookable than are vulnerable to first basing, but dealers against whom you can use this technique do come along every now and then.

**Technique No. 7: Front loading.** This is by far the most effective way to beat blackjack, but it is only effective in a hand-held game. Front loading is the art of seeing the dealer's hole card before the dealer has finished setting it on the table. Due to faulty dealing procedures, some dealer's will quickly flash the card allowing someone with a "fast eye" to get a glimpse of it. There are five distinct types of front loaders, and depending on the type you happen to be up against, the position at the table from which you can see the flash will be different.

Knowing the dealer's hole card is a gigantic advantage that dramatically affects the correct playing strategy. Basically, if the dealer holds a strong hand, hit all your weaker hands and do not double down or split anything. If the dealer holds a stiff, make sure you do not bust, and remember to split and double down on everything that you can. The mere fact that your insurance decisions will always be right is worth 2½ percent. However, also make sure that you do not make any plays that will give you away. An obvious example would be to hit a total of 19 when the dealer holds a total of 20. (The house might not suspect you of taking advantage of a front loader, but it definitely would suspect you of taking advantage of something.)[34] Front loaders are not as common as they once were due to improved casino procedures, but they can still occasionally be found. Again, this is easily the most powerful technique discussed since you will *always* have knowledge of the dealer's hole card, not just those times when he checks to see if he has made a blackjack. Also, because of the different strategy that you will use, having knowledge of the dealer's hole card will make your play look strange to anyone observing you. In fact, unless the pit recognizes that you might be front loading, they will think that you are an awful player.

The best discussion of front loading, where the five different types of front loaders are described, appears in *Blackjack Essays* by Mason Malmuth. But don't expect to learn this technique overnight. It takes a great deal of practice.

**Special note:** For those of you who think using some of the above techniques are unethical — even if they are not illegal — we won't quarrel with that viewpoint. Our personal stance is that casinos that treat their customers fairly and honestly rather than like "suckers to be fleeced" probably don't deserve to be taken advantage of in this way. We don't feel this charitable to all casinos, however. A good test might be to see how casinos treat their obviously drunk patrons. If they try to take advantage of that weakness, we have no qualms about taking advantage of theirs.

---

[34] A detailed discussion of front loading playing strategy can be found in Ken Uston's book, *Million Dollar Blackjack*.

# Double Exposure Blackjack

To be complete we want to mention double exposure blackjack. This is a form of blackjack where both dealer cards are dealt face up. The catch is that the dealer wins all ties, and you are only paid even money on blackjack. (The one exception is that if both you and the dealer have blackjack, you win.)

Double exposure achieved a fair amount of popularity in the early 1980s, but most of the games have died out. However, it is still played in a small number of places and seems to have an occasional resurgence.

Basic strategy for double exposure is actually more complicated than what it is for standard blackjack. Because of that we won't give it here. But like standard blackjack, with correct basic strategy, double exposure is essentially an even game. However, double exposure does have one advantage over standard blackjack in that the removal of cards from the deck have more of an impact than they do in standard blackjack. Thus counting is even more effective.

An excellent write-up of both appropriate basic strategy and card counting for double exposure appear in Stanford Wong's book *Professional Blackjack*.

# In Closing

As you can see blackjack is a very beatable game, and there are many ways to beat it. But for most people, standard card counting is the way to go. You can make a very good living playing blackjack, and a small number of people do just that. As we have stressed many times, however, it can also be quite frustrating.

Both authors of this text have played a great deal of serious blackjack, and we can testify that it is not easy. You must be able to play perfectly, and you must be able to play quickly and make it look natural. To beat blackjack in today's casino environment takes a lot of work, and anyone who undertakes this endeavor needs a complete and well-thought-out strategy. This section will get you started on the correct path to winning play.

We also recommend that the aspiring player read and research the current literature as much as possible. Unlike some other forms of gambling, there are many good blackjack books available. Some of these were mentioned in the text, and others are listed in the recommended reading at the back of this book.

But don't forget to play as well as read. True winning blackjack is a balance between study, good counting and playing technique, a good casino "act," and practical experience. Be patient, and slowly you can become a winning player. Don't expect to become a top player overnight. It takes time and dedication, but it is worth it.

# Part Two

# Betting Sports

# Betting Sports

# Introduction

Later on we say that the most popular form of *casino* gambling is slot machines. However, we believe the most popular form of gambling in general is sports betting. Whether it's a small bet between two friends, an office pool, a bet with the "neighborhood bookie," or a bet in a casino sports book, virtually everyone has at one time or another made a bet on their favorite team.

But can you bet sports for long-term profit? Is it possible to get the best of it at this game? Many people don't think so. They point out that the bookie's usual edge of 4.54 percent is a very difficult percentage to overcome. To support this argument they point to some of the casino games such as craps and baccarat that have a much smaller house vig and which are unbeatable. It turns out, however, that they are wrong. First of all, odds on a sporting event are a matter of opinion, unlike craps or baccarat. Secondly, sports like the horses is a "no ante game." That is, you only have to bet on those situations where you have an edge. These edges do occur, and they occur often enough that an astute person who is willing to work hard enough can make a good living. In fact, the most successful gamblers are the big sports bettors.

There is an obvious reason for this. Sports betting is the only "game" where you can increase your bets in proportion to your bankroll and still have virtually the same edge. You can't do this at the racetrack without dropping your odds. Increase your bet size in blackjack and expect more "heat" and a less profitable game. Move up to bigger stakes in poker and you run into other pros who will cut down your potential win rate dramatically. In the case of slots, promotions, and tournaments the prizes usually stay fixed regardless of your ability to gamble higher. Such is not the case in sports (unless you are betting such huge amounts of money that you move the line; in Vegas this would take about $50,000 per game if you spread your bets around).

So if you really do learn to beat sports, do your homework, watch as many games as you can, keep records, and treat it like a business, you can forget about that measly $100,000 a year we promised you. In sports, the sky's the limit.

# You Don't Have to Bet

It's important to understand that the line (sometimes called the "Pointspread") that the bookie puts up is usually "correct."[35] When this is the case, you shouldn't make a bet. Since you normally have to lay $110 to win $100, the line must be significantly "off" for your bet to be profitable. If you bet lots of games where the bookie's line is approximately right, you will slowly lose your money no matter how knowledgeable you happen to be.

Fortunately, you don't have to make a bet. The fact that there might be a mathematical edge against you if you bet *all* the games isn't a big deal if you are able to restrict yourself to only those games where you have reason to believe that the bookie's line is wrong. *That is, don't make bets just to make bets.* Once again, you must understand that there is no guarantee that there is a good bet on any particular game. You must remember that the line is usually correct, and if the line is right, neither side of a bet is a good bet.

It may seem that we are putting a lot of emphasis on something that should be obvious. Of course you shouldn't make bad bets. Everyone knows that. But it is our experience that the desire to be in action and "sweat" the games is what undoes most potential sports bettors. The experts, on the other hand, will pass on most games. On some days, they may not bet at all.

---

[35] When we say that the bookie's line is correct we mean that it has reflected the true odds of the game in this particular situation. That is, if the game could somehow be played many times over, the luck involved in the sport would be such that a gambler who bet *either* team (laying 11-to-10 each time) would be losing. The correct line does *not* mean a line that will get equal action on both sides even though this is what bookies usually strive for. (It would be better for them if they stuck with the correct line.) *A correct line cannot be beaten.* A sufficiently incorrect line (including some that do in fact split the action) can.

For there to be a good bet the line has to be off more than just a little bit. If we are talking football or basketball, the line normally needs to be off by at least two points. If we are talking baseball the line would have to be off by 20 or 30 cents.[36] If the line the bookie puts up is within that distance from the theoretically correct line, *you have no bet.*

---

[36] If you are not sure as to what we mean when we say 2 points or 20 or 30 cents we recommend that you read the chapter entitled "The Mathematics of Sports Betting" in *Getting the Best of It* by David Sklansky.

# Why the Line May Be Off

As we said, the bookie's line needs to be off by a fair amount for any bet to be profitable. You might think this will only happen on very rare occasions, but that is not the case. There are many situations where the bookie's line is inaccurate, and a good bet is available. Here are some examples and the reasons behind them:

First, the line may be off when the bookie has misevaluated at least one of the teams playing. He may have underrated it, producing a bet on it, or he's overrated it producing a bet against it. You may know this simply because you know your sports.

This isn't something that we can discuss in detail because, as just stated, it is a matter of knowing your sport and your team. But it is possible for you to know some things better than the bookie does. On the other hand, you should be hesitant to really believe that you are more of an expert than the bookie. In general, bookies have access to a lot of information, and they ought to know how good a team is at least as well as you do. When they don't, it is more likely to occur in obscure college basketball games or sometimes in a college football game.

But there are other reasons why the bookie's line may be off. The second reason has to do with how the public evaluates a team. It may be that the line is off not because the bookie misevaluates a game but rather the public does.

One weakness that bookies frequently exhibit is that they become obsessed with balancing their books so they will get approximately equal action on both sides of a bet (and thus guarantee a profit no matter who wins). Because they do this they allow the public money to influence their line, and sometimes their eventual betting line will be something that they themselves don't believe is correct. But unlike the rest of us, most bookies don't want to gamble on their opinions. They would rather balance their books.

So this is one time when you may use your skills to find a line that is wrong because of the fact that the *public* might not know what they are doing. What's interesting is that bookies will be aware that they are offering a good bet, but they won't care as long as their books remain balanced.

The third reason the line may be off is related to the method that is usually used to calculate lines. In general — at least in the case of basketball and football — every team is given a numerical rating known as a "power rating." When two teams play against each other the rating of one team is subtracted from the rating of the other team. Then an adjustment is made to account for the home team advantage. Thus the line is produced.

For example, if one team is rated 103 and another team is rated 95 that would make the 103 team an 8-point favorite on a neutral court.

$$8 = 103 - 95$$

Next an adjustment is made for the home court. This adjustment will vary depending on the sport and what kind of home court they have. For instance, if it is a professional basketball game where 4 points is typically the home court advantage, the 103 team becomes a 12-point favorite if they are at home, but would be only a 4-point favorite if they are on the road.

This method usually works reasonably well. But flaws do develop in some cases. And occasionally lines will be offered that are off by the required two or more points to make it a good bet.[37]

One important flaw in the power rating system of developing lines is that it does not take psychological factors into account. It may turn out that a particular game may deserve to have a point

---

[37] Though you normally need the line to be off by at least 2 points for a bet to be profitable, it doesn't need to be that much if a frequently hit number such as 3 or 7 in football is involved. For example, if the correct line is 6 and the bookie posts 7½, you probably have a good bet on the underdog, taking the points.

spread quite a bit different from what the power ratings would imply. Usually these situations come up when one team is "fired up" for the game and the other team isn't. When this occurs, it is frequently worthwhile to bet on the team that you can deduce (or feel) is hyped. (The major exception to this concept occurs when there is large disparity in talent. Extra adrenaline can only change outcomes when the innate talent is close. *For this and other reasons it is rarely correct to bet the underdog when the point spread is very high.*)

There are at least three examples of automatic type bets that take advantage of this situation. One occurs in college basketball when a top ten team is on the road playing a team that's not too bad but isn't quite good enough to make the national rankings. Typically the top ten team is favored by a few points. Historically, the underdog home team has done very well in these cases. The principle that makes it work is the fact that the favorite doesn't really expect a particularly tough game because they are quite a bit better. But they are not completely in a different class. Meanwhile, the home team is sky high to make a mark at home by beating a nationally ranked team. If the line is under 10 take the points.[38]

Another automatic bet that takes advantage of this syndrome occurs in the NBA playoffs where in a best of seven series two games are played at one team's court and then the next two games are on the other team's court. If the home team has won their first two games (meaning that they lead the series two games to nothing), you should bet against them when they become the visiting team.

---

[38] These bets were originally discussed in *Getting the Best of It* by David Sklansky. The fact that twenty-five teams are now ranked rather than twenty as was true in the past may have an impact on the strength of this bet. So check it out before betting. Of course, there is no guarantee that any automatic type bet that has shown a profit *in the past* will continue to do so. There is always the chance that the bookie will get wise and adjust the line. (Unfortunately the existence of this book may increase that chance.)

That is, you want to bet that the team behind will make the series two-to-one.[39]

Again, the principle is that the team that is up two-to-nothing has a slight psychological letdown, and the other team, which has its back against the wall, is fired up in front of their home fans. Historically, this bet has done much better than 50 percent. This is true even if you are laying the points (and they usually will be the favorite). One warning, however: Bookies have become wise to this situation and now usually adjust the line a couple of points, so it is not as strong as it once was.

A third example of an almost automatic bet occurs in professional football where a team that has not been in contention for the Superbowl or the playoffs, starts off their year winning their first two games and then in their third game they play a team that was much better than them the previous year. Usually, they will be so hyped up (and the other team relatively complacent) that they are a good bet. This is especially true if they are playing a team that has also won their first two games, and the bet is even better if they are at home and are a small dog. That is, it is frequently worthwhile to make bets the third or fourth game of the year where an undefeated team is playing another undefeated team but one of the teams is a surprise, at home, but still a couple of points underdog.[40]

---

[39] Again, the exception occurs when there is a very large talent discrepancy.

[40] There is a situation that comes up at the end of the year that is almost the exact converse. We are speaking of pro football playoffs. With the game as important as it is, the favorite never takes the game lightly and thus always plays its best even when it knows it is the better team. Furthermore, it is not nearly as apt to let up even when it has a comfortable lead. This is very important. Many times during the regular season a team that could win by 14 points if it had to, wins by less because it gives up a last-minute score when virtually assured of a win. Bookies take this into account and put up a line of 10 or 11 rather that the aforementioned 14. However in the

Here's our final example of a psychological situation that sometimes occurs at the end of the college football season where most teams play eleven games. If one team has a record of five and five, winning or losing this last game may make a big difference in their season, especially if the team was not expected to have a winning season before the year began. This team will usually be up for the game. If they are against a better team with a winning record, but one that does not completely outclass them, the bet will be even better. If the superior team is looking ahead to a minor bowl they may come out flat, and the bet is better still. And, of course, you would like the team with the five and five record to be a small home dog.[41] [42]

Now we recognize that these automatic plays are not enough to keep you in good bets. Therefore it is important to develop an instinctive feel for other similar situations. That is, from a psychological point of view, you must be able to put yourself in the

---

playoffs, they *will* put up 14. Many bettors will take the points knowing that same matchup would have had a lower point spread during the season. They think the higher line is simply caused by unknowledgeable fans betting the favorite. We think that they are wrong and that we gave the real reason for the inflated line. So don't be so fast to jump on those few extra points.

[41] A classic example of this bet occurred at the end of the 1990 college football season. Virginia Tech, with a 5-5 record, was playing their archrival Virginia, currently 8-2. Virginia Tech was at home, they were a small dog, the game was on national TV, and their third year coach, Frank Beamer, who had only won four games the two previous seasons, needed to win to be sure that he would keep his job. Needless to say, the (Va Tech) Hokies were an easy winner.

[42] If the team was expected to do much better than just break even, then they may view their season as already ruined, and not be up for the game.

place of these teams. In other words, if you can feel the adrenaline running, the players on a particular team will also have the same type of intensity. However, keep in mind that this only works for basketball and football where adrenaline intensity counts a lot. It doesn't mean as much in baseball where pure skill rather than strength and speed is the greater factor.

Another reason why the point spread may be wrong when it is based solely on power ratings has to do with a more in depth knowledge of the teams. Specifically, you have to realize that most sports are not like weightlifting. If Person A can lift 20 more pounds than Person B and Person B can lift 30 more pounds than Person C, then A is obviously a 50-pound favorite over C. But the same is not necessarily true in sports. Power ratings, however, incorrectly imply that this is the case.

The fact is, in sports like football or basketball you might even have a situation where Team A is favored over Team B and Team B is favored over Team C but C should be favored over A! Though that situation is rare it *is* common where A is a 5-point favorite over B and B is a 5-point favorite over C, but A should only be a 6-point favorite over C. There are many different reasons why this could be true. If you really understand your teams and where their strengths and weaknesses lie, you should be able to spot these situations. (If you can spot them in conjunction with psychological situations you might have really found a great bet!)

Some of the best examples of the above concept involve teams that are very good mainly because they have a good defense, or in the case of baseball, a good pitcher. When a team has a good defense (or a good pitcher), this strength, which on average is worth X points, is worth even more when they are up against a team that features a normally high-scoring offense that they are good at defending against. In other words, a very good defensive team would find itself even more valuable in comparison to its power ratings when playing a good offensive team and should be bet on if the bookie hasn't adjusted from the pure power rating line.

The opposite is also true. Ironically, a good defensive team when it is playing a lousy offensive team might very well be overrated as far as the power ratings are concerned. For instance, to take an extreme example, suppose there is a football team that is known to reduce their opponents normal score by an average of 20 points. Now they are playing a team that doesn't even score 10 points per game. In this case their strength, which has been worth 20 points in the past, *can't* be worth 20 points. At best it can be worth 10 points. Thus you should probably bet against them. When a great defensive team is playing a team not known for its offensive ability, you should usually bet the weaker team. Similarly, if you have a great pitcher against a weak hitting team, betting on the favorite is probably a very bad bet especially given the big odds that you would probably have to lay. Bet the underdog or not at all.

The matchup concept doesn't always have to involve the whole team. If you have a team where one or two of its players are great defensive players and they are being matched up against a team where they will be defending against non-offensive type players, again that defensive team might be overrated because of these matchups in the sense that the technique of just adding and subtracting power ratings will give you incorrect results. (We suspect it would have been right to take the points against the great Boston Celtics years ago when they were playing a team with a low-scoring center. Since Bill Russell's biggest contribution was his defense, he wouldn't have helped his team as much as usual in these situations.)

An example from football might occur when a team has a couple of great pass rushers who are very good at getting to the quarterback. If they are playing a team that doesn't throw much, then this edge is frequently negated, and a good bet may appear on the nonpassing team.

As you become more experienced you should get better at recognizing these situations. However, we need to mention two things. First, as previously stated, these bets become stronger when you can couple a favorable matchup with a favorable psychological situation. Second, and more importantly, make sure you are evaluating the situation correctly. The desire to be in action has been the downfall of many potential sports bettors.

# Other Ways of
# Finding Good Bets

So far we have mainly been discussing those times when the point spread might have been incorrectly calculated due to a reliance on power ratings. But there are other reasons why a line may be wrong and you therefore have a good bet. One example is when the results of the last few games may have been fluky. When a team wins, its power rating is generally increased a little bit, when it loses its rating is usually dropped by a small amount. Thus, when a team is on a streak, its power rating may be inaccurate.

For instance, suppose a basketball team wins most of their early season games but you notice that they have been hitting 50 percent of their three-point shots. Even though they are playing great, you also know that no team can maintain that type of shooting percentage. Thus, you might be able to bet against this team because the bookies may not be taking this into account. They may only be looking at the win/loss record of this team and may have overrated it.

Similarly, if a football team has been losing because of devastating fumbles, you may find that it is being underrated. Again, this is because most people are only looking at its win/loss record and are not considering how they lost the games. Remember, even if the bookies don't get confused by this, the public is very apt to, and since bookies move lines according to the action they receive, they may wind up at the end of the week with a line that is advantageous (to you).

In fact, in professional sports — especially professional football — if a line moves from the beginning of the week to the end of the week it is probably better to bet *against* the move. This is not necessarily true in college sports where a line moving might indicate a sharp bettor who has information that most people don't have. But since information is so well known in pro sports, when a line moves you probably should bet against the move if you are going to bet the game at all. In other words, when betting the pros, you want to bet against the public and simply take the extra couple of points that is now available to you.

For example, suppose the Dallas Cowboys open up as a 2-point favorite over their arch rival San Francisco. If, by the end of the week, the line has moved to 4 making the Forty-Niners a bigger underdog, you should consider betting San Francisco. In the NFL the opening lines are generally correct, but the public will often overbet one of the sides.[43]

This brings up the idea of the "trap" game. The trap occurs when you see what appears to be an odd line, different from what you expected the public would make a particular game, and where therefore it seems that there is an obvious way to bet. If you are going to bet at all you should bet the opposite way.

The trap game is analogous to the situation in horse racing where the odds themselves are related to the odds of the horse race. If there is a strange number and it seems like the public will be betting in one direction, yet the bookies are keeping that strange number up there, it is either because they have a strong reason to believe that the other direction is a good bet or because there are

---

[43] This is a common occurrence when one team is a small favorite (1 to 4 points). The public discounts the mathematical importance of a point or two and is apt to drive the line up while saying to its collective self something like "Well, if I think the team will win what do I care if I lay 3 rather than 2 points." So a 2-point favorite turns into a 3½-point favorite. If you were leaning at all toward taking the 2 points you *must* take 3½. In the long run this is almost a 10 percent edge purely for mathematical reasons. You can probably win money just hanging around a sports book before the games start as there will often be a last-minute rise on the point spread of small favorites. This is especially true of TV games. Automatically taking the (inflated) points in this spot would probably result in a small profit even if you had no other insights to help you decide whether to bet.

some very big bettors who are betting the other way. Either explanation should tell us to bet the nonobvious way if we bet at all. You must always keep in mind that bookies don't like to gamble. Generally they want equal action on both sides. But occasionally a line will appear where it is apparent that the books won't get equal action on both sides. (This is especially true for illegal hometown bookies). The most likely justification for this line is that the books have a strong suspicion that the majority of money will be bet on the side that will lose. When this is the case, if you are going to bet, bet against the public.

# Looking at the
# Past (Carefully)

Some profitable bets fall into general categories. For instance, it may be that a pro basketball team that plays three consecutive days on the road will only cover the spread 42 percent of those third games. It may be that a pro football team will cover 57 percent of its games after it has lost by 30 or more the previous week. Super Bowl winners may be good to bet against the *second* game of the following year.

At this moment we have no idea whether any of the above is true. The three statements are all plausible but it would be silly to run out and bet money on them. The far better thing to do would be to *check them out.* In other words, check out a betting theory's performance in the past. That will take a bit of work since you need not only past scores but also point spreads. But it must be done.

As a professional sports better you ought to be finding good bets through many routes. One might involve insight for a particular game only. Another route would involve finding discrepancies in the line. A third way is to take advantage of situational bets like the ones mentioned in this chapter or others that you know about. Many bets will involve a combination of these three routes. The fourth route to a good bet should come from your research into the past.

There is almost no doubt that there are general recurring situations that affect outcomes of games in ways the bookie doesn't know about. Some may be stronger than the ones mentioned in this chapter. In fact they are almost certainly stronger if they have not been put into print. It is your job to find them (and keep the information to yourself).

But there is a problem. And it could be a big one. So read carefully.

In a nutshell it's this: If you look at past data in enough different ways you are bound to find patterns that indicate good bets but are actually worthless. For example, suppose a certain situation has arisen in the past where the favorite covered 16 out of 20 times. The chances that this would happen by luck alone is about 1 out of 150. Is this strong evidence that you have found a good bet? Maybe, maybe not. There are two other factors involved. One is how many other patterns have you looked at. If you have already checked out 200 scenarios and this is the first one that looked promising your results were irrelevant. After all with 200 samples it should be expected that one of them would be lucky enough to have a 150-to-1 shot come in. (Had the bet gone 18 and 2 that would have been a different story.)

The other factor has to do with whether or not the plausibility of the pattern you found is really meaningful. If you found that certain underdogs are good bets on leap years we would be skeptical even if the sample results were 1,000-to-1 to occur this way by chance. (On the other hand if you get outlandish results such as 50 wins and 6 losses we would have to seriously consider that there was something about leap years that correlated to [if not caused] this result.)

The bottom line is this: When you find a pattern that has shown a nice profit against the bookie in the past you need to put it into one of three categories and act accordingly.
1. If you have come up with a plausible theory based on your insight (or someone else's) and you now go check into past results, moderately strong confirmation may be good enough. In other words if the winning results of the past could only happen by chance 1 percent of the time you probably have something.
2. If you (or a computer) have simply been checking through a large number of scenarios and finally find one that shows a profit you must be skeptical of what you have found. Without trying to be precise we will say that you can't put much stock in this newfound system unless it is both plausible and the results from the past would happen very rarely due to chance alone.

3.  If the winning scenario from the past makes little sense at all (teams wearing red uniforms beat the spread on Wednesday) the situation from the past would be such that these occurences by chance would be in the millions-to-1 before you would start taking it seriously.

When you do find a pattern that indicates a good betting situation it may be wise, especially in marginal situations, to watch for the same situation in the future without betting on it. Of course, whether you start betting it right away or not, you need to put these new games in your data base to see whether you have truly added one more good betting situation into your arsenal.

Note: There is some difficult math involved in evaluating the probability of results occurring by chance. Some of it is covered in *Getting the Best of It* by David Sklansky, but to be fully informed you need a basic statistics book.

# Half-Time Bets

Another opportunity for making money at sports involves what is known as half-time bets. These are bets on the outcome of the second half only. They have become very popular in recent years, especially in the sports books of Nevada. They work like this: The bookie will put a line on most TV games as soon as the first half ends. So you have about twenty minutes to make a decision.

There are two reasons why half-time lines can be easy to beat if you know your sports. The first is that the bookies have to make the line on the spur of the moment. They don't have access to the normal amount of research, and while they do have experts coming up with that line, you may have noticed something while watching the game that those experts didn't.

The second reason why the half-time line could be profitable has to do with the fact that, as usual, the bookies are out to balance their books and thus normally try to put out a number that they think will get equal action. There will be many times when the bookie will *not* put up what he thinks is the proper line. He will put up the line that he thinks will split the action. And for half-time bets that line could be far different from the true line. This is the case because there are prospective hedgers out there who have made a bet on the game and now want to guarantee a profit on the bet.

To understand, let's look at an example. Suppose Team A is a 10-point favorite over Team B and at the half the score is B 10 and A 3. The people who have bet on B are in great shape, but they still could conceivably lose. At this point the book might post a half-time line making Team A somewhere around a 7-point favorite (for the second half only). There are a few reasons for this. Presumably Team A is still the better team. If the 10-point line is right it would seem that the half-time line should be about 5. The fact that team A needs to win the second half by more than 5 to win the game could be a justification for making the line higher. But the biggest reason the half-time number is 7 could well be because the books know higher. But the biggest reason the half-time number is 7 could well be because the books know that they will get action on Team A from those who bet on Team B at the beginning of the game! This is because some players will think that it is smart to "hedge." By betting the opposite way at the half they can cut down their loss to almost nothing regardless of the outcome. At the same time they will win both bets if Team A wins the second half by more than 7 and less than 17.

The above scenario might indicate a profitable bet for you because there are times when Team A deserves to be nowhere near a 7-point favorite. After all, they were outplayed in the first half. An astute game watcher should be able to tell when this is the case.

So what do you do? The answer should be obvious. You seriously consider betting Team B. The bookie puts up a number knowing that even though the number may be wrong he's going to get a lot of people hedging to ensure a profit. You bet the opposite way of the hedgers because the number has been inflated to charge the hedgers a maximum amount.[44]

---

[44] Needless to say *you* should never make bets just to hedge a previous bet. The side you bet on a half-time bet should never have any relation to where you stand on previous bets on the game. If you spot a good half-time bet you make it regardless if you're betting the same way as before the game or not.

# Mathematical Bets

In places such as Las Vegas where there are many sport books to choose from, there are going to be games where the player is not bucking a house edge. This is because various bookies will not all have the same line. (Even if they do at first, the betting action may change that by the end of the week.) Thus a football team that is a 2-point favorite may become a 3-point favorite by the end of the week at one book but still be a 2-point favorite at another book. Thus, you can lay 2 points if you like the favorite or take 3 if you like the dog which easily makes up for the 11-to-10 "vig."

In baseball, if you take the best price you can lay on the favorite and the best price you can take on the underdog you might even be able to make money at no risk. Suppose one book has the favorite -$1.40 and the underdog +1.30, and some other book has the favorite -$1.55 and the underdog +$1.45. Then that means you can lay $1.40 and take $1.45. Notice that you cannot lose with this bet if you bet your money on both sides in the right proportions.

Figuring out that optimal mathematical bet is difficult to do. But if you take the midpoint of the two figures and lay that on the favorite while laying 1 unit on the dog you will be betting approximately the correct amount on each side to guarantee a profit. For example, if your unit bet is $100 you would lay $142.50 on the favorite and $100 on the dog. You will win $1.79 if the favorite wins and $2.50 if the dog wins.

In the case of football or basketball, purely mathematical bets will occur if one bookie's line differs from another bookie's line by approximately 2 points. It could be as little as 1½ points if the number involved is an often hit number such as 3 or 7 (in football). The idea is to bet both ways. These bets are known as "middles."

Certainly a 2-point middle such as laying 5½ and getting 7½ in football would clearly be a profitable bet. If you take both sides of this bet you are getting 20-to-1 odds that it comes in 6 or 7. If you lay $110 on both sides you either win $200 or lose $10.

But betting a middle might not be as good as betting just one side. Though a middle figures to have a positive expectation, sometimes only one of the two bets really has the best of it. If you feel you are a good enough handicapper that you know which is the good bet and which isn't, you might not want to bet the middle but rather bet one side only. So if there are lines of 5½ points and 7½ points and you think that 5 is the correct number then you might just go ahead and take only the 7½ rather than both lay the 5½ and take the 7½. This way you won't make both a good bet and a bad bet in order to hit the middle (even though the middle *combination* is a good bet.) You'll theoretically earn more if you put the same amount of (total) money on just the one side that you like.

However, there's a problem with this. *Are* you going to put the same amount of total money on it? Because of the size of your bankroll, you may not want to gamble it all on one side. But you certainly can afford to put that same total amount on both sides. For instance, if you have $1100 to your name and are trying to decide whether to take the 7½ for $1100 or take both sides of the bet for $550, the answer is simple. You cannot afford to risk it all on one bet. But you can afford to put it all on both sides of the bet. When the game is over, even if you lose — that is, you didn't hit the middle — you only lose $50, not $1100.

So the bottom line is when you find a bookie's line out of whack, what you do depends on your bankroll and your knowledge of the game. Going for a middle can never be that bad.[45] It is only when you can easily afford the bookie's limit and you know which side to take that you should bet one side only.

There is one point that must be stressed: Even if you are a great handicapper you should always have the math working for you. Just as in horse racing, if you like a horse, you shouldn't always bet it to

---

[45] If you are trying to catch middles in Nevada, you must be quick. You may need some partners with cellular phones. This is because when the point spread gets out of line between two bookies someone usually jumps on it right away. This is less true if at least one of your bookies is not in Nevada. Now the problem is the law.

win. You might be better off putting it on top in an exacta if the average price is going to be higher, or betting it in the place or show pool. By the same token, if you like a team you should always take that team with the best possible odds or point spread, keeping in mind that 1 point will come up approximately 3 percent of the time.[46] That is, the additional point whether you get it or no longer have to lay it, will increase your chances of being successful, since it will sometimes make the difference between winning, (or tying), and losing. Thus, it obviously goes without saying that no matter how great a handicapper you are, you make an effort to get the best number.

---

[46] Understand that winning 3 percent more often is a 6 percent edge. If you win a coin flip for a dollar 53 percent of the time, you will be ahead $6 after a hundred flips.

# Totals

Also known as *over/under* bets, the idea is to bet whether a particular game will go over or under a certain total score. The bookie, of course, comes up with this number. As in regular point spreads the line can move. And, as in regular point spreads the line can be wrong. Once again, the bookie's desire to balance the action can be the reason behind an incorrect line. His lack of knowledge about the game is another.

But there are a couple of problems with betting on totals. First, it is unlikely that you will have insights that the bookie doesn't have. The mathematical principle for a correct total line now seems to be well understood. This, of course, allows for fewer good bets.

The second problem is potentially more serious: The total score for football and, to a lesser extent basketball can easily be manipulated. For instance, how often the two teams will be passing rather than running is the single most important factor regarding whether a football total will go over or under. If someone with inside information is betting a total the opposite way as you, we like his side.

That being said, the fact is that there are people who beat totals. They do this by taking into account weather, matchups, and other factors that we frankly are not fully conversant with. We do know, however, their edge has decreased over the years as bookies have smartened up.

There is one piece of information about over/unders that we can give you that you might turn into money. It concerns middles. The discrepancy that you must find to have a good bet is no more than it would be for a regular point spread. This surprising statement stems from the fact that the standard deviation of the *sum* of two independent random variables is the same as the standard deviation for the *difference* of these two variables. Thus, a 2-point discrepancy should give you an edge. (Actually you need slightly *less* of a discrepancy in over/under lines to have a good bet or a good middle than you do for the regular point spread. This is because the two scores are not completely independent variables. The more one team scores the less the other team figures to in the allotted amount of time. This makes the sum of the two scores slightly more likely to fall near the mean and thus between the two bookies' lines.)

# Regression to the Mean

One principle that we need to discuss is what is known as "regression to the mean." It is a statistical concept that occurs in virtually all aspects of gambling. In layman terms it is the idea that whenever your results for some recent period of time happen to be extremely good or extremely bad, you can expect them to move closer to the middle in the future.

A simple example would be a poker player who has won a lot of money in the last three months. It is highly unlikely this is solely due to skill. His results during the next three months will probably not be as good. That is, he will tend to regress toward the mean and do closer to what is expected.

Another example is sport betting services. These are outfits which, for a fee, will give you their picks. Since there are so many of these "services" it is inevitable that a small number of them will do very well in one particular year. However, this was almost certainly simply because they were lucky. Probability tells us that a small number are supposed to get lucky. Of course their future results usually regress back toward the mean and their subscribers pay the price.

Here's an example from baseball. If you pick a random baseball player and want to predict his batting average next year based on his average this year, then you would normally predict that it would be about the same. But suppose his batting average is extremely high. Now you should almost certainly predict that his next year's average would go down because he was almost certainly getting lucky. This syndrome is a common occurrence. If a guy wins the batting championship you can bet that the next year his batting average will take a dip.

Along similar lines is the phenomenon of the "sophomore slump." It applies to players who had a great rookie year and then don't do as well their second year. Again this is just regression to the mean. Our rookie star probably played above his head, and luck had something to do with his success. The fact that he might have been Rookie of the Year doesn't mean that his next year will be as good. Expect to see his results diminish.

Why are we telling you all this? One reason is because we don't want you to assume that a team on a streak is better than it truly is. More likely it has gotten lucky (especially in baseball). Yet the bookie will adjust the line while a team is on that streak. He does this because many people believe that teams on streaks are good bets. But you as a professional gambler will know that the better bet is probably *against* the team on the streak. You'll be getting better odds than you would normally against this team, and your money will be on regression to the mean.[47]

Regression to the mean also frequently comes into play when evaluating teams that had a great record the previous year. It is frequently correct to bet *against* them the next year, especially at the beginning of the season. If you can find a bookie that puts up a total season win line betting *under* on that team, is something to be considered. (See the section on "Future Bets.") The well-known fact that Super Bowl winners are usually poor bets the next year is a simple example of regression to the mean.

A third reason to bring this up has to do with your own betting streaks. *No one* can have more than about a 20 percent edge betting sports as long as they bet more than a few games a year. If your results start off better than this we *guarantee* that they will regress. If you don't realize this you can go broke by over betting your bankroll. (See the section "How Much Do You Need" in the "Putting it All Together" chapter.) On the other side of the coin, poor results do not prove that you are destined to lose. You will certainly regress to doing better. (However your results can be analyzed statistically to see what the chances are you really are a

---

[47] However, please do not think that regression to the mean is similar to the following long "due" idea. If a 60 percent team is winning 90 percent of their games, we aren't saying that it will start winning 50 percent or less for awhile. Only that it will revert back to 60 percent.

winning player. Also, there is a second less technical technique that can be helpful. That is, notice the scores. If you are losing all the close ones and winning big on the others, that is strong evidence that things will eventually turn around. The converse is also true.)

# Notes on Baseball

We are devoting a separate section to baseball since it is so different from football or basketball as far as handicapping and betting are concerned. The problem with baseball is that you cannot use some of the techniques that work for those other sports. As we have shown, one reason why football and basketball are beatable is because simply using power ratings, as they do in those games, is frequently not the best way to get a line on a game. Because of the matchup concepts and/or psychological situations that sometimes occur, one team will occasionally figure to play above its rating while the other team might do the opposite.

In baseball, psychology means much less because of the fact that being extremely "up" for a game doesn't translate into a significantly higher chance of winning. Adrenaline, strength, and speed, which are most affected by emotions, are not nearly as important as they are in football and basketball. Baseball is more about reflexes and quickness. It is not as related to those things that are helped by adrenaline. (The exception might be pitching.)

On the other hand, there is much more luck in baseball than the other two games. Only in baseball, for instance, could a college team sometimes beat a pro team. This is partly true because whether or not a ball becomes a hit is a matter of an eighth of an inch on the bat. If the ball is hit solidly, it's a hit, and if the bat is a little bit too high or too low it's either a grounder or a pop up. Of course, the more skillful players do better in the long run as far as these eighth of an inches are concerned. But in the short run, anything can happen.

That being said, there is one very nice aspect to betting baseball. It is the fact that nowadays many Las Vegas books offer 10-cent lines. (In football or basketball laying 11-to-10 is the equivalent to a 20-cent line.) However, 10-cent lines are at least twice as good or (perhaps a better way of stating this) half as bad as 20-cent lines, and in many cases without going into detail, it's even better than that.[48] On average, 10-cent lines are only about a 2 percent disadvantage to the player. Furthermore, those players who have access to more than one bookie may find that they are able to bet into essentially what is for them a nickel line or even a "zero cent line" (no disadvantage at all). (See the section on "Making Money on Mathematical Bets.") In other words, baseball has a very small inherent disadvantage so you don't have to find as big a flaw in a bookie's number to find a good bet.

So how do you beat baseball if adrenaline and those entities relating to adrenaline don't have much impact? One way involves pitchers and matchups. For instance, it is well known that right handed pitchers are tougher against righthanded hitters. Thus, if you have a righthanded pitcher going against a team that has many righthanded hitters, you may have a pitcher who in this particular game deserves more than his usual amount of credit. In this case, that team may deserve to be the favorite even if both teams are normally about equal or even if the righthander's team is normally a little worse. So if the bookie has not recognized this situation and adjusted for it you have a good bet. (Another baseball matchup situation, where you bet *against* the good pitcher, was mentioned earlier in the section "Why the Line May Be Off.)

There is another method to beat baseball that has been recently tried by some computer whizzes. We are speaking of *game simulations.* Since baseball is so statistical, these computer experts have programmed each player's batting average, what percentage of his hits are singles, doubles, triples, and home runs, how often he walks or gets on base by an error, and so on. They also program the pitcher stats. They then have the computer "play" thousands of simulated games and the results determine the price between two teams. If the computer price is far enough away from the bookie's line they have a bet. Obviously this is a very time-consuming method that takes a lot of expertise (don't forget regression to the

---

[48] See *Getting the Best of It* by David Sklansky.

mean when you are plugging in batting averages as well as other stats). However, those who have pulled this off have been well rewarded. Even without a computer, there are many rabid baseball fans who probably have the talent to "watch" two teams play "in their minds" taking into account the idiosyncracies of all the players and how they match up. Our righthanded hitter example was fairly trivial. Not being baseball experts we can only show you the general concept. But if you can find other, perhaps more subtle, methods to think of similar ways to find "bad" lines, then a fortune may await you.

# Future Bets

Future bets are bets offered by a bookie that have to do with the outcome of a team's season. For example, you might bet on a particular team finishing first in their league or division, or you might bet on how many games you expect them to win in that season. If before the season starts you know your teams better than the bookie does, you might find a good bet. But as we have cautioned before, a lot of people falsely believe that they are great handicappers and forget that the bookies have also done their homework. You have to guard against fooling yourself into thinking that you are certainly right when you have a different opinion on a team than the bookie.

However, in the case of finishing first in their league or division, you can sometimes find a mathematical sure thing. What you need to do is go to all the various books that you have access to and note the best odds available on each team and see if this produces over 100 percent payback. Clearly no individual bookie will be paying back more than he takes in, but by taking the best odds you can find on each team among many different books you may be able to guarantee yourself a profit.

Here's a simple example. Suppose ten teams are in some particular league. If everyone of these teams is 12-to-1 *somewhere*, you could make a profit by betting on each of the teams at that book where it is 12-to-1.

Of course, the numbers will not be that simple and obvious. In practice what you need to do after you have gotten the best odds for every team is to change those odds to percentages. (See the probability appendix.) Then add up these percentages. If your total comes to less than 100 percent you have an edge.[49] You can then

---

[49] That's right, less than 100 percent is correct. If your total comes up to more than 100 percent the bookie is not paying back more than he is taking in.

bet every single team in such a way that it guarantees you the same payback regardless of who wins. This payback will give you a profit at the end of the year. If that profit is enough to make it worth tying up your money for six months or so then you should go for it.

You can also occasionally have a mathematical edge with another kind of future bet. Many bookies now put up a line for each team as to how many wins they will have at the end of the season. You can bet over or under. The edge comes from the fact that the total of wins that *all* the teams will have will add up to half the total games played. So should the total of the bookies line, but they often don't.

For instance, suppose there are 10 teams in a league and they each have a 12-game schedule. Then the average number of wins per team will be 6. If you add up the totals for all the wins in the league the number should be 60.

$$60 = (\tfrac{1}{2})(10)(12)$$

But suppose that when you add up the totals that the *bookie* offers it comes to 66 instead of 60. This means that if you bet every single team *under* you ought to show a profit at the end of the year. (It isn't always a cinch but it's the favorite.)[50]

What's most interesting about this situation is that it is actually quite common to see, even when just looking at one bookie. This is because the typical bettor bets over, not under, and thus moves the line up.

---

[50] Actually the totals of the bookie's line don't have to add up to *exactly* half of the total games to be correct. That is because the lines are what statisticians call *medians* rather than *means*. While it must be true that the mean of the total is the total of the means, the same need not be true of medians. However, this is a fine point that will almost never affect the profitability of the techniques given above.

Of course, if you were doing it right you wouldn't just go to one bookie and see if the totals that he offers are too high. You would go to all the bookies that you have access to and look at the numbers they have on each team, and then add up the highest numbers that you found. If that total was too high, you would then go back to each book that offers the highest number on some particular team and proceed to bet those teams under.[51] Keep in mind, once again, however, that this play is not worth doing if it ties up money that you could more profitably use elsewhere.

One final note concerning future bets. After the season starts, bookies will let you continue to make these bets. But most bookies will now lower the odds on the teams that are winning without significantly raising them on the teams that are losing. This is stupid on their part but it is what is usually done. Thus, if you are going to bet future bets, you should usually bet them the day they become available because unlike normal bookie bets, future bet lines usually only get worse as time goes by.

---

[51] Theoretically the various lines could be too low on total, thus giving you an edge on the "over" bet. But in practice this would probably never happen as fans move the lines on their favorite teams up.

# Parlays

A parlay is simply a bet that two or more events will all occur. These events might be that two or more teams all beat the point spread, or it could be that a team not only beats the spread but that the game goes over the total as well. A parlay is not normally a particularly good bet. If you like two teams there is really no reason to parlay them. You should generally bet them both individually. But there are times that you should parlay.

One time when it might be right to parlay is if you are betting a parlay card where the numbers on the card are not the same as what the point spread is on the board. That is, the line has moved since the parlay card was printed, and you can get a little bit the better of a number on the card. Even if it is just one game that is off on the card, it is mathematically better to bet the card as long as you are getting a good parlay price. And a good parlay price means 2.6-to-1 (or 13-to-5) on two teams, 6-to-1 on three teams, and about 12-to-1 on four teams. If you can get those odds then you would be better off parlaying it if the parlay allows you to get better point spreads. (Keep in mind that parlay cards usually use "for one" terminology: 7-for-1 is only 6-to-1; 12-to-1 means 13-for-1.)

The second time when it would be right to parlay is if bookies allow you to couple events that are not totally independent. This would typically involve parlaying the pointspread of a game with its over/under total. When they let you do that there are going to be some cases where it makes sense to parlay. To take an extreme case, suppose a football team is a very big favorite, let's say 35 points, and the over/under is 43 points. If you can parlay the favorite with the "over," you are getting 13-to-5 on something that is much less than a 13-to-5 shot. This is because of the approximately 50 percent of the time that a 35-point favorite covers the spread, common sense says that a vast majority of those times the total score will be above 43 points. If they allow you to parlay such situations it could be worth doing even if you don't particularly like one or even both of the bets. (This is similar to the rubber band concept we will talk about in the horse racing section.) If you do in fact like one or both of the bets, then that's even better.

# Teasers

A teaser is a bet where you get extra points in exchange for lower odds. They apply mainly to football or basketball. For instance, if you bet what is normally a 10-point favorite in a 6-point teaser, you only lay 4 points. If you bet the underdog you would get 16 points. Since each point occurs about 3 percent of the time, 6 extra points should make your bet about a 65 percent shot (in football). The bookie might make you lay 5-to-2 odds. However, what is usually done to disguise the high price you are laying is to make you bet two or more games (and win them all) in the teaser. For example, for a 6-point teaser the bookie might pay even money for two teams, 9-to-5 for three teams, and 5-to-2 for four teams. But if each game is 65 percent, a two teamer will win

$$(.65)^2 = 42.5\,percent,$$

a three teamer will win

$$(.65)^3 = 27.46\,percent,$$

and a four teamer will win

$$(.65)^4 = 17.85\,percent.$$

The true odds are about 7-to-5, 5-to-2, and 9-to-2 respectively.

Generally speaking, your inherent disadvantage when betting teasers is over 10 percent. Because of this we do not recommend that you pursue them. There are better ways to "invest" your money.

# In Closing

There is no question that sports betting is a beatable "game." In fact, for the reasons noted earlier, the wealthiest professional gamblers are the successful sports bettors. (We know quite a few poker players who gave up very profitable cardplaying careers to pursue sports.) The bookie's vigorish does not guarantee failure as it does in nonskillful, independent trial games. The main reasons why sports betting can be beaten are:

1. You can choose which game to bet or not to bet.
2. You can shop around for the best line.
3. The bookie is not always striving for the perfect line but rather for one that splits the action.
4. The bookie's line is usually arrived at in a rather robotic way that sometimes doesn't adequately take into account emotions or matchups.

However, the fact is that few sports bettors win in the long run. One of the reasons is of course talent. Not everyone can evaluate sports. Being lazy and unwilling to do research is another. But the biggest reason is probably a lack of discipline and too much ego. To beat sports you can only bet those games where you are sure you have an edge. If, for instance, you rationalize a reason to bet a game whenever it happens to be on TV you are heading for trouble. To be a professional gambler you must *treat* it like a profession. Your fun comes from spending your winnings, not from gambling.

# Part Three

# Horse Racing

# Horse Racing

# Introduction

Many of you will be surprised to see a section on horse racing in this book. In fact, many so-called authorities on gambling will tell you that "the ponies can't be beat." They give horse racing's high "take out" as their reason. Usually the take out is in the neighborhood of 18 percent, 20 percent if you consider the "breakage"[52] This is a lot higher than what the house takes on baccarat — 1.1 percent; or on craps — 1.4 percent; or on roulette — 5.4 percent, and we all know that it is not possible to attain an edge in these games. Even the theoretically beatable "game" of sports betting has a lot less of an initial disadvantage (about 4½ percent), yet few people beat it. So it seems to many people that 20 percent is too gigantic an initial disadvantage to buck and that those who think they can do it are just fooling themselves. But they are wrong. In spite of what they might think, horse racing is beatable.

There are many reasons why a 20 percent disadvantage on horses is not as bad as it seems. The first reason of course is that horses are not inanimate objects like dice where past results have no bearing on future results and where the odds on any result are perfectly known. Another reason is this: You are not forced to wager on a race when you don't think that there is a good bet. In poker, for instance, if they raked 20 percent (or even 5 percent) from the pot the games would be virtually unbeatable unless you

---

[52] Breakage is the extra money the track keeps because it doesn't pay off exactly according to what is bet on your horse. Instead it rounds the payment downward to the nearest 20 cents. Thus if a horse should pay $8.79 it will only pay $8.60 ($8.70 at a few tracks), and the tracks keep the extra money. This is especially significant when the payoff is small as it usually is for place or show bets.

were against truly horrible players. Even the best players would lose in such a game because they are *forced to play every hand* — to at least ante or to post a blind bet that acts like an ante.

But there is no ante in horse racing. There are some trivial expenses when you go to a track (parking and admission fees). However, if you do your betting in a casino horse racing book even these small fees vanish. (In fact, if you consider the comps that you might earn, the casino may be paying you to play.) So this allows you to have an edge even if you only rarely find a good bet.

Before we get into the techniques that can give you an edge at the horses, we want to point out some historical facts that should help convince you that the 20 percent is not an insurmountable number. First, 20 percent is what you expect to lose only if you were to bet horses with no regard to anything — in other words, if you were to bet simply randomly. But this is not taking into account the historical fact that the public does not bet in strict relation to a horse's chances. Rather, they tend to overbet the longshots. Bets on very high priced horses have historically had a 50 percent disadvantage, returning only about half of what was bet on them in the long run. (For example, 40-to-1 shots win about once in 80 times.)

What this means for you is that with just this little bit of knowledge you do not have a 20 percent edge to overcome. Though you would be bucking the 20 percent if you were to bet randomly, if you just bet the favorites your disadvantage would be more like 10 percent. In fact, if you were to limit your bets to very-short priced favorites you have a gamble that is approximately dead even.

So we see horse racing isn't such a bad bet after all, and the fact is, there are methods to find good bets — bets that will win (in the long run) in spite of the house edge, which we now see can be made to be much less than 20 percent.

We will also see that finding a good bet does not necessarily involve much handicapping skill or knowing horses. Admittedly, this is one area of expertise that the authors have never fully developed, especially when it comes to the "flats," although there are a few handicapping hints we will give. One of the authors

(Sklansky) does have some handicapping skill in harness racing, and we will mention a few ideas later in this section. However, as you will see, there are other ways to get an edge in horse racing that don't involve handicapping. They are more of a mathematical nature.

Of course, handicapping skills are certainly beneficial. And if you do have handicapping skills you should combine them with the mathematical techniques we are about to show you. There are also some handicapping books available, and we will recommend a couple at the end of this section. However we are a little hesitant in doing so because we are not completely sure that everything they say is correct. So keep this in mind while reading them.

# Parimutuel and Nonparimutuel Race Books

When you go to a track, you will typically have about ten races to choose from. If you follow our advice, you will be able to find a good bet on most days. On some days you'll even find two bets, and on a rare day you may find as many as three. But there will also be a fair number of days where there won't be any good bets at all. On those days you'll just have to enjoy the scenery and appreciate the competition and the beauty of the animals.

But there is another approach. Besides a racetrack you could go to a horse racing book, usually located in a major casino. The advantage of this is that you will now have many tracks to choose from, meaning that instead of nine or ten races a day from which to pick, you can easily have as many as two hundred. This translates into many good bets on a typical day if you follow our methods. (We need to note that there are now some race tracks such as Hollywood Park in Inglewood, California that also offer betting on races from other tracks. You still won't have as many races to bet as you would at a casino race book, but it is better than playing a track that offers only its own race card to choose from.)

It used to be in the old days in Nevada that when you bet on a horse you got the same price as the track paid, but your bet wouldn't affect the odds. This, of course, isn't true if you are at the track. Bets made at the track go into the parimutuel pool and thus can conceivably reduce the payoff that you get if you win. If you are a small bettor this is unlikely, but if you are betting a few hundred dollars you could easily lower the payoff by 20 cents. For example, betting $300 at a track might reduce the payoff from $8.60 to $8.40, or perhaps even more at a small track where the handle is not very large. This is especially true in the place and show pools where less money is bet than in the win pool. But as we said, this disadvantage didn't affect you when you made your bet at a Nevada race book.

105

Nowadays, however, there is a new type of horse racing book. These are books that are actually *in* with the track. This means that the money you bet at the race book goes directly into the track pool. So, again, if you are betting any kind of serious money you reduce your own odds. Notice that these books do not risk their own money. They are nothing more than an agent for the track.

A nonparimutuel book is different. Now the casino's money is at risk and your bet will have no effect on the track odds. That is, your bet, no matter how much it is, will not affect what the payoffs are. From a casino's point of view, the advantage of being nonparimutuel is that they do not have to share their expected profit. The track is cut out. But the disadvantage is that smart bettors might be able to beat them out of their cash.

From the bettor's standpoint there are some drawbacks to playing at nonparimutuel books. Because of the inherent risk that they must assume, these books will limit the amount that you can bet or will limit the amount that they will pay out, or sometimes they will refuse to take certain bets. A parimutuel house on the other hand will take all bets. In addition, some nonparimutuel books have been known to bar skillful players, just like many casinos do at their blackjack tables. Fortunately, this is a very rare event.

Even with these small drawbacks, having two hundred races a day to choose from and not having your bets affect the track pool makes a lot of difference. So, as long as the nonparimutuel books will take your bets, this is where you should probably play if you can. But there are some exceptions. One reason *to* bet at a parimutuel race book is when you really like a bet and want to bet more than the nonparimutuel book will take. Another reason would be that there is a worthwhile promotion going on. At the time of this writing there is a small parimutuel book in Las Vegas — currently getting a lot of business — that is paying a 9 percent rebate to the people who are betting there. At the end of the day, win or lose, you get 9 percent of your total action back. So if, for example, you bet $5,000 for the day, they give you back $450 in cash. Thus, unless you are betting an awful lot (which would drop your payoff by more than the 9 percent rebate helps you) you are better off betting parimutuel at this establishment than betting nonparimutuel. (By the way, their deal is actually a win-win situation for both the player and the book. Since the book gets a flat percentage of about 13 percent from the tracks it still does okay. Even though it is giving more than half of its profit back to the players, it still makes a lot more than it would without the promotion as it now gets far more action than it would otherwise.)

One last reason to consider betting at a parimutuel book is if you want to take advantage of high paying exotic bets like the Pick Six that can't be offered by nonparimutuel books for obvious reasons. More on these bets later.

# Overlays

Many authors will tell you that one of the ways to beat horses is by finding "overlays." What they usually mean by this is to find a horse with moderately high odds that has a good chance of winning. An example would be to identify a horse that goes off at 10-to-1 but whose true odds should be closer to 5-to-1. This would not be the best horse in the race but a horse that has a good chance to win and which, for some reason, is underrated.

There is no question that this is a good bet and that it is an overlay. But the authors are wrong when they imply that this is the only definition of an overlay and that an overlay is but one way to beat the races. All good bets are overlays.[53] In order to have the best of it on any bet, that bet must be an overlay. An overlay can appear on any horse, including the favorite. Favorites too can go off at odds that are too high when compared to their real chances of winning. When this happens you have an overlay. You must always keep in mind that in order for a bet to be a good bet it has to be an overlay in the same sense that any other gambling bet has to be an overlay if it is to have positive expectation. In other words, it has to be one where the odds that you are getting are higher than the odds that it deserves. This could be an 80-to-1 shot that you think will win 1 out of 50 times, it could be an exacta that's paying 30-to-1 that you think will come in 1 out of 20, or it could be a favorite that goes off as a 1-to-2 shot that you think will win three-fourths of the time.

---

[53] There is one possible exception. It is when you make two simultaneous bets where you know that at least one of them is good. An example would be hedging a win bet with an exacta bet. In this case you may be making one bad bet. But the *combination* of bets is profitable and it is this combination that can be called an overlay. (A simple example would be "middling" a sports bet.)

# House Quinellas

Many of the race books in Nevada, even those that are parimutuel in general, will offer some bets that they book themselves. One of these is known as the quinella bet. It is simply a bet that a particular two horses will finish first and second in a race but their order of finish relative to each other does not matter.

There are a few tracks that offer this bet themselves on a parimutuel basis, but most don't. If a particular race does include a parimutuel quinella there is usually no house quinella offered. (The reason we say usually is that there is one race book that we know of that will give you the higher of the two payoffs if there was in fact a track quinella. Needless to say, this is a very nice deal. If you are betting quinellas and you know of a race book that offers this option you should certainly be doing your quinella betting there.) Parimutuel quinellas can be a good bet if you are a good handicapper or see a discrepancy in the quinella pool. But when there are house quinellas offered you can occasionally find truly great bets.

To see how this occurs you must understand the way that house quinellas are calculated in Nevada. What the books do is take the win price of the winner, multiply it times the place price of the second place horse and divide by 2. This is the quinella payoff for a $2 bet.

Here's an example. Suppose the horse that finishes first pays $5.60 to win and the horse that comes in second pays $3.00 to place. Then the house quinella will pay $8.40.

$$\frac{(5.60)(3.00)}{2} = 8.40$$

In general, this method of calculation will result in a payoff that gives the house a nice advantage. However, there is a situation where house quinellas can be highly advantageous to the player. To show you why we will look at an extreme case. Imagine that there are two horses in a ten-horse race that are almost dead equal but are far, far above the rest of the horses in the race. (A good example was Sunday Silence and Easy Goer. An even better example was Affirmed and Alydar.) In this case, a win bet on either of these two horses would pay about even money or less. You might find them both 4-to-5. Because of the almost certainty of them coming in first and second, the winning horse will pay about $3.60 and the place price of the second horse could be as little as $2.10. This will produce a house quinella of $3.80. *But the quinella truly should pay only about $2.20 because there are no other horses that can compete with either of these horses in this race.*

So in this situation you are getting approximately even money on something that could be as much as a 1-to-10 favorite. However, for the quinella bet to have a nice edge the situation doesn't have to be this extreme. The general rule is that if there are two horses that are quite a bit better than the third horse and approximately equal to each other, the house quinella — if they will accept it — is advantageous, and you need to know almost nothing about the horses except their odds.

It would be helpful if you were a handicapper and were able to see that this is in fact a race where these two horses deserve their odds. But even if you don't have any handicapping skills and you just automatically bet every quinella where both horses were 8-to-5 or less you will have an edge. In addition, if there is a race where there are three horses at 5-to-2 or less and you bet all three combinations that are available, you will have a small edge. (We will leave the math to those readers who are so inclined.)

Now if you are a handicapper, you can extend the envelope. It might be possible to find a few more good quinella bets that take advantage of this syndrome as long as you bet two horses that are relatively short prices. However, once the odds of the horses go significantly higher than 8-to-5, it is no longer an automatic bet.

Now even if you really like two horses, you may be better off betting an exacta in both directions. When the horses odds get above what we recommend, house quinellas are not usually worth messing with.

(One exception occurs where you see a horse significantly underbet in the place pool. It may work out that the best way to take advantage of this is by betting it with other horses in a house quinella rather than by simply betting it to place. This is especially true if your place bet would be a large one at a parimutuel book. This strategy would take advantage of the good place price without your bet knocking it down. Place prices are discussed in the next section.)

# Place and Show Bets

Another simple mathematical way to get an edge at horse racing is by betting to place or to show. In general, like most horse bets, place and show are not good bets. But it can occur that you can find a good place or show bet even without handicapping. This will happen when the place price (or show price) is particularly high when compared to the win price. It turns out that you can predict whether this will occur.

The way to do it is quite easy. All you do is to look at the place and show pools. If the amount bet on the place pool or the show pool is less than *half of what it should be* when compared to the win pool you usually have a good bet. For instance, suppose there is $40,000 total bet in the win pool and $20,000 total bet in the place pool. This means that whatever amount of money is bet on an individual horse in the win pool you would expect to see approximately half that amount bet on the same horse in the place pool since $20,000 is half of $40,000. In fact, you expect to see approximately this ratio all the way down the line. Let's suppose that there was a horse that had $7,000 bet on it to win. You would now expect to find approximately $3,500 bet on it in the place pool. If in fact it had only $1,700 bet on it to place it will almost definitely be a good place bet, as long as this ratio doesn't change.

Before going any further we need to point out that this is the one time that you would be better off being at the track because typically the place and the show pool is flashed on the TV screen two minutes before race time. Unfortunately, during the last two minutes a lot can happen. It can occur that money gets bet on the horses that were underbet in the place or show pool up to that point in time. So it would be better to be at the track where you can wait until the absolute last second to make your decision.

If you can't be at the track, you obviously would prefer to be at a nonparimutuel race book. But there is a problem. Many nonparimutuel race books will limit your action on place and show bets. On the other hand, if you avoid this problem by going to a parimutuel book where you can bet what you want, you have to worry that your own bet will reduce your payoff price especially at a small track. The perfect solution of course, would be to find a nonparimutuel book that accepts big action on place and show bets.[54]

There are some other pitfalls. If you are a reasonable handicapper you might want to avoid some of these place and show bets. There are certain horses, typically front runners, who go to the front and sometimes hang on and sometimes quit badly. Horses like this are almost always either winning the race or finishing out of the money. This type of horse should pay almost as much to place as to win, and you would almost never want to make a place or show bet on a winner/quitter. For instance, a horse that would pay $8.00 to win and $5.60 to place is normally a nice place bet. But if you have some knowledge of its form and happen to know that this is a horse that would rarely come in precisely second it wouldn't be right to bet to place.

On the other hand the opposite type of situation can occur. Suppose you have a horse that runs a good (by the standards of the other horses in the race) but highly predictable time. In other words it is very consistent from race to race. Further, let's suppose there are quite a few other horses in the race that run erratic times. This consistent horse, even though it is the best horse in the race, may very likely have a better chance to come in precisely second than it does to win.

To see why, let's look at an example. Suppose there are five horses in a particular race. Furthermore, let's suppose that one of the horses, which we will call Horse A, runs a very steady predictable time every race. The other horses are more erratic, but

---

[54] The Sport of Kings, a Las Vegas race book that opened a couple of years ago with much fanfare, did accept "any reasonable bet,"and it was nonparimutuel. Is it any wonder that after a few months it went out of business? The book got destroyed by some smart bettors, including one of the authors of this text.

all about equal. Suppose further that this time is good enough to finish ahead of any particular other horse 7 out of 10 times. Is this horse more likely to finish first or second?

The probability that Horse A will win is .7 to the fourth power or .2401. That is the chances are that it will beat every one of the other horses. Thus it is about a 3-to-1 shot. Figuring the probability that this horse will finish precisely second is a little more complicated. It is given by the following equation.

$$Pr. \ of \ finishing \ second \ = \ (4)(.3)(.7)^3$$

$$= \ .4116$$

Where

    4 is the number of different ways that Horse A can finish second,[55]

    .3 is the probability of finishing behind a particular horse, and

    .7 is the probability of finishing ahead of a different particular horse.

In essence this equation figures out the total probability of the four different ways Horse A will beat three horses and lose to one. The answer is 41.16 percent. This is approximately 3-to-2. In other words, even though Horse A is clearly the best horse in the race it is much more likely to finish second as it is to finish first. This phenomenon is moderately common. Horses like this will run second very frequently and are often, as the example shows, more likely to come in precisely second than precisely first. These are the opposite kind of horse mentioned previously that will either win or do nothing, and a bet on them to place could be a very good bet. (In this case the probability that Horse A will finish first or second is about 65 percent. This means a $3.20 place price is an overlay even

---

[55] It can run second to Horse B, Horse C, Horse D, or Horse E.

while an $8.00 win price is not.) A possibly even better bet with these type of horses is to bet exactas where the horse is bet only for second with various other contenders bet to win.[56]

Here is a trick that you can sometimes use to avoid the problem of cutting your own price when you make place or show bets at some parimutuel books. It is to bet what is known as a place or show parlay. That is you bet two (or more) horses to show. (The two horses are running in two different races and they must both show for you to collect.) When they book a parlay, the bet is not entered into the parimutuel pool. The parlay price is based on the prices on the board. The problem with this trick is that the second horse that you parlay with the horse you really want to bet may not be an overlay by itself. You may still want to do it, especially if you really like a particular place or show bet and you want to bet enough on it (perhaps a few hundred) that a parimutuel bet would have caused your odds to go down significantly. However, unless you simultaneously see a second place or show bet you really like, what you are gaining by not putting your money into the pool you may be losing by having to bet a second show bet that is just random.

There is a final point we would like to make about horses that are underbet in the place and show pool. That is, the fact that there is less money than there should be in these pools may in of itself be an indication that this horse is ready to run. In other words there may be a discrepancy because someone with inside information is betting to win. In this case, the place and show pools are about what was expected, and it is really the excess win money that is causing this discrepancy. However, betting to place in these situations is still

---

[56] This concept also comes up in poker where you have a hand of medium strength that is unlikely to improve and are against several players who have "drawing" hands or hands that have little immediate value but have some chance to improve to a very strong holding. Notice that even though you may be a significant favorite against any one of your opponents, collectively you can be a money dog in the pot. For more discussion see "Another Gambling Paradox" in *Getting the Best Of it* by David Sklansky.

probably the right play. You are now betting on a "hot" horse without having to accept a lower price.

The bottom line is that horses are underbet in the place pool for one of three reasons:

1. Simple statistical fluctuations. (This will not occur at tracks that actually show prospective place and show *payoffs* on the board. When only the place and show *pools* are shown, discrepancies are frequently overlooked.)
2. The horse is the kind of runner that figures to either win or run out of the money.
3. The horse is "hot," and the smart money is betting only to win.

With no handicapping skills you should have an edge betting on all place and show overlays you see. But this edge can be substantially increased if you don't bet in situation No. 2 above. One guideline to identify this situation is to be aware of front runners who often quit, horses coming off a long layoff, or horses shipping in from another track. These horses are best avoided where place and show bets are concerned.

# Exactas

There are three ways to possibly get an edge on exactas even when you don't know much about the horses or have any handicapping skills. The first two methods would involve comparing the prospective exacta prices that are on the tote board with the win odds on a particular horse to see if they are out of line. The third method, which we call the "rubber band" concept, will be explained shortly.

How do you know if the prospective exacta prices are out of line? There are basically two ways. One is to compare the total money bet on a particular horse in the win pool with the total money bet on the same horse in the exacta pool with that horse on top. For instance, suppose one-fourth of all the money in the win pool is bet on a particular horse. This would mean that an estimate of its true odds are 3-to-1. (Although the toteboard will show 2-to-1 because of the takeout.) But now further suppose that only 10 percent of the money in the exacta pool was bet on combinations that had this horse on top. Clearly this is a significant discrepancy, and at least some exacta combinations with this horse on top are good bets as long as we believe the win odds are close to being accurate.

There is one problem with this method. Most books will not show the aforementioned information on their screens. However, there is another way you can find these discrepancies. You can compare exacta payback prices to which horse is favored in the win pool.

Here's an example. Suppose the One horse on top of the Three horse is paying $17 and the Two horse on top of the Three horse is paying $31. Meanwhile the One horse on top of the Four horse is paying $82 and the Two horse on top of the Four horse is paying $157, and it is going like this in most of the other combinations involving horse One and horse Two. Then, clearly, horse One is favored over horse Two in the exacta pool. But if horse Two is going off at lower odds in the win pool than horse One, something is out of kilter. You have found a discrepancy and may have a good exacta bet on horse Two (or a good win bet on horse One, or both).

So if the horse that is the favorite in the exacta pool has significantly higher win odds than the horse that is the favorite in the win pool, then you should probably bet the horse that is the favorite in the exacta pool in the win column. But you should probably also bet the horse that is the favorite in the win pool on top in some exactas.

What we are saying is that if there is a major discrepancy between the win pool and the exacta pool, there ought to be a good bet somewhere. It will be either the exacta favorite in the win category or the win favorite in the exacta category. You know that at least one of them, and perhaps both, are probably good bets.

A similar mathematical technique would involve picking out precise exacta combinations that seem underbet. The fair price on an exacta can usually be estimated by adding 1 to the price of each horse, multiplying them together, and then doubling the total. Thus a 4-to-1 shot and a 7-to-1 shot should pay about $80 (a little less if the 4-to-1 shot wins, and a little more if the 7-to-1 shot wins).

$$80 = (2)[(4+1)(7+1)]$$

(This method however loses some accuracy when a short-priced horse is involved.)

You will find that prospective exacta prices that are flashed on the toteboard will rarely pay this much (because of the house take). When they do pay significantly more than this you usually have a good bet (as long as big longshots are not involved.) The converse is also true, of course. If many prospective exacta prices involving a particular horse are paying far less than the win odds would imply, you may have a good bet to win or place on the horse in question. (If the strangely low exacta prices involve some horse in the second spot it might well be that a place bet is better, especially if the place pool also indicates a bet. [See the previous discussion on place and show bets.])

The third way you can get an edge in exactas involves a mathematical concept but also takes a little handicapping skill. What you do is look for horses that ran very close to each other in a recent race. If you find them you may have a good exacta bet (with its reverse). Typically an exacta on two horses is related only to their win odds. A 4-to-1 shot on top of a 5-to-1 shot would pay in the neighborhood of $50 for a $2 exacta win. Using the method above we would need about a $60 exacta price 5x6x2 before this bet starts to look good. But it can occur that even though you wouldn't particularly want to bet either of these horses to win, the $50 exacta price on the two horses can be a good bet. This is because in certain circumstances the chances of one horse coming in second has changed if in fact the other horse comes in first.

This would occur when the two horses have, in their most recent outing or in one of their most recent outings (and the last time they ran together), come in very close to each other. The idea becomes particularly good if they were both in the money.[57] For example, one came in first and the other second or perhaps third and there was very little distance between them. If that has happened and these two horses are competing again in a race where the other horses are coming off different races, then the exacta, in both directions, can be a good bet. This is because if, in fact, one of the horses does win there is a good chance that the other horse will be right there with him. Specifically, if the 4-to-1 shot finishes first, it might now be even money that the 5-to-1 shot, which has previously just run next to it, finishes second. *In this case even a $30 exacta price would be an overlay.* (Of course, before making a bet like this you should *check the toteboard* to make sure the public hasn't caught on and driven the price down. Also consider

---

[57] That's because each jockey is probably trying and the horses are running optimally. There will be more discussion on this idea later in the text.

the parimutuel quinella if the track offers it.[58] If the quinella is a lot higher than half of the average of the two exactas, it is probably better to bet it than to bet the exacta and the reverse.)

This is what we call a "rubber band." In a sense, it's like these two horses have a rubber band around them. We don't believe that most bettors take this kind of information into account. Thus, rubber bands can produce an occasional good exacta bet.

---

[58] We don't recommend the house quinella in this spot because we would typically be dealing with two non-favorites. As previously explained, the higher the odds the worse the house quinella disadvantage would be as compared to the track quinella or an exacta with its reverse.

# Pick Sixes and Other Exotic Bets

The last mathematical bet that we will talk about are bets on combinations of events that are very hard to pick perfectly. They come under the heading of "pick sixes," "place nines," or perhaps another name. But the bottom line is that you bet on something that is extremely tough to pick, and if you get lucky enough to hit it, you can win a wheelbarrel full of money. In itself these bets are normally not good bets, especially if you don't have handicapping skills. But occasionally it can occur that the mathematics can turn bets in your favor usually because of what is known as "carryovers." What happens is, when no one picks every winner, a portion of the pool (usually half) is carried over to be won the next day. (The other half of the pool, after the takeout of course, is paid back as a consolation prize to those who have picked the most winners. This consolation prize is paid out [to those who have five winners] even if there are six of six winners.) So if there were no winning tickets yesterday, this means that you can be shooting at money that wasn't bet today but rather was bet the previous day or days.

This doesn't mean that you necessarily have the best of it. Remember, the track still takes its cut. So it's still likely that even with the carryover the total amount paid out may still be less than the total amount of money bet that day. This is because carryovers usually produce much bigger betting the next day.

Here's an example: Suppose there is a $100,000 carryover — they throw $100,000 into the pool the next day. But on the next day a total of $500,000 is bet making the total pool (including the carryover) $600,000. If the track cuts 20 percent it will take $120,000, leaving only $480,000 in the pool, less than what was bet that day. This means that a small carryover is unlikely to produce an edge. But on days when there is a large carryover, you may have a situation where the amount of money bet that day is less than the amount of money eligible to be given back.

Still, even on these days, the amount of money paid out is not necessarily more than the amount of money bet unless in fact that there is a big winner. If no one holds a perfect winning ticket, then half the money in the (pick six) pool is carried over again, including what was bet that day as well as what was previously carried over. So even a large carryover may not be that great an opportunity.

There are, however, occasional days — typically on the last day of a meet at a particular track — where they guarantee to give *all the money back* (less the take). If no one has a perfect ticket the next best tickets share all of the pool. If this day is also coupled with a big carryover, you truly have a nice mathematical edge. But you can't just close your eyes, bet at random, and have the best of it.

Let's look at a highly simplified example. We are betting a "pick one." Suppose the carryover is $1 and there was no track take. Further, let's suppose that you and another person were the only ones to bet on a two-horse race where this $1 carryover will appear and we will assume (to keep this example simple) that the two horses are an even match. You bet $10 on horse One, while the other person bets $10 on horse One and another $10 on horse Two. This puts $31 in the pool. The track is taking in $30 and they will give back $31.

If horse Two wins, you lose $10. But if horse One finishes first you only win $5.50. (Because you split the $11 profit.) So even though the track is giving back more than it took in, you are making a losing bet.

Generalizing, the point we are making is that even when the amount of money given back is significantly larger than the amount of money taken in, if you know that some of your competitors are betting every reasonable combination and you are not, you may not have a positive expectation bet. That is, you may still be taking the worst of it.

Another well-known author in this field tried to argue this point.[59] He stated that if there is a set of bets that shows a positive expectation there must be a subset of bets that also shows a profit, and you should therefore attempt to find that subset. But the problem is that the subset may be dependent upon what you bet. Your own bet can turn the winning subset into a different subset as can clearly be seen by our example. If you bet horse One and your opponent bets both horses you have made a losing bet. The same would be true if you had bet only horse Two. There is no subset that you can pick where you have the best of it. You will be at a disadvantage to the person (or syndicate of persons) who bets all reasonable combinations while you don't. (Though this doesn't mean that you don't have an edge when there is a large carryover and there is a syndicate operating against you, it does mean that the edge isn't as great as it might appear.)

There is another idea concerning the "pick six" that we want to mention because it will save many of you some money. Typically, those who want to bet many combinations will fill out a ticket where they choose varying numbers of horses for each race. This produces a lot of combinations. For example, let's say they choose one horse in two races, three horses in two races, four horses in one race, and five horses in one race. They will now have a ticket with 180 combinations

$$180 = 1 x 1 x 3 x 3 x 4 x 5$$

which at $2 a combination will cost $360.

But this is a wasteful method of betting, especially if you start going deep down the odds board. Specifically, let's say that in three different races you are willing to give a 30-to-1 shot enough of a chance that you include them. But do you really want to include combinations that would have more than 1 of these 30-to-1 shots winning?

---

[59] See *Betting Cheap Claimers* by Stanford Wong.

In other words, when you put in a ticket with a lot of horses in each race you are being wasteful because you will be including some combinations that are too farfetched to bother with. If you want to include a slight chance horse because you think it is possible that that horse can come in, put that slight chance horse only in tickets involving shorter priced horses. Don't waste a lot of extra money by coupling a bunch of horses that are at high odds. You should break out the ticket into separate tickets.

To give a simple example, let's say it was a pick three instead of a pick six. It's usually a mistake to bet a ticket that includes five horses in each race. You would probably be better off to bet a ticket that has five horses from the first race and perhaps the best three horses in the second race and the best three horses in the third race. Then bet a second ticket that has the two longest odds horses in the second race with the best three horses in the first race and the third race, and bet a third ticket that has the two longest odds horses in the third race with the best three horses in the first race and the second race. This scheme will reduce your combinations by 44 from 125 to 81. It will save you $88.

Doing things this way is more difficult, but as our example shows, it saves a lot of money unless you truly thought that there was a reasonable chance that all the longshots could win together. But there is another reason why you don't need combinations that feature all the longshots. If only a couple of them win you wouldn't care who won the other race because you would now automatically have a good chance to win the consolation pool.

Again, the point that we are trying to make is that many people throw away some of their cash because they are not willing to break up their pick six tickets into rational combinations. They unwittingly include ridiculously farfetched ones. If you are a horse bettor and this is the only concept that you get out of this book, it has more than paid for itself.

# How to Pick Winners

Now that we have labeled this section we will go on to say that this is actually the wrong title. What we really plan to show you — as we have stressed before — is how to pick good bets, not necessarily the horse most likely to win. Though it doesn't hurt to be able to have a good opinion on who will win the race, the important thing is to be able to assess any particular horse's chances of winning. It is then a simple matter to find a good bet either in the win pool, or possibly the place pool, the show pool, or the exacta pool. Or perhaps you like two horses that are both being rated properly in the win pool, but the combination of the two is underrated in the exacta or quinella pools. This, of course, all assumes that you know how to assess a horse's chances.

Though this is not our field of expertise, we can give you some guidelines. First, keep in mind that in order to find a good bet it is necessary that your opinion of the horse not only be accurate, but that it be significantly higher than the public's. Generally speaking, just being able to evaluate a horse's chances isn't good enough to find a bet because most of time the public will evaluate the horse about the same as you, and with the house take you won't have the best of it. As a rule of thumb, you will probably have a good bet only if there is less than half the amount of money bet on a horse compared to what you think *should* be bet on the horse. This means that you have to have a much stronger opinion of the horse than the public.

Even this unfortunately is not always enough. If the public's opinion of the odds at which the horse is going off at is significantly higher than *you* think are the fair odds, this in itself is a negative factor. Why? Because there are people out there who have some sort of inside information who may be staying away from your horse and betting some other horse.[60] Thus, when you evaluate what you think are the chances of a horse winning, one of the factors is the toteboard odds themselves.

This means that in order to find a good bet — especially a simple win bet — you not only need to find a horse whose odds are significantly higher than what you think are his true odds, but you have to find a horse that has a plausible reason for going off at those odds. This usually means that you expected this horse to go off at those higher odds. For example, if you thought a horse had a 20 percent chance of winning — meaning that the fair odds would be 4-to-1 — and *unexpectedly* you see this horse going off at 8-to-1, this could easily be a bad bet. It seems like a great bet, yet you probably should not make it because these *unexpected* high odds may indicate something that you know nothing about. The only time you should really like a win bet is if you knew before the race that this horse was going to have much higher odds than it deserved. (Because the factors that make it a good bet are not readily understood by the public.)

The bottom line is that in order to find a good win bet that isn't simply for mathematical reasons, but rather for handicapping reasons, you must perceive something about this horse that you know the public doesn't see. If you can't do that the bet may be no good. In other words, if the information you like about this horse is rather shallow — for example, it won its last two races and had a great time — you should often pass on the bet. You must keep in mind that everyone will have this same information. To repeat, *if a horse is going off at higher odds than you thought it would, you have to worry that it's for reasons that you don't know.*

Again, the only time that you can be sure you have a good bet is if the reason why you are making this horse's chances higher than the public's are for reasons that the public doesn't know or hasn't taken into account. In the next section we will discuss some of these possible overlooked points.

---

[60] See *Getting the Best of It* by David Sklansky for more discussion.

By the way, if you do have handicapping ability you might want to list each horse and put next to it what you think the true odds of that horse are — making sure that when you add up all the odds they add up to approximately 100 percent.[61] (This will not be true of the odds on the board. They will add up to more than 100 percent because the track is taking its cut.)

We also recommend that you write down what you think are the odds each horse will go off at. If a horse is going off at *surprisingly* high odds it is probably not a good bet. The very best bets occur when a horse is going off at higher odds than you *think* it should be, but at slightly lower odds than what you *expected* it to be. This would imply that knowledgeable people are betting the horse lower than you expected, but it is still at higher odds than what you think it truly deserves.[62]

---

[61] You don't actually add up the odds. You must first convert them into percentage and then add these percentages together.

[62] Again see *Getting the Best of It* by David Sklansky.

# Eliminating the Favorite

There is one excellent way to combine mathematical and handicapping techniques at the races. This occurs when you the handicapper come to the conclusion that the favorite (or possibly a short-priced second choice) is highly overrated by the public and therefore highly overbet. If you are right in this assessment then it follows that at least one other horse in the race must be a good bet. Even if you aren't sure what other horse to bet on, you can have a profitable play by betting every other horse that has a good chance or even every other horse in the race! If you bet an amount that is approximately inversely proportional to the odds on each horse you will show a small profit no matter who wins as long as it isn't the one you eliminated. (Keep in mind the warning in the previous section however. If the horse you hate is *unexpectedly* much lower odds than you thought it would be, this is not a horse to be eliminated. Only when you came to the track expecting the horse to be highly overbet can you use this technique.)

If you trust your handicapping skills the idea is to find a horse whose odds, when translated to percentages, is 30 percent higher than the percentage chance you give it to win. An even-money shot (50 percent) that you think should be 4-to-1 (20 percent) would be an example. Eliminating a 2-to-1 shot altogether would be another. A 2-to-5 shot (70 percent) that you think should be 3-to-2 (40 percent) would also work. (Notice that giving a 3-to-1 shot absolutely no chance still does not guarantee a good bet elsewhere. Such is the strength of the house take. However, if you *could* eliminate a 3-to-1 shot it is much more likely that there is a good bet to be found.)

Since for professional gamblers missing good bets is just as dumb as making bad bets, there is no excuse for not playing a race where your handicapping skills can virtually eliminate a short-priced horse. If you can do that in a race where you can't assess all the horses, you simply take your handicapping hat off and put your mathematical hat on to find a bunch of win, place, exacta, or quinella bets. This must give you an edge.

# Watching the Races

If you want to have a significant edge by handicapping, you must watch the races. This is especially true for harness racing, but is also important at the flats. If you watch a race carefully and see something that won't be shown in the program next week, you may have gained an edge. Generally, this means you are looking for a horse that was actually better than the results of the race will show. Typically this will happen if it was blocked, had traffic problems, or was wide around a turn, and then did poorly. But *you* saw that it was ready to run. For instance, when a horse is forced far out from the rail around one full turn the total extra distance it has to run is $\pi$ (3.14) times the distance it was from the inside horses. (Of course, these problems are sometimes mentioned or shown in the program, and if they are, the information is no longer very useful.)

In addition, the jockey may compound a horses seemingly poor performance. Once the jockey or harness driver is caught in these problems — either having to go very wide or being blocked — he will frequently realize that he now has no chance of coming in the money. Consequently the jockey will often make no effort to improve his position. So you might see a horse that because of early problems finished poorly and has a subpar time. His poor performance may partly be due to the problems and partly be due to the fact that the jockey quit trying because he knew that he was completely out of it. (This also can occur if the horse was involved in a speed duel and has now run out of gas. The jockey will often mercifully let up on an exhausted horse rather than try to hold on for fifth or sixth place.)

A horse like this ought to be a good bet the next race and sometimes is a good bet for more than one race. But if you don't watch, you won't see these events. It's very important that you see whether there are horses that had a good excuse for doing poorly, especially when the public doesn't know about these extenuating circumstances.

One concept that is especially important in harness racing but also true in the flats has to do with physics. More precisely the formula

$$e = \frac{mv^2}{2}$$

where
e is energy,
m is mass, and
v is velocity.

Or put another way, the amount of energy that you use is proportional to the *square* of your velocity. And for our purposes (and without going into detailed math) this means if a horse was trying to run its best time it should run at a nearly steady speed all the way through. If it was to run any section of a race significantly faster it will use up so much energy that it will have to slow down so much in the other parts of the race that its average total speed will drop.[63] For small discrepancies there won't be much effect. But

---

[63] This idea also applies to people. If you are striving to run a four-minute mile, your best strategy is to run each quarter in 60 seconds. If you try to run one of the quarters in 55 seconds, it will cause you to run the remaining three-quarters of a mile in more than 3 minutes and 5 seconds. (This is especially true for the first three-quarters of the race where "finishing kick" doesn't come into play.)

once you make a horse go a quarter mile significantly faster than what is optimal, its final time will be impacted.[64, 65]

So what does this have to do with handicapping? If you can find a horse that is forced to run a small section of a race exceedingly fast you should expect that horse to fade. And if he doesn't fade badly, even if he comes in fifth or sixth, this may be an impressive performance.

Here's an example. In the first quarter of a mile race suppose a horse gets caught on the outside but when the quarter is over is one of the leaders. The horse had to run faster since it had to cover more ground. If it fades, but not too badly, you may have a good future bet. Even if it fades badly, it may be that the jockey has decided not to push the horse in a hopeless cause. This may be a better bet still.

Here's another example. In harness racing if a horse decides to make its move on the outside during the fastest quarter of the race and then fails and falls back, it will appear to most people that it ran a very poor race. Yet, it isn't nearly as bad as it seems. Without knowing about the other horses in the race, it is very likely that betting on this horse the next time will be an overlay as long as the odds are not ridiculously high.[66] (Remember higher odds horses

---

[64] It was this physics concept that did in Cigar in his bid to win his seventeenth consecutive race. He ran the first mile of a mile-and-a-quarter race in near world record time while a lesser horse behind him ran a steady speed and caught him in the stretch.

[65] Almost all horses do run their first quarter mile a little faster than average in order to achieve position. This is actually a good strategy as long as it doesn't go overboard.

[66] The converse is also true. If you notice a horse did well in its last race but had an "easy trip," this might be a good horse to bet against, especially if it is the favorite. By an easy trip we mean not being blocked or going wide around a turn as well as no especially fast quarters. Examples would be a front runner who was never

have an inherent disadvantage because the public likes to overbet the longshots.)

There are two other ideas concerning the flats that we want to mention. These are what are known as track biases and jockey biases.[67] At some tracks the inside horses may have a big edge, while at other tracks this edge may go to the horses on the outside. Secondly, the better jockeys, even though they are bet down more than typical jockeys would be on the same horse, may still be good bets. According to Wong, good jockeys are not taken into account enough. This is probably also true of the best drivers in harness racing.

---

pushed or a stretch runner who kept a steady pace and only passed horses because they had earlier dueled for the lead.

[67] See *Betting Cheap Claimers* by Stanford Wong for more discussion.

# Analyzing Past Results

If you really plan to be a serious or professional horseplayer, you should constantly be striving to find new "angles" or methods that will result in good bets. The best way to do this is to use past results to find or check out a winning method. But you have to be careful. There are some subtle mathematical reasons why the past may mislead you. This was explained in more detail in the previous chapter on sports. We don't want to repeat ourselves. But if you haven't read it already please read the section in the previous chapter called "Looking at the Past (Carefully)." The words apply just as much to horse betting, so please don't ignore them.

# Handicapping Tournaments

Occasionally a horse book will offer the opportunity to enter a handicapping tournament. They can be very profitable, as we know from personal experiences. Perhaps the most interesting aspect of handicapping tournaments is that knowledge of finding good bets and knowledge of horses may both be irrelevant. What's important is to know the rules of the tournament and what is required to win. This may very well mean something a lot different than finding good horse bets. We will discuss these tournaments in our tournament chapter.

# In Closing

Horse racing can definitely be beaten. This is true whether you are betting at the track or at a race book. The advantage of going to the track is that you can see the place, show, and other pools up to the very last minute. You may also gain more insights by watching a race in person rather than on television. On the other hand, a race book gives you far more races to choose from. It also hopefully offers house quinellas and parlay bets that are not parimutuel. Some books are not parimutuel at all. On balance we think the advantage of betting at a race book as opposed to at the track outweighs the disadvantages.

To find good bets at the races you use mathematics or handicapping skills or some combination of both. Mathematical bets include place or show overlays and certain house quinellas. Exacta discrepancies are another example. (Remember also to bet Pick Sixes efficiently as we showed you.) Bets involving handicapping include finding horses in trouble in previous races, analyzing fractional times, noticing track biases, and other concepts not mentioned here but explained in the books we recommend (or discovered by you when analyzing past results *properly*). Bets combining mathematics and handicapping include betting against highly overrated favorites and the "rubber band" concept. But keep in mind that factors that appear to make for a good bet are never worth it if everyone else knows them too.

# Part Four

# Slots and Poker Machines

# Slots and Poker Machines

# Introduction

Without a doubt the most popular form of casino gambling is slot machines. There are many reasons for this. First, they are fun to play. Second, they offer the possibility of a big payoff. Third, they are simple to play, and thus the intimidation factor is low. (This is particularly important to those people who are relatively new to gambling.) Fourth, they play very quickly, and most gamblers like fast-paced games. And finally, many people prefer the exciting, less serious atmosphere in the slot area of the casinos as opposed to the regular gaming pit.

The casinos also love slot machines. They are a low-maintenance item, and it's not necessary to hire a lot of personnel to run them. In addition, the variety of slot machines helps to make a casino a more interesting place.

No wonder slot machines are such a large money maker for the industry. In fact, in most jurisdictions where casino gambling is offered, the slots produce the majority of a casino's income. That is, casinos make more money from the slots than they do from all other games combined. Yet despite this, some of these machines are quite beatable.

In fact, as difficult as this might be for you to believe, there are lots of people out there who are making a living by playing some of these machines, (usually, but not always poker machines). If you live in the right part of the country, you can too.

# Progressive Machines

The reason you can win at slots for the most part has to do with a particular type of machine called a progressive machine. Some nonprogressive machines can also be beaten, but by far, the big money is being won on the progressive machines.

So what is a progressive machine? It is a machine offering a jackpot that increases as people play and do not hit the jackpot. It starts off at a certain amount and increases as coins are pumped into it. Exactly how it increases depends on how it is set. For example, in some cases the jackpot might increase one penny for every dollar that's put into the machine. Other machines will increase at different rates. But the point is that it continues to increase until someone hits the jackpot. Then it returns to the initial setting.[68]

Sometimes progressive machines are "stand alone" machines. That is the jackpot that they show, can be hit only on that particular machine. Other times progressive machines are linked together which means that all machines in the group will share the same progressive jackpot. If any one of these machines is hit, the jackpot for all the machines (hooked up together) is reset to its starting point. A system like Megabucks has thousands of machines throughout Nevada. When any one of these is hit the gigantic jackpot is reset.

---

[68] Though slot machines will allow you to play only one coin at a time, in order to be eligible for the progressive jackpot you must play the maximum number. Depending on the machine this is usually three or five coins. (If you play less than the maximum number of coins you are still contributing to the increase of the progressive jackpot even though you cannot win it. If you do hit the royal flush or whatever symbol combination is necessary to hit the jackpot, you will win a much lesser amount while the progressive jackpot meter rolls merrily along.)

(Before we go any further, since we just mentioned Megabucks let us state that you as a professional slot player will just about never want to play one of these machines. There are two reasons for this. First, the jackpot, even though it is huge, is almost never going to get high enough for your play to be theoretically profitable. Second, even if the jackpot gets technically high enough, the probability of hitting it would be so minuscule that you could easily go for hundreds of years before you got lucky. This certainly wouldn't be a very secure way of making a living.)

# The Underlying Theory

The underlying theory behind beating either a progressive poker or slot machine is that when the jackpot has reached a certain amount, the machine will pay out, on average from that point forward (until the jackpot is hit) more than it will take in. The machine will temporarily be over a 100 percent average payback machine (if you include the jackpot). The typical slot machine pays back an average of 90 to 95 percent of what is put into it, and the typical poker machine pays back a little more.[69] In either case you are doomed to lose if you play these machines, no matter how knowledgeable you may be. But progressive machines can have progressive jackpots that have grown to the point that you will have an advantage. Sometimes this advantage is large enough that you can expect to make some decent money playing it.

Take a progressive poker machine. There are many people who have won a lot of money off these machines. Some of them are far, far ahead of it. In fact, there are even a few millionaires who were created by video poker. (These millionaires didn't do all the playing themselves. They hired other people to play. We will get to that later.) Progressive poker machines can reach points where the jackpot is high enough that they give you an edge.

At this point we have to do a little math. Assuming you are playing the proper strategy, you can expect to hit a royal flush one time out of (approximately) 40,000 plays.[70] If you happen to be on

---

[69] As already mentioned there are some nonprogressive poker machines that also pay back over 100 percent (if you know how to play them correctly). They will be discussed later in the text.

[70] It is important to understand that this 1 out of 40,000 comes up totally randomly. If, for example, someone hit a machine five minutes ago it has no effect on when it will hit next. It does not mean that you have to wait another 40,000 hands before another

a typical quarter machine that requires five coins to hit the jackpot you expect to "pour" on average $50,000 into the machine to get that royal ($1.25 x 40,000 = $50,000).

Fortunately, this doesn't mean that the jackpot has to be over $50,000 for you to be happy about playing this machine. This is because the machine pays back on many hands besides a royal flush. In fact, the typical poker machine, even without paying out the royal flush jackpot will pay back in the neighborhood of 95 percent or 96 percent of what you put in. That is, the machine will win — assuming you play correctly, only about 5 percent of your "coins in." Consequently, after you have invested $50,000 you expect to be behind somewhere around $2,500.

Now suppose the royal flush paid $2,500. Then when you hit it, you should be about even. That is approximately the situation that occurs for poker machines in Las Vegas. When their jackpots get higher than $2,500, the professional slot players actually have the best of it.

---

jackpot occurs. Every individual play is about 40,000-to-1 shot. This 40,000 figure also assumes normal good strategy. If you were to go for the royal every time, you would hit it almost twice as often. But that strategy would eliminate almost all other paybacks and would eat you alive.

# The Payoff Schedule

We need to be very clear about a couple of things regarding the aforementioned progressive poker machines. First, the payoff schedule is such that you will be getting back about 95 percent of what you bet, without the royal flush. Second, you need to be playing your hands properly, so that you are obtaining the optimal return while you are waiting for that elusive royal. (Optimal strategy may change depending on the payback schedule and the size of the royal flush jackpot.)

If you don't play perfectly, you will need a higher jackpot to have the best of it. For example, if you don't always draw to your hands correctly and this costs you just 1 percent in expectation, then after you have put in $50,000 you will have had $500 less returned to you than what you should have. That is, if you are playing a machine that could pay back 95 percent without the royal, to *you* it pays back only 94 percent. This means that you need a $3,000 jackpot to break even rather than a $2,500 jackpot. Notice that just a small error in your playing strategy can be very expensive.

In standard Jacks-or-Better poker machines — no wild cards and no special bonuses for certain hands other than the royal flush — the progressives are usually what are called "8-5" machines. That means for each coin played they pay back eight coins for a full house and five for a flush. The other payoffs (for each coin played) are typically one for a pair of jacks through aces, two for two pair, three for three of a kind, four for a straight, twenty-five for four of a kind, fifty for a straight flush, and the progressive jackpot for a royal flush. For example, if you play four coins and make two pair you will get eight coins back. (Don't forget, however, that you need to play five coins to be eligible for the royal flush jackpot.)

For this payoff schedule there is an optimal way to play your hands. (Some tips will follow later in the text.) If you vary from what is correct, your expected return from the machine will be lower than what it should be and you will need a higher jackpot to be at the break-even point. (You also need a higher jackpot to have the best of it, even with perfect play, if the payback schedule is worse than "8-5." On the other hand, the jackpot need not even be $2,300 if you can find a progressive machine with better paybacks. This might be a 9-6 machine. It also might be a double bonus machine that pays 1, 1, 3, 5, 7, 9, 50, 80, 160, 50, 800 where the 50, 80, 160 refers to four fives - kings; four deuces, treys, and fours; and four aces respectively.)

# Your Profit Potential

Assuming you know how to play perfectly, it has been calculated that a progressive jackpot of about $2,300 is a break-even situation for the standard quarter progressive poker machine. So what does that mean? It means that when you finally hit the royal flush you will be down, on average, $2,300. So if you find a machine that has a $3,300 jackpot, this means that when you hit your royal flush, on average, it will have put you ahead $1,000, since it costs you an expected $2,300 to hit it.

Thus, theoretically you will make $1,000 by playing this machine. How long will it take you to hit the royal and earn this $1,000? It probably won't take you as long as you think. Nowadays most machines can hold credits. This means that instead of putting in coins for every play you can quickly hit a credit button that will automatically play five coins for you. Experienced players can easily play 8 to 10 hands a minute or as many as 600 hands an hour. Since a royal flush should occur once in about 40,000 hands, a fast player could hit one in an average of seventy hours. Therefore he would be able to beat this machine for an average of about $14 per hour.

$$\frac{3,300 - 2,300}{70} = 14.29$$

If you can find a machine whose jackpot is $4,300, you can expect to earn about $29 an hour.[71]

$$\frac{4,300 - 2,300}{70} = 28.57$$

This is the general principle behind playing poker machines. But this book is supposed to tell you how to make $100,000 a year gambling. Furthermore, we have already talked about people becoming millionaires from playing poker machines. And, of course, you can't do that at $14 an hour. However, that kind of money can theoretically be made if you hire other people to play for you. The going rate is usually $6 or $7 an hour, plus a small bonus — $200 would be reasonable — if and when the royal flush is hit.[72] Of course, if you do this you have to be able to trust the people you hire and you have to make sure they play close to perfectly. If your "team" is playing machines with a $3,300 jackpot, you're only making yourself about $5 to $7 an hour per hired player after you subtract their salary. This doesn't leave room for many mistakes.

We should point out that poker machines with high jackpots are not as easy to find as they once were. However, we feel that if you do decide to become a professional gambler, even if poker machines aren't the only gambling that you are doing, you should be aware that progressive machines will sometimes reach a point where there is a nice positive expectation, and you should be ready to take advantage of them when they come along.

---

[71] This is not taking into account the fact that the jackpot will be rising somewhat as you are playing. That is, if you can find a machine whose jackpot is $4,300 when you start, you expect it to be a bit more when you actually hit it.

[72] The bonus would go only to the player that hits the royal, not to everyone on the team.

# Jacks-or-Better Strategy Tips

To point you in the right direction, here are a few tips for playing the standard Jacks-or-Better poker machines. These guidelines will get you started, but they are not quite optimal play. Three sources that can give you expert advice are *Winning Strategies for Video Poker* by Lenny Frome, *Professional Video Poker* by Stanford Wong, and *9-6 Jacks or Better Video Poker* by Bob Dancer. For other recommended reading, see the appendix at the end of this book.

**Tip No. 1:** If your hand contains one or two high cards, jacks or better, but has no other value, draw to the high cards.

**Tip No. 2:** If your no pair hand contains three high cards of different suits, jacks or better, hold only the non-ace high cards.

**Tip No. 3:** If your hand contains no pair but has two to a royal flush, draw three to the two-card royal, even when your hand contains a third high card.

**Tip No. 4:** When drawing to a small pair, never keep a kicker.

**Tip No. 5:** If your hand contains a small pair but also has four cards to a flush or three cards to a royal flush, discard the pair.

**Tip No. 6:** If your hand contains a small pair but also has four cards to a straight, you still draw three cards to the pair.

**Tip No. 7:** If your hand contains four cards to a flush but also has a high pair, (jacks or better) draw three cards to the pair.

**Tip No. 8:** If you have four cards to a royal flush, always draw to the royal regardless of what your fifth card may be (unless it is the nine of the same suit, giving you a pat straight flush).

**Tip No. 9:** If you have nothing reasonable to draw to, you have to draw five new cards. It is better to do this than to draw to an inside straight or to draw 2 cards to a small flush. A two card draw to a *straight flush* is, however, better than a total redraw.

# Standard Slot Machines

As you can see, some video poker machines can be beaten, but what about the standard "one-armed bandits?" Well, the answer here is yes and no. There is no question that a progressive slot machine jackpot can rise to a point where it is worth playing, but the problem is in figuring out when this point is reached. It wasn't always this way. In the old days it was a simple matter to figure out the probability of not only hitting any jackpot, but of getting any payoff, because it was related to the symbols on each wheel of the slot machine.[73]

Unfortunately, today's modern slot machine works very differently. They are made with something called "virtual reels," where hitting each symbol on a reel is no longer "equally likely." It is random, but the probability of any particular symbol appearing can be different from any other symbol. A random number generator is used but some symbols will come up much less often than others. Thus it's much harder to determine how much a machine pays back while you are waiting for the jackpot, and it is also much harder to determine what the probability of hitting the jackpot is.

For those of you who are confused by this, here is a quick explanation of how virtual reels work. To keep things simple, let's say that a reel only has four symbols. Let's call them *seven, orange no. 1, cherry,* and *orange no. 2.* Further, lets assume that the machine has the capability of making 200 "stops" per wheel. What it will do is pick a random number from 1 through 200. If it comes up specifically number 1 it will be the *seven,*[74] from 2 to 35 it will be *orange no. 1,* 36 to 48 will correspond to the *cherry,* and the

---

[73] See *Getting the Best of It* by David Sklansky.

[74] The symbols corresponding to the jackpot, usually a seven, will in general only have one opportunity to appear.

remaining numbers will mean that *orange no. 2* will appear. That is, today's modern machine will generate a random number and then find the matching symbol.

As you can see, it can be very difficult to figure out what these machines are paying back between jackpots and what the probability of hitting a jackpot is. You could do a statistical analysis based on the results of the machine. That is, you might want to pull the handle five or ten thousand times to see approximately the frequency of each symbol coming up on each reel. But because of what is known as sampling error, even though you might get a good idea, it won't be perfect.

Also, there is one overriding fact. Even if you could do the statistical analysis very accurately, you would only rarely discover that you have the best of it. (Virtual reel progressive slots hardly ever reach over 100 percent payback.) And some of those times, as we stated before, the jackpot would be such a rare event that it still wouldn't be worth playing as long as you are interested in producing a "steady income."

At the time of the writing a new type of slot machine that builds up "equity" and occasionally pays mini bonuses has been introduced. These machines can be beaten if you look around for those that have been "abandoned" by others even though a bonus is likely to hit shortly. But this is a horrible way to make a lousy living and the situation may dry up quickly. We mention it only for completeness.

# Slot Clubs

One of the recent concepts in casino marketing is what is known as "slot clubs." Most casinos now offer them. In exchange for membership you have your play "tracked," and you receive various comps and in some cases cash back. If you are playing slots seriously, these clubs are a "must join."

After you sign up you will receive a card that looks and feels a lot like a credit card. When you play, you stick your card into the machine and accumulate points, which you then exchange for either comps or cash, or sometimes prizes. The more you play the more points you earn and the more you qualify for.

Casinos do this not only to encourage customers to play, but also to track how people are doing, how much they are betting, which machines are most popular, and so forth. The clubs also allow the casinos to make their marketing decisions more accurately. In short, casinos like their slot clubs. We also like them because they can add significantly to our profits.

The reason for this is that the rebate is usually in the neighborhood of ½ of 1 percent of what you bet. Put another way, if you have a machine where you have an edge, the slot club is just going to add to that edge. Now, in general, the slot club by itself — if you are playing a machine that has a disadvantage — isn't going to kick back enough to you to turn your disadvantage into an advantage. But it could be a significant figure when you do have the best of it.

For example, getting back to the standard quarter poker machine, we said that the break-even jackpot figure is $2,300 and that to hit the jackpot you expect to play approximately 40,000 hands, and put in $50,000. During this time you expect to earn from the typical slot club a $250 rebate.

$$250 = (.005)(50,000)$$

That's like adding $250 to the size of the jackpot. Sometimes it gets even better than that. For instance, at one major strip casino their slot club is worth 0.65 percent, which reduces the break-even point on their dollar machines from $9,200 to $7,900. This same casino also has a $5 progressive machine that pays 9 on the full house, 6 on the flush, with all other payouts standard. With perfect play and the slot club, you will always have at least a small edge on this machine. If they took the slot club away, this would not be true. *So always join the slot club.*

# Beating Nonprogressive Poker Machines

Earlier we mentioned that you could also make money from some nonprogressive poker machines. There are actually a small number of nonprogressive machines in Nevada which with perfect play, will pay back over 100 percent.[75] The expected return is usually somewhere between 100.2 and 100.8 percent. This isn't much of an edge, but it is better than nothing.

Frequently these machines are wild card poker games. The reason some of them have slightly over 100 percent payback is partly because when they were originally invented, the inventor didn't realize the optimal payback, and partly because it is no big deal anyway. Wild card machines require a more complex strategy for perfect play. Thus, the typical gambler plays them worse than he would a standard poker machine and loses at a faster rate. But if *you* play them and you are a member of the slot club they might pay back as much as 101 percent. But you must play them perfectly.[76]

Now what does a 1 percent edge turn into on a 25 cent machine? Well, we already showed that you can play extremely quickly — with practice perhaps as much as 10 hands per minute or 600 hands per hour at $1.25 per hand. That is equivalent to $750 an hour of action, so your expected profit is approximately $7.50 per

---

[75] As far as we know, nonprogressive poker machines that offer a positive expectation do not exist in any other locations.

[76] Again we recommend *Winning Strategies for Video Poker* by Lenny Frome, and two other reports by Bob Dancer: *Deuces Wild Video Poker* and *10-7 Double Bonus Video Poker*.

hour (counting the slot club, remember).

$$750 = (1.25)(600)$$

$$7.50 = (.01)(750)$$

So if you are ever desperate, you could play this nonprogressive machine and make $7.50 per hour. However, there is one thing that you must remember. That $7.50 includes hitting the royal flush. You're not making $7.50 an hour until you hit the elusive royal, and since it will take you 70 or 80 hours on average to hit it, you can be down quite a bit until you do. This of course would be even more true if you were playing a 100+ percent dollar machine. On the other hand that machine could be worth as much as $30 per hour.

In Las Vegas, some casinos have a deuces wild machine whose expected payback with perfect play is 100.6 percent. They also have a dollar version of deuces wild on the floor, but it pays back less than 100 percent. This used to be unheard of. Generally speaking, higher denomination slots always paid back at least as much as the lower denomination slots. But this particular dollar machine doesn't pay as much because the casino knows that while expert players aren't going to bother with a 100.6 percent quarter machine, they will play a similar dollar machine. $7.50 an hour (including the slot club) won't pay the bills — but $30 an hour will. Most casinos are smart enough to realize that they will get less than experts playing (and thus have to pay back less than 100 percent) on their super loose machines only if the expected hourly "earn" to an expert is small. Thus the dollar machines cannot be as good. If they were they would be filled with pros. But casinos are not always this smart. So you should always be on the lookout for dollar or five-dollar poker machines that pay over 100½ percent. (As of this writing this includes "double bonus machines" that pay 1, 1, 3, 5, 7, 10, 50, 80, 160, 50, 800, for respectively jacks or better, two pairs, trips, straight, flush, full house, four 5 - Ks, four 2,3,4s, four aces, straight flush, and royal flush. (The key here is 10 for the full house). This machine pays only a tiny bit over 100 percent, but may be worth if if you include the slot club. However, the correct strategy is quite complicated.

# Deuces Wild Strategy Tips

If you are interested in playing a wild card machine, here are a few tips for playing deuces wild. Again, we want to warn you that this advice is not all encompassing and that deuces wild requires a more complex strategy than jacks-or-better. (See the books by Lenny Frome and the deuces wild report by Bob Dancer.)

**Tip No. 1:** If your hand contains no deuces but you have two pair, throw one pair away.

**Tip No. 2:** If your hand contains no deuces but you have either four to a straight flush or a three-card royal, discard a pair if you have it.

**Tip No. 3:** If your hand is a completed straight or flush that also contains four to a consecutive straight flush, draw one card to the straight flush if your hand contains a deuce. Otherwise keep the pat hand.

**Tip No. 4:** If you have a four-card royal, always draw one even if you have a straight or flush made. (This is true if you have no deuces, one deuce, or two deuces. With three deuces, go for four of them.)

**Tip No. 5:** If your hand contains two deuces, draw three cards unless your hand is four or five of a kind, a straight flush, or a one-card royal draw.

**Tip No. 6:** If you have three deuces, draw two cards unless you already have five-of-a-kind or a royal flush (and four deuces pays 200-for-1 or less; machines that pay a lot higher for four deuces are common; with them you draw to three deuces no matter what).

# In Closing

As we have seen, playing the slots can be quite profitable. As of now this usually means playing the video poker machines, and specifically it usually means playing the poker machines that have a progressive jackpot that has reached a profitable level.

But many people will say that they want to play a standard slot machine with a huge jackpot. They would like to win $1 million or more. Well, we agree that winning this much would be nice, but as we pointed out in the text it's very unlikely that you can get an edge on these machines, and even if you did you could go for years before you hit. That is, you could easily be broke before your sevens come home.

We again want to mention that there are some people out there who have made a great deal of money from playing machines. Both of the authors know some people who only play video poker, have no other source of income, have done it for years, and are quite successful. This form of gambling has been good for a long time, and we expect it to remain good in the future.

Remember that the best machines are mostly found in Nevada. One well-known writer in the field refers to Las Vegas as "Video Heaven." He's right, but there are also many opportunities throughout Nevada and maybe even in other places.

.

# Part Five

# (Usually) Unbeatable Games

# (Usually) Unbeatable Games
# Introduction

This book is here to show you how to truly make a living gambling. So, unlike other authors who only dabble in the field, we will not have much to say about games where you cannot get an edge. That includes baccarat, craps, keno, and roulette, as well as some of the newer games like Let It Ride and Caribbean Stud. We are not going to give detailed explanations of why these games are unbeatable except to say that they involve gambling on events that involve no skill and that the odds don't change as the game goes on.

Other games are beatable because the opposite is true. Horses and sports involve skill. Blackjack and poker involve both skill and changing odds. But in games like craps and roulette, each time you bet, you are essentially playing a brand new game. Statisticians refer to these events as *independent* trials since the results of previous trials have nothing to do with the current outcome. We know that there will be some of you who don't see why this automatically means you can't have an edge. However, take our word for it. This is not something that is a matter of debate. There is no chance that you can have an edge if you play these type of games in an honest and normal manner no matter what you may read or may hear.

What about betting systems? There is a widespread fallacious idea that you can beat otherwise unbeatable games by using a betting system. Some of these systems generally involve betting more when you're winning, and others involve betting more when you're losing. But it makes no difference. Each individual bet is a separate bet, and as long as each bet has a disadvantage the sum total has to have a disadvantage in the same way that you could not add up a bunch of negative numbers and still get a positive number.

For example, suppose you are playing one of these games and are following a betting system where you bet more when you are losing in an effort to recover your losses. This presents a serious problem: If you have a prolonged losing streak — and the laws of probability state that if you play long enough, you eventually will — you will get wiped out.[77]

If it was possible to beat games like this using some kind of betting system, don't you think you would have heard of somebody doing that? After all the house has only a tiny advantage at some of these games. But, you know of no one beating these games using a betting system. That is because there is nobody who can honestly claim that he makes his living playing baccarat, craps, or roulette, providing that he is playing in the normal manner.[78]

That being said, it is still important that you have some idea of the rules of these games and how they work so that you can take advantage of promotions that might alter the normal rules in order to bring in customers. Casinos have been known to make mistakes, and when one of these errors is made, you want to know when it occurs. Let us now look at these games one by one.

---

[77] If you were playing the same system at a game where you had a constant *advantage* rather than disadvantage, your accumulated winnings would on average be large enough to weather these bad streaks.

[78] By "normal," we mean playing by the normal rules (as opposed to rules associated with a tournament or a special promotion) and not obtaining some "physical" advantage by cheating or other means.

# Roulette

We mention roulette first because it is the one game that could conceivably afford you the possibility of beating it even without taking advantage of a tournament or a promotion. But we're not talking about playing it in a normal manner. When you do play normally you must have a disadvantage simply because of the zero or zeroes on the wheel. The reason why those two zeroes give you a disadvantage is *not* because you must lose when they come up. The fact is, you could bet on the zero and/or double zero. It has to do with the fact that your payoffs on the roulette wheel would be fair only if the zero (and double zero) did not exist.

All the payoffs on the roulette wheel pay as if there are only thirty-six numbers (with one exception). For example, if you bet on a single number you get 35-to-1. If you split your bet on two numbers you get 17-to-1. These would be the fair payoffs if there were only thirty-six numbers on the wheel. In a nutshell, roulette has a disadvantage because when you win they pay you less than they should, given the number of numbers on the wheel. When there is a zero and double zero, the disadvantage on all of your bets with that one (even worse) exception noted below is a bit over 5 percent.[79] If you are "lucky" enough to find a single zero wheel, your disadvantage is about 2⅔ percent.

In many European casinos, and in a very few casinos in the United States, that disadvantage is cut in half yet again for even money bets only. In these places when you bet on red-or-black, odd-or-even, or first eighteen versus last eighteen, you don't immediately lose if it falls on the zero. Instead the casino spins the

---

[79] The one exception is a bet that on the next spin the ball will land on either 0, 00, 1, 2, or 3. This is sometimes called the "house special" and pays off at 6-to-1. Since the true odds are 33-to-5, you figure to be losing three bets after thirty-eight such bets. This is a disadvantage of 7.9 percent.

wheel again. If you win your bet the second time you don't actually win anything but you do get your money back. This has the net effect of only putting "half a zero" on the wheel, and when this option is offered the house advantage is only 1.3 percent on even money bets.

Of course, that's all probably irrelevant because you still have a disadvantage. To have an advantage you have to be paid more than you deserve. If you come upon a promotion where they are, for instance, advertising that they are going to be paying 40-to-1 on a number, then of course you would go and play the roulette wheel. But don't hold your breath waiting for this to happen.[80]

However, there is a way to beat roulette in theory. Actually there are two ways. One way is to find a wheel where certain numbers for some physical reason are coming up more often than the 1 in 36 times necessary for you to have an edge. If the wheel was perfect and it was a two-zero wheel, each number would come up 1 in 38. If it was a single zero wheel each number would come up 1 in 37. But no wheel is perfect and an imperfection might be enough to give you an edge. That is, on some wheels a particular number might come up more often than 1 in 36. But for the situation to really be worthwhile that number would have to be hit at least 1 in 34. If you could find a roulette wheel like that it would be worth playing because 1 in 34 translates to a 5 percent edge.

So how does one find one a wheel like that? The idea is to go to a wheel and "clock it," which means making careful note of how often each number comes up.[81] However there are two problems with this method. Number one is the extremely large number of

---

[80] Casino managers are often stupid, but not that stupid. Promotions that give the player the edge usually involve more subtle mathematics, and they are usually not as strong as the 8 percent advantage 40-to-1 on a number would give. (See the chapter on "Casino Promotions.")

[81] For a terrific writeup of some people who attempted to do this see *The Casino Gambler's Guide* by Allan Wilson.

spins you would have to watch and record to be relatively sure that
a number was coming up more than it should for reasons other than
pure chance. Number two is simply the fact that most wheels are
not "off" by enough, and you have wasted all of that time.[82]

Finally, we need to point out that the newer, modern casinos
are almost certainly buying wheels that are highly calibrated and are
very unlikely to be sufficiently biased. It is conceivable that if you
are dealing with an older casino that may have bought an older
wheel then just maybe you might be able to find a biased wheel.[83]
But you still have the two problems that we just mentioned. In
addition, you also have to worry about the casino itself. That is, if
you are tracking the wheel, betting the same number every time, and
winning, they just might change the wheel. So we really only
mention this method for completeness. We would be surprised if
you are able to find and exploit biased roulette wheels even though
it has been done in the past.

The other way to beat the wheel involves physics and is illegal
in many places. It takes advantage of the fact that the ball spinning
around the rim of the wheel always has the same "escape velocity"
and thus will leave the rim at the same speed every time. This
means that theoretically if you had a computer and possibly a laser
beam you could build a device that would predict where the ball
would fall. Again this is something that would require (1) a possibly

---

[82] See *Getting the Best of It* by David Sklansky on some
guidelines on how often a number needs to come up in order to
conclude that you have probably found a biased wheel that will
produce the desired results.

[83] A few years ago a new casino opened in downtown Las
Vegas. What was unusual about this casino was that it featured all
sorts of antiques, including some very old roulette wheels. It went
out of business a few months later, and we have always wondered
if their pretty, but ancient wheels contributed to their demise.

illegal device and (2) a lot of subterfuge, and so forth. But we do want to mention that it is something that conceivably can be done.[84]

So the fact remains that with the possible exception of a casino promotion or tournament, roulette is not something that any serious gambler, that is, someone who intends to make money gambling, is going to mess with. If you don't understand and believe this, you may as well kiss your money goodbye now.

---

[84] There was a book detailing the adventures of some brilliant young scientists who attempted to do this called the *Eudemic Pie* by Thomas Bass. They failed, but that was twenty years ago. We do know of a group that was successful doing this in the mid-1980s. However, because of changed laws the devices that they used are now illegal in many states.

# Craps

    Craps should really be divided into two categories — the bad bets and the not-so-bad bets. Though the not-so-bad bets are, of course, still bad in that if you were to make enough of them you would eventually lose all of your money, we call them not-so-bad because they lose at a much lower rate than the truly bad bets, which we will discuss first.

    When you are at the crap table there are opportunities to make what are known as *proposition* bets. For instance, you can bet that the next roll will be double sixes. This is a 35-to-1 shot, but the typical crap table pays only 30-to-1 or 31-to-1. This is an example of what we call bad bets. Most of them have a house edge of 9 percent or more. Speaking plainly, people who make these bets are hopeless. The only reason to know the odds on them is because of the chance there will be a promotion where they are paying too much.

    To give another example of a bad bet, let's take the case of the "hard 8." When you bet on hard 8 you are betting that two 4s will come up before either a 7 or an "easy 8." Since there is only one way to roll two 4s, six ways to roll a 7, and four ways to roll an easy 8, the chances that your number comes up before the other ones is 10-to-1 against you, or 1 out of 11. The crap table will pay you 9-to-1 (although they will call it 10-*for*-1). If you make this bet you will win 1 out of 11 and after eleven bets will find yourself down one bet so you have about a 9.1 percent disadvantage. All other crap propositions are figured along the same lines.

The not-so-bad bets are the pass line bet, the don't pass line bet, the come bet,[85] and the don't come bet.[86] If you bet on the pass line you win immediately if the player throws a 7 or 11 and you lose immediately if he throws a 2, 3, or 12. If he rolls any other number it is his "point," and the player continues to roll until he either rolls his point and thus wins or until he rolls a 7, in which case he (and you) loses. The player expects to win his pass line bet about 49.3 percent of the time.[87] This means that a bet on the pass line has a disadvantage of 1.4 percent.

$$1.4 = 50.7 - 49.3$$

Now to some of you 1.4 percent may not seem like much but it is still a pretty significant disadvantage. However, it turns out that you can obviate this disadvantage by making what is called the *odds* bet. If you make a pass line bet and the shooter throws a number other than a 2, 3, 7, 11, or 12, and thus establishes a point, you can now make a second bet that the shooter will hit this number before a 7. And on this second bet the casino pays off at fair odds. It pays 2-to-1 for a 4 or 10, 3-to-2 for a 5 or 9, and 6-to-5 for a 6 or 8. By doing this you take the disadvantage on the total amount that you

---

[85] *Come bets are just like* pass line bets except they can be made at any time.

[86] Place bets on the six and the eight may also fall into the not-so-bad category since the house edge on these bets is only 1.515 percent.

[87] If you bet "don't pass" you would win 50.7 percent of the time *except* that casinos won't pay you if the come-out roll is 12 (or in some casinos 2). Since this happens about 2.8 percent of the time you only win 47.9 percent, while losing 49.3 percent.

bet down to under 1 percent as long as you bet at least the same amount on your odds bet as you do on your pass line bet.

More liberal casinos allow your odds bet to be twice the amount or more of your pass line bet. For example, you can bet $10 on the pass line and then take $20 odds. Recently there has been a major war, so to speak, among casinos, where the odds that they are allowing you have escalated far higher. At the time of this writing there are four places in Las Vegas that are offering 100 times odds, where you can bet, for instance, $5 on the pass line and take $500 odds.

When you take 100 times odds, your disadvantage is so minuscule (about 2/100 of 1 percent, even less if you are a "don't" bettor) as to be almost irrelevant. That doesn't mean that you could start playing craps for a living. But the truth of the matter is if you made only pass, don't pass, come, or don't come bets, and constantly took 100 times odds you actually would have a small advantage in practice. This is true as long as you were willing to take the money when the dealer made a mistake in your favor and to point it out to him when he made a mistake in his favor. If you are astute enough not to make any errors yourself and complicate matters by betting odd amounts you would almost certainly have the best of it when playing craps at one of these 100 times odds places. Still, that edge would be very small and would involve giant swings. So we don't recommend it.

One other reason, however, why 100 times odds could be something to think about is if there was ever any kind of promotion that added to your advantage. This could be as little as getting a comp for your room or a few free meals. Then taking 100 times odds might be worth doing. The same might even be true for 20 times odds. (Of course this would only work if the casino was dumb enough to count your odds bet in their rating system.)

Still, with all this being said, there is no way to beat craps even when your disadvantage is tiny. There is no gambling method that will turn that slight disadvantage into an advantage. It just can't be done. For those of you who wish to learn more about craps and all the different possible bets, we recommend the *Fundamentals of*

*Craps* by Mason Malmuth and Lynne Loomis. This small booklet should tell you everything that you may want to know. Another good discussion of craps appears in *The New Gambler's Bible* by Arthur Reber.

# Keno

Keno has a rather terrible disadvantage. For every dollar bet you get back about 70 cents. The only reasons to know any of the details of keno is to take advantage of an advantageous keno tournament or if there is a promotion where they decide to offer you much more than normal. This, in fact, has happened in the past and so it could be helpful if you knew the exact odds regarding any keno ticket. The mathematics are somewhat complicated so we won't go into that here. What we will do is simply reprint the complete keno odds as they appear in *Getting the Best of It* by David Sklansky.

## One Spot
In 4 trials you will average hitting:

| | | |
|---|---|---|
| 1 number | - | 1 time |
| 0 numbers | - | 3 times |

## Two Spot
In 16⅔ trials you will average hitting:

| | | |
|---|---|---|
| 2 numbers | - | 1 time |
| 1 number | - | 6⅓ times |
| 0 numbers | - | 9⅓ times |

## Three Spot
In 72 trials you will average hitting:

| | | |
|---|---|---|
| 3 numbers | - | 1 time |
| 2 numbers | - | 10 times |
| 1 number | - | 31 times |
| 0 numbers | - | 30 times |

## Four Spot
In 326 trials you will average hitting:

| | | |
|---|---|---|
| 4 numbers | - | 1 time |
| 3 numbers | - | 14 times |
| 2 numbers | - | 69 times |
| 1 number | - | 141 times |
| 0 numbers | - | 101 times |

## Five Spot
In 1,551 trials you will average hitting:

| | | |
|---|---|---|
| 5 numbers | - | 1 time |
| 4 numbers | - | 18¾ times |
| 3 numbers | - | 130¼ times |
| 2 numbers | - | 419½ times |
| 1 number | - | 629 times |
| 0 numbers | - | 352½ times |

## Six Spot
In 7,752 trials you will average hitting:

| | | |
|---|---|---|
| 6 numbers | - | 1 time |
| 5 numbers | - | 24 times |
| 4 numbers | - | 221 times |
| 3 numbers | - | 1,006 times |
| 2 numbers | - | 2,390 times |
| 1 number | - | 2,818 times |
| 0 numbers | - | 1,292 times |

## Seven Spot

In 40,980 trials you will average hitting:

| | | |
|---|---|---|
| 7 numbers | - | 1 time |
| 6 numbers | - | 30 times |
| 5 numbers | - | 354 times |
| 4 numbers | - | 2,139 times |
| 3 numbers | - | 7,172 times |
| 2 numbers | - | 13,386 times |
| 1 number | - | 12,916 times |
| 0 numbers | - | 4,982 times |

## Eight Spot

In 230,116 trials you will average hitting:

| | | |
|---|---|---|
| 8 numbers | - | 1 time |
| 7 numbers | - | 37 times |
| 6 numbers | - | 545 times |
| 5 numbers | - | 4,212 times |
| 4 numbers | - | 18,755 times |
| 3 numbers | - | 49,425 times |
| 2 numbers | - | 75,512 times |
| 1 number | - | 61,317 times |
| 0 numbers | - | 20,312 times |

## Nine Spot

In 1,380,700 trials you will average hitting:

| | | |
|---|---|---|
| 9 numbers | - | 1 time |
| 8 numbers | - | 45 times |
| 7 numbers | - | 817 times |
| 6 numbers | - | 7,897 times |
| 5 numbers | - | 45,013 times |
| 4 numbers | - | 157,460 times |
| 3 numbers | - | 339,800 times |
| 2 numbers | - | 436,900 times |
| 1 number | - | 304,700 times |
| 0 numbers | - | 88,020 times |

## Ten Spot

In 8,912,000 trials you will average hitting:

| | | |
|---|---|---|
| 10 numbers | - | 1 time |
| 9 numbers | - | 55 times |
| 8 numbers | - | 1,207 times |
| 7 numbers | - | 14,359 times |
| 6 numbers | - | 102,310 times |
| 5 numbers | - | 458,340 times |
| 4 numbers | - | 1,312,900 times |
| 3 numbers | - | 2,383,100 times |
| 2 numbers | - | 2,631,400 times |
| 1 number | - | 1,600,300 times |
| 0 numbers | - | 408,100 times |

## Eleven Spot

In 62,382,000 trials you will average hitting:

| | | |
|---|---|---|
| 11 numbers | - | 1 time |
| 10 numbers | - | 66 times |
| 9 numbers | - | 1,770 times |
| 8 numbers | - | 25,665 times |
| 7 numbers | - | 225,062 times |
| 6 numbers | - | 1,260,350 times |
| 5 numbers | - | 4,621,300 times |
| 4 numbers | - | 11,140,600 times |
| 3 numbers | - | 17,366,200 times |
| 2 numbers | - | 16,723,000 times |
| 1 number | - | 8,977,700 times |
| 0 numbers | - | 2,040,400 times |

### Twelve Spot

In 478,264,000 trials you will average hitting:

| | | |
|---|---|---|
| 12 numbers | - | 1 time |
| 11 numbers | - | 80 times |
| 10 numbers | - | 2,596 times |
| 9 numbers | - | 45,627 times |
| 8 numbers | - | 487,640 times |
| 7 numbers | - | 3,361,000 times |
| 6 numbers | - | 15,404,000 times |
| 5 numbers | - | 47,533,000 times |
| 4 numbers | - | 98,410,000 times |
| 3 numbers | - | 133,784,000 times |
| 2 numbers | - | 113,717,000 times |
| 1 number | - | 54,410,000 times |
| 0 numbers | - | 11,108,700 times |

### Thirteen Spot

In 4,065,200,000 trials you will average hitting:

| | | |
|---|---|---|
| 13 numbers | - | 1 time |
| 12 numbers | - | 97½ times |
| 11 numbers | - | 3,835 times |
| 10 numbers | - | 81,558 times |
| 9 numbers | - | 1,056,540 times |
| 8 numbers | - | 8,875,000 times |
| 7 numbers | - | 50,064,000 times |
| 6 numbers | - | 193,103,000 times |
| 5 numbers | - | 511,724,000 times |
| 4 numbers | - | 923,946,000 times |
| 3 numbers | - | 1,108,736,000 times |
| 2 numbers | - | 839,951,000 times |
| 1 number | - | 361,032,000 times |
| 0 numbers | - | 66,652,000 times |

### Fourteen Spot

In 38,910,000,000 trials you will average hitting:

| | | |
|---|---|---|
| 14 numbers | - | 1 time |
| 13 numbers | - | 120 times |
| 12 numbers | - | 5,752½ times |
| 11 numbers | - | 148,287 times |
| 10 numbers | - | 2,324,400 times |
| 9 numbers | - | 23,667,000 times |
| 8 numbers | - | 162,708,000 times |
| 7 numbers | - | 772,414,000 times |
| 6 numbers | - | 2,558,620,000 times |
| 5 numbers | - | 5,913,260,000 times |
| 4 numbers | - | 9,424,250,000 times |
| 3 numbers | - | 10,079,420,000 times |
| 2 numbers | - | 6,859,600,000 times |
| 1 number | - | 2,666,100,000 times |
| 0 numbers | - | 447,521,000 times |

### Fifteen Spot

In 428,010,000,000 trials you will average hitting:

| | | |
|---|---|---|
| 15 numbers | - | 1 time |
| 14 numbers | - | 150 times |
| 13 numbers | - | 8,850 times |
| 12 numbers | - | 278,038 times |
| 11 numbers | - | 5,282,712 times |
| 10 numbers | - | 65,083,000 times |
| 9 numbers | - | 542,358,000 times |
| 8 numbers | - | 3,137,931,000 times |
| 7 numbers | - | 12,793,100,000 times |
| 6 numbers | - | 36,957,840,000 times |
| 5 numbers | - | 75,394,000,000 times |
| 4 numbers | - | 107,003,400,000 times |
| 3 numbers | - | 102,894,000,000 times |
| 2 numbers | - | 63,319,400,000 times |
| 1 number | - | 22,376,000,000 times |
| 0 numbers | - | 3,430,990,000 times |

# Baccarat

Baccarat is a very silly game. It's sort of amazing that so much money changes hands in this game. It used to be considered fairly liberal because the house edge is only slightly over 1 percent. But it should no longer be considered that liberal. The disadvantage in blackjack, even for a basic strategy player who doesn't count cards, is far less than 1 percent. Likewise for a craps player who takes the odds. And the fact is that 1 percent the worst of it on even money type bets is actually a fairly significant disadvantage.[88]

But we will use baccarat to show a mathematical concept. First, understand that the game involves getting as close to 9 as possible. Tens count as zero, and if your total is 10 or higher you drop your first digit. So a total of 14 is the same as a total of 4. Sometimes you use only two cards. If your first two cards total 7, 8, or 9 you always stand with it. If they total 0, 1, or 2 you always

---

[88] Percentage edge (or disadvantage) is not really a perfect measure of the strength of a bet. "Longshots" don't really get a completely fair shake when evaluated this way. As an example, let's say you were playing a game where you were getting even money and your chances of winning were 49½ percent. If there were no possible ties, each bet would have a 1 percent disadvantage. Suppose, however, that your plan was to either lose \$1 or to let your winnings ride until you had \$64. To do this you must win six bets in a row. The probability of this is $(.495)^6$ which is .0147 or 1 in 68. You are in reality getting 63-to-1 odds on a 67-to-1 shot. But a one-time bet on a 67-to-1 shot that pays off at 63-to-1 would be calculated as a bet with a 5.9 percent disadvantage! You would thus be better off taking a one-time bet where you were laid 63-to-1 on a 66-to-1 shot (a 4.5 percent "disadvantage") than trying to get to the same result using 1 percent "disadvantage" bets.

The upshot of all this is that a small percentage disadvantage is actually quite strong when applied to even money bets.

hit. The "player" always hits 4 or 5 also (and stands on 6). The "bank" may or may not hit totals between 3 or 6. Whether he does depends on specifically the *third card* that the player draws.

Since the rules are not exactly symmetrical, the so-called bank wins more often than the player. The bank will win about 50.7 percent of the time. Therefore if you bet on the player side you have about a 1.4 percent disadvantage.[89]

$$1.4 = 50.7 - 49.3$$

Hence, if you bet on the bank you might think you would have a 1.4 percent advantage. However, since casinos are in the business to make money, what they do to negate this edge is to charge a *5 percent "commission."* Now some people might think that that is a terrible price to pay and that betting on the bank ought to now have a very big disadvantage. But they are wrong, and the reason is because the commission is only paid when the bank wins, which is approximately half the time. Therefore, a bank bettor is not really charged 5 percent but rather an average of 2.5 percent. Furthermore, since he started out with a 1.4 percent advantage, the charge produces only a 1.1 percentage disadvantage.

$$-1.1 = 1.4 - 2.5$$

Again, however, this is of no real consequence. There is no way you can beat the game. One of the authors once wrote about situations that could conceivably come up where if you were

---

[89] We are ignoring ties for the sake of simplicity. Thus, our figures are slightly inaccurate.

counting cards you could have a big advantage.[90] For instance, if half the cards left in the shoe were deuces and the other half were treys a bet on the player would have a gigantic advantage. Those of you who know the rules would see that the player would always make at least 6 and the bank would frequently lose because it often stands on 5.

However, these situations are so few and far between that you cannot in practice get an edge by knowing about them. So for all practical purposes baccarat is just like craps. That is, you should consider it a series of independent trials each with a significant negative expectation.[91]

---

[90] See the chapter entitled "Card Counting and Baccarat" in *Getting the Best of It* by David Sklansky.

[91] For more information on the futility of card counting as applied to baccarat see *The Theory of Blackjack* by Peter Griffin.

# Other Games

Even though we have covered most of the (usually) unbeatable games that casinos offer, new ones are appearing all the time. Most of the other games like Let It Ride and Caribbean Stud normally have big disadvantages. The only time that you could have an advantage in Caribbean Stud, besides when there is a special promotion, is when the progressive jackpot gets to be extremely high. We are hesitant to say what that figure would be because it depends very much on what their smaller payoffs are. You would have to learn how to calculate it yourself. We will say that using the payoffs that are offered in many casinos at this time, the figure is in the $250,000 range. But it might be more than that depending on what you are required to put up on the initial bet. Let's just say it has to be a minimum of $250,000, and even that might not be enough.

There is one other game that should be mentioned. It is Pai Gow Poker. In theory it is beatable whether you are in a Nevada or a California casino. But we are not going to go into detail about it here because we are not really all that thrilled with this game.[92] There is no reason to give an in-depth analysis of it, however, we will say that if you are in a situation where you think that you want to consider playing Pai Gow Poker seriously, anything that you might need to know about the game is almost certainly going to be covered in Stanford Wong's book *Optimal Strategy for Pai Gow Poker*.

---

[92] The edge in Nevada is tiny, so California is, as of this writing, the only viable place to play. However, there are "logistical" problems that we won't go into here.

# In Closing

As you can see we did not spend much time on any of these games. There is no reason to. Despite what you may sometimes read or hear, these games are not beatable as long as you play them honestly and normally.

This doesn't mean that you should never bounce the dice off the back wall of the crap table or place a wager on the whirling ball. If you do this sort of thing for fun and are aware that you are taking the worst of it, we have no quarrel with that. But this isn't always the case with semi-knowledgeable gamblers. We have watched too many otherwise successful poker players and sports bettors have one of those inevitable bad nights and then spend time in the pit trying to get even quickly. This is suicide, and they eventually get what they deserve. We mention this only because the purpose of this book is to show you how you can make a good living gambling — and spending your quality time in the pit playing independent trial games with a fixed house advantage won't get the job done.

So remember, if you want to play a game like craps, play it for fun and don't bet your serious money. Look elsewhere in this book to find where the bets that produce real "income" are.

# Part Six

# Casino Promotions

# Casino Promotions

# Introduction

To win at gambling you must find games where you have an edge. If you don't, you have no hope of being a successful professional gambler. Fortunately, there are many games where if you know what you are doing you can get a small edge. Furthermore, by playing these games on a steady basis you can make a good living, frequently $100,000 a year or more.

On the other hand, you cannot expect to find a game where you have a *big* edge at least on a day in and day out basis. There's an obvious reason for this. If a game that good existed, it would immediately be taken advantage of, and it wouldn't last long. The casinos would "wake up" quickly. However, there are times, when you just might get that big edge. These situations come at intermittent intervals so you can't count on them. But over the years they have popped up many times and we expect them to continue to do so.

What situations are we talking about? They are promotions, advertising ploys, and special events where the casino has decided to change the rules of a particular game or betting proposition to make it better for their patrons than it usually is. In general, when these "props" occur, casinos are trying to attract new customers.

You would think that when a casino does this they would have enough sense to do it in a way that the player is not getting a huge edge. But that's not always the case. Over the years we have taken advantage of many promotions that were ridiculously good. In fact, some of them still seem hard to believe. The only explanation for these events is that, in general, casino management is not very strong in the mathematics of gambling.[93]

---

[93] Yes, when we make this statement we are being polite.

How valuable are these promotions? Well, we don't think you should be devoting your full gambling time to them since you can never be sure when they will come up. On the other hand, if you have decided to become a professional gambler, you ought to be on the lookout at all times for promotions where it might be worth your time to suspend all other gambling activities temporaily and take advantage of an outlandishly good deal.

How do you recognize these occasional outstanding opportunities, and what skills are required to be adept at taking advantage of them? The answer is, you must have a good understanding of basic probability theory as it applies to gambling.

Notice that this is not really the case when you are trying to master some of the other games that we have talked about. If you were simply trying to become an expert at blackjack, horses, or sports you could get away with being only mildly familiar with probability and still be very successful. For example, in the case of blackjack you could just memorize a good (published) count strategy and follow the casino composure advice that we (and other authors) have talked about. You don't need to do the probability work. Other experts have already done it for you. All you need to do is follow their instructions. Even in poker, you don't have to be that adept at figuring out precise probabilities.

However, if you are going to take advantage of promotions, especially new promotions that have not already been analyzed, you need to learn some simple probability because the edges come from the mathematical errors that the casinos make. To start you should read the probability appendix in this book. Next we recommend that you read "The Mathematics of Gambling" section in *Getting the Best of It* by David Sklansky. If you understand this material you should be able to analyze most casino promotions that you will come across correctly. (In addition, if you want to learn more about gambling math, you may also want to read *Gambling Theory and Other Topics* by Mason Malmuth, as well as a basic statistics text.)

There is no way we can tell you about every possible promotion that has come up in the past or may come up in the future. As just stated, you must know how to be able to evaluate them yourself. But we will give you some examples of highly profitable promotions that actually did happen and a few hypothetical examples so that we can demonstrate the correct technique to analyze them.

# Blackjack

The first promotion we will discuss is one that does occur rather frequently even to this day. It is when the casino offers a 2-to-1 payoff on a blackjack rather than the normal 3-to-2 payoff. Let's see how this affects your game.

The first thing you need to know is the probability that you will be dealt a blackjack. In a single deck game one way to calculate it goes like this: The chance that the first card dealt to you is an ace is 4/52. Given that your first card is an ace, the chances that the second card is a 10-value card is 16/51. Thus the probability that you will be dealt a blackjack this way is .0241.

$$.0241 = \left( \frac{4}{52} \right) \left( \frac{16}{51} \right)$$

But there is a second way of being dealt a blackjack. It occurs when the first card is a 10 value card (16/52), and the second card is an ace (4/51). Notice that this will produce the same probability of .0241.

$$.0241 = \left( \frac{16}{52} \right) \left( \frac{4}{51} \right)$$

To get the probability of being dealt a blackjack all you need to do is add the two probabilities together. This produces .0482 or almost 5 percent.

$$.0482 = .0241 + .0241$$

If you did this calculation for more than one deck the numbers would be clumsier but you would get almost the exact same answer. The bottom line is that you are going to be dealt a blackjack approximately 5 percent of the time and except for those few times when you push with the dealer (when he also has a blackjack) you will be paid your bonus. This means that if you are being paid 2-to-1 on blackjack you will win an extra half a bet almost once in twenty times. In a hundred hands you expect to get an extra half a bet almost five times. That means almost two and a half bets extra will be paid to you on average every hundred hands you play. So being paid 2-to-1 on blackjack adds approximately 2 percent to your results.[94] If you are just a basic strategy player this should give you an edge of about 2 percent in a single-deck game with favorable rules and an edge of at least 1½ percent in most other games. And as we've said this particular promotion still occurs fairly frequently.[95]

A second example of a blackjack promotion occurred many years ago at the Fremont Hotel and Casino in downtown Las Vegas. In an attempt to attract customers, management inserted a joker into their double-deck game. If the player received the joker, it was wild.[96] If the dealer received the joker it was discarded and he would have to take another card. So what would this do to a blackjack game?

---

[94] Again, the reason it doesn't add a full 2½ percent to your results is because of the occasional blackjack ties.

[95] Recently this promotion has been occurring a lot in the California Indian casinos. However, in these casinos there is typically a fee per hand, and if this fee is significant it serves to reduce the advantage that this promotion offers. Generally the fee is about 1 percent so this would cut the edge down to below 1 percent for the basic strategy player.

[96] Except that joker-ten counted only as a regular 21 rather than a blackjack.

Clearly this gave the player an edge, but how big an advantage was it? Without being totally precise we will show you that it is a very nice edge indeed. First, you must realize that if the player gets the joker (and the dealer doesn't have blackjack) he will always make 21. (If you don't see this, pause and think a bit.) So the joker is an almost guaranteed win. Second, you need to realize that the average hand is approximately a push (in a mathematical sense) for the basic strategy player. Remember in the blackjack chapter we showed that the basic strategy player plays almost dead even with the house. Thus, when you get the joker it is gaining you, on average, almost one whole bet. (It doesn't gain quite one bet because you will occasionally push or even lose with your joker hand.) Third, you need to know that the average blackjack hand contains about 3 cards, and since a double deck with the joker will contain 105 cards you should get an almost automatic winner about 1 in every 35 hands. That's about 3 percent of the time and that, in fact, is what this promotion was worth to the player. It was a 3 percent edge.

Now let's consider a hypothetical blackjack promotion. Suppose a casino gives you an opportunity to surrender your hand for only 25 percent of your bet. Common sense tells you that this is a giant edge. To calculate the exact edge is extremely laborious, so we won't do it here. The more important question is how would you take full advantage of this obviously profitable situation? The idea would be to surrender every time you expected to lose at least 25 percent of your bet if you played your hand. Basically this would mean that you should surrender as long as your chances of winning were less than 37½ percent. (Do you see why?) To do this accurately, what you would need would be a top-quality blackjack book that has charts that show what your expected value is in every situation. You then would surrender all of those hands that have an expected value worse than -25 cents per dollar bet.[97]

---

[97] The best book for this kind of information is probably *Professional Blackjack* by Stanford Wong.

Our final blackjack example actually occurred just a few weeks before this writing. A small casino in Las Vegas called the Klondike offered something called a "free ride." It went like this: When you were dealt a blackjack you would be given a small plastic button known as a "lammer" with the amount of your bet imprinted on it. Then on a subsequent hand where you bet no more than that amount, you could turn your lammer in after receiving your first two cards and get your money back.

For example, suppose you bet $50, were dealt a total of 16, and the dealer had a ten showing. If you had a lammer for $50 or more, you could turn it in and get your money back. With a little reflection the astute reader should see that this option is giving you about the same thing as paying 2-to-1 on blackjack. Can you see why? Remember that a 2-to-1 blackjack promotion is giving you an extra half a bet every time you are dealt a blackjack (except for pushes). This promotion is also giving you approximately half a bet extra on each blackjack. The extra half a bet is not an immediate payoff but rather a delayed payoff on a future hand. The idea is to use your free rides on hands that you would normally surrender. Since these hands (such as a total of 16 versus a dealer's ten) have an expected value of negative 50 cents or more per dollar bet, the opportunity to call them a push saves you more than half a bet. So each blackjack that you are dealt now saves a half a bet down the road. The bottom line is about a 2 percent edge to the non-counting basic strategy player.

# Craps

Many years ago an incredible craps promotion took place at the Rainbow Casino in Henderson, Nevada. The casino made one simple change in the rules: If you bet the pass line and your come out roll was a 7 or 11, you would be paid 3-to-2 odds rather than your normal even money. So what kind of edge is this?[98]

Well, an 11 has two ways of being rolled and a 7 has six ways of being rolled, so the probability of rolling one or the other is 8 out of 36, which is 2 out of 9, or approximately 22.2 percent.

$$0.2222 = \frac{8}{36} = \frac{2}{9}$$

Thus, on 22.2. percent of your come out rolls you will win this bonus of a half a bet. Now as we already know, if you make a pass line bet your normal disadvantage is 1.4 percent. But the Rainbow Casino was offering a half a bet 22.2 percent of the time, which gave you 11.1 percent the best of it above normal. Since normal means to lose at a 1.4 percent rate, this amazing dice proposition gave the player a 9.7 percent edge on pass line bets.

$$9.7 = 11.1 - 1.4$$

Needless to say this promotion didn't last very long, and yes, there sometimes is a pot of gold at the end of the rainbow.

---

[98] When this promotion occurred David Sklansky was there to take advantage of it. Mason Malmuth was out of town and is still jealous to this day.

Let's now look at a hypothetical craps promotion. Suppose a casino decided to give pass line bettors a push when rolling a total of 3 on the come out roll. Normally you lose your bet when this happens so you can see that this hypothetical promotion will save you a bet whenever you "shoot" a total of 3 on your starting roll.

This is a fairly simple one to figure. And it might come up some day. A total of 3 is expected to come up 2 out of every 36 times that the dice are thrown. This is about 5.6 percent.

$$\frac{2}{36} = .056$$

Now, since you are saving a bet 5.6 percent of the time and the initial disadvantage is 1.4 percent, a promotion like this, which might seem to a mathematically naive person as no big deal, would in fact give about a 4.2 percent edge to the pass line bettor. If it ever happens, you should get there and play for as long as the casino will let you. (As an exercise to the reader, can you see why offering a push on a total of 2 rather than 3 is only about a 1.4 percent edge, while offering a *win* on 3 rather than a loss or push would bring the edge up to about 9.7 percent?)

# Sports Betting

Without a doubt the ultimate promotion that has ever come along was in the area of sports betting parlay cards. This particular promotion was so mindboggling that even to this day when we tell mathematicians about it they think we're making it up. Mathematicians find it especially difficult to believe that not only could one casino be that stupid, but that *four* were. Yet the fact is that this promotion was offered by the Stardust and the Fremont Hotels in Las Vegas, and then a week later by the Golden Nugget and the now defunct Churchill Downs sports book.

What was it? Simply a parlay card that paid in the following manner for a "ten teamer." If you won all ten you were paid 160-for-1. If you hit nine out of ten you were paid 60-for-1. And if you won eight out of ten you were paid 20-for-1.

Now suppose you bet every possible combination. You would have to buy 1024 tickets. That's simply 2 to the 10th power.

$$1024 = (2)^{10}$$

If you bet \$1 per ticket, then one of these combinations would contain all winners and thus be worth \$160. You would also have ten tickets with only one loser. That is you would have a ticket that won every game except for the first one, a ticket that won every game except for the second one, a ticket that won every game except the third one, and so on down the line. Each would return \$60. But the real killer is how many tickets you would have that had two losers and eight winners. You would have a ticket that had a loser on the first game and the second game, a ticket that had a loser on the first game and the third game, a ticket that had a loser on the fifth and seventh game, and so forth. Altogether there are forty-five different tickets with exactly two losers. (This is a simple combination problem involving choosing two out of ten. The number of ways is 45.)

$$45 = \frac{(10)(9)}{(2)(1)}$$

See the appendix on probability or see *Getting the Best of It* by David Sklansky for a further explanation.) So out of your 1024 $1 tickets, you would have one ticket that was worth $160, 10 tickets worth $60, and 45 tickets worth $20. For your initial $1024 investment you would be getting back $160, plus 10 times $60, plus 45 times $20. This comes out to $1660!

$$\$1660 = \$160 + (10)(\$60) + (45)(\$20)$$

And you have absolutely no risk! This promotion really did happen, and one of the authors made a ton of money on it. Every $1,024 turned into $1,660. All because many casinos don't even have a cursory knowledge of simple probability.

We want to talk a little more about parlay cards because other errors sometimes appear on them, particularly if only one game is involved. And when we say one game we are frequently referring to the Super Bowl. (Parlay cards usually involve betting on three or more games. However, for big games like the Super Bowl, cards are printed offering many different proposition bets on just the one game.)

There have been many errors in Super Bowl parlay cards, but the most obvious one appeared at Circus Circus a few years back. This one was so ridiculous it was funny. The Circus offered a card where, among other things, you could bet on the game, you could bet on the winner of the first half, and you could bet on the winner of the second half. But these bets could all be part of a parlay!

Specifically, your first bet could have been that Team A won the first half, your second bet could have been that Team A won the second half, and your third bet could have been that Team A won the game. But if Team A wins both the first and the second half, they *must win* the game. The bottom line is that you were paid the three team parlay price (6-to-1) on what in reality was only a 3-to-1 two teamer.

Of course, it was correct to bet both A, A, and A, and B, B, and B. Since the parlay paid 6-to-1 you would risk $2 in an attempt to get $7 back. That is, you would either lose $2 or win $5. This means that you got 2½-to-1 whenever the team that won the first half also won the second half. The Circus didn't know it but they were paying 2½-to-1 on an approximately even money shot.

Here's another similar error that actually appeared on a Super Bowl parlay card. A Las Vegas casino allowed you to parlay "who scores the first field goal" with "who scores the most field goals." Obviously with this parlay, if you won one of the bets, you are a big favorite to win the other. (If you have trouble seeing this, think about what happens if only one field goal is kicked in the game.) Yet the parlay paid as if both events were independent (13-to-5).

# Video Poker

You always need to be on the lookout for promotions that involve slots and, even more likely, video poker. In fact, at the time of this writing there are numerous video poker promotions all over town (Las Vegas). Since video poker machines are already very close to an even bet, any promotion that affects them has the potential to be worthwhile. Given that management does not always understand the math, it is easy for them to slip into a promotion that could be very advantageous for the player.

For example, let's say a casino offered to pay double on any four of a kind. On a standard machine this gives you an average of 25 extra bets for every (approximately) 420 hands. This is about 6 percent extra. If the machine was normally a 99 percent machine, you would now have a 105 percent machine.

A recent similar promotion that we were told about was even better than this. At the Ramada Express Hotel and Casino in Laughlin, Nevada, there was a coupon readily available that entitled you to collect double on four of a kind. What really made it strong was that this casino had some machines known as bonus four of a kind where the normal payoff for quads was at least 50-to-1. With the coupon you got double that. (Some of the other paybacks are lowered to make up for it.) They thus produced a machine where the player with these coupons had an edge of over 10 percent.

Let us also use video poker to illustrate how some promotions that seem great really are no big deal. For instance, "Reversible Royals." This fairly common promotion involves paying a bonus for hitting a royal flush in sequence. Some casinos pay if the sequence is in either direction, namely ten-jack-queen-king-ace or ace-king-queen-jack-ten. The typical bonus is $10,000 for a quarter machine (with 5 coins played).

The calculation for this proposition is actually rather simple. (If it is beyond your capabilities, you need to change that if you expect to make money via promotions.) First, you should realize that there

are 120 ways to arrange the 5 cards of a royal flush. This is simply
(5)(4)(3)(2)(1) also called 5 factorial and denoted by the symbol 5!.
Two of these ways are reversible royals. So only one out of 60
royals qualifies for the bonus. Since the probability of hitting a royal
flush is usually about 1 in 40,000, a reversible royal is about a 2½
million-to-1 shot. It thus takes about $3 million worth of quarters,
on average, to be inserted into the machine for each reversible royal
hit. Note that $10,000 extra for every $3 million bet is one-third of
one percent.

$$.003333 = \frac{10,000}{3,000,000}$$

This is a nice bonus, but nothing to write home about even if you
pay no taxes on it.

# Other Games

There was a great keno promotion that once appeared at the Sahara Hotel and Casino in Lake Tahoe. (The Sahara is now The Horizon.) The promotion was that on a $2 ten spot keno ticket, if you hit 7 or more they gave you a Krugerand in addition to your normal winnings.[99] At the time a Krugerand was worth approximately $200, so in reality they added $200 to the payoff for 7, 8, 9, or 10.

But a funny thing happened. Their keno play didn't increase much. As the table that appears in the keno section in this text shows, getting 7 or more hits on a ten spot ticket just doesn't happen very often. Even the Krugerand did not make keno attractive since the Krugerand was only rarely being given away. So someone in casino management came up with a "brilliant" idea. They would drop the requirements on the Krugerand from 7 to 6 hits for a ten spot ticket.

Well, this makes all the difference in the world. Adding $200 to the payback for 6 out of 10 as well as 7 or more out of 10 made this a very profitable promotion for the player. In fact, the player's advantage was now about 100 percent. We will leave it to the reader to verify these numbers, but needless to say keno became a very popular game in Lake Tahoe for a short period of time.

There have also been profitable promotions involving baccarat. The most obvious one, done a couple of years ago at the Sahara Hotel and Casino in Las Vegas, was to offer the player the opportunity to bet on the bank with no commission. How they could believe that they could make money doing that is beyond us. As we mentioned elsewhere in the text, commissionless baccarat would give someone who bets on the bank almost a 1.4 percent advantage. He would now expect to win at exactly the same rate that the "player" is supposed to lose at. Again, as with most other

---

[99] A Krugerand is a South African gold piece.

promotions of this sort, when a casino gives away the bank, the promotion doesn't last very long, and this one went for just a few days. (This illustrates why it is very important to "keep on top" of things in the gambling world. The best way to do this is by reading all the publications that have casino ads. This normally means newspapers and publications like *Card Player*. By perusing ads you often know about promotions *before* they happen. If you wait to hear about promotions from other people or from gambling newsletters that tell about them, you will probably have missed the boat.)

There was even a ridiculous promotion involving the Big Six Wheel. In fact it was the first promotion that either one of us ever took advantage of. Twenty years ago the Union Plaza in Las Vegas let you purchase $10.00 worth of Big Six bets for $7.50. So it cost you 75¢ to make a dollar bet. As bad a bet as the Big Six usually is this promotion gave you an edge. For instance, of the fifty-four stops on the wheel, four of them are "ten-dollar bills." The odds on hitting one of them is 50-to-4 or 12½-to-1. But if you could make a dollar bet on the ten with a 75¢ coupon, then you would figure to be ahead $2.50 after fifty-four spins.

$$\$2.50 \ = \ (4)(\$10) - (50)(\$.75)$$

And you could bet up to twenty coupons per spin! So the Union Plaza was nice enough to give one of the authors (Sklansky) about $2,000 before calling it quits.

# Coupons

Very often promotions are related to coupons. A coupon is possibly going to offer you something that adds up to significant money. We already gave an example of a valuable coupon that doubled the payouts when making four of a kind at a Laughlin casino. The MGM in Las Vegas recently gave out a valuable coupon to their high-limit pit players. If you were a rated player and had given this casino enough action, you would have received a coupon in the mail which you could exchange for a $1,000 chip or $1,000 in slot tokens. We know of one person who has received three of these in the past year and a half.

Of course, coupons aren't always this valuable. For instance, a coupon that offers you the opportunity to bet it along with a dollar and then get paid $2 is worth 50 cents and no more. But if the coupon allowed you to bet *any amount* and get paid 2-to-1 then obviously that coupon would be worth a lot. And such coupons do appear every now and then.

There are coupons that can be used only once, and other coupons that can be saved until a winning combination comes up. Many casinos don't know the difference, but there is an incredible difference. For instance, a (hypothetical) coupon that offers you the opportunity to get 50-to-1 on a number in roulette or 50-to-1 on double sixes in craps is merely okay if you can use it only once and if you must present it when you make your bet. But if, instead, they tell you that the coupon can be brought out when you hit your winner rather than when you place your bet, it becomes extremely valuable if you are allowed to bet a large amount. For those who don't see why, it works like this: A $100 bet on double sixes that pays 50-to-1 has a positive expectation of $41.67. You have a 1-in-

36 chance of winning $5,000 and a 35-in-36 chance of losing $100.

$$\$41.67 \ = \ \left(\frac{1}{36}\right)(5,000) - \left(\frac{35}{36}\right)(100)$$

However, if you don't have to present the coupon until you actually hit double sixes, this means that the $5,000 is *guaranteed* to be paid to you. Since it will take an average of 36 rolls to hit your number you will be losing on average $3,500 at the time you get your $5,000 payoff. Thus this coupon is worth an average of $1,500, which is a lot more than the $41.67 of the one-time coupon.

# In Closing

The bottom line of all of this is that casinos are to this day coming up with promotions, which can be quite profitable to the player. Sometimes the casino will willingly give up a little bit. However, the really juicy times are when the casino doesn't know what they are doing. When this happens, there is tremendous money to be made.

In this chapter we have given a few examples of what you might expect. Furthermore, with more and more casinos out there and with top quality casino management being spread thin, it is probably more likely than ever before that you will find one that is offering an advantageous promotion.[100] They might not be as ridiculous or as insanely profitable as some of the examples that we gave. But if you are already a good player the promotion may only need to be just okay for you to want to take advantage of it. This is especially true if you were going to play anyway.

Finally, we again want to emphasize that taking advantage of promotions should probably not be the sole source of your gambling income since you can never be sure when they will occur. But if you are going to seriously consider being a professional gambler you should constantly be perusing the literature, the advertisements, and the papers to see what is out there. And hopefully you will have learned enough about probability that you will be able to evaluate and take advantage of a promotion where you have much the best of it. You won't be sorry if you do.

---

[100] As of this writing some casinos are wise enough to retain Sklansky Casino Consulting to design mathematically sound promotions that sound great, but still let the casinos do okay. So you will have to confine your search to those that aren't.

# Part Seven

# Casino Tournaments

# Casino Tournaments

# Introduction

Another popular form of gambling offering the astute player good money-making opportunities is casino tournaments. In fact, it may even be possible to make a living solely from gambling on the tournament trail. Many casinos occasionally hold tournaments for all their various games. They do this to attract customers and to increase the overall action in their pits. Typically tournaments are held in poker, blackjack, craps, slots, video poker, horse racing, and keno.

When there is a tournament the smart player can usually get enough of an edge where he will show a long-run profit. Sometimes this edge is significant, depending on how big the tournament is, which game it is, the rules of the tournament, and the strength of the competition. Ironically, it doesn't depend very much on the house advantage. The fact of the matter is, you get your advantages in tournaments via methods that have very little to do with whether or not your individual bets have an edge.

Why is this so? Because to win a tournament or to win one of the  top prizes in the tournament you must do better than your opponents. Thus, what matters is not your absolute results, but your results in comparison to the other entrants. Because of this, you have many opportunities to use logic and advanced tournament strategies to give yourself a far better chance than the average player. That is what is unique about these events. They essentially require *tournament* skills as opposed to *playing* skills. For example, in a blackjack tournament there is virtually no need to count.

We will discuss poker tournaments at the end of the poker section. This section will discuss all the other kinds of tournaments.

# What Is Involved
# in a Tournament

Before we go into the details of some specific tournaments, let's explain some things that are normally part of any tournament. In general, the casino asks you for two things: an entry fee and a buy-in. (In some cases they offer the opporunity to make more than one buy-in.)

Usually the casino will have all of the tournament participants play with their own money.[101] Then the results are recorded. Those who do the best not only keep the money they have won at the tables, but win prize money as well.[102]

The total prize money is usually at least as much as the total of the entry fees, so the casino does not usually make a profit from the entry fees. In other words, they give back as much as they take in. In some cases, they give back more. They can do this because they make their money from the players gambling both during the tournament and at other times during their stay.

---

[101] Occasionally a tournament only requires play money. This is rare, however, because the casino usually holds these tournaments in order to get you to gamble where they have an edge.

[102] In most cases, tournaments are separated into rounds. For instance, you may have to have one of the best results in each round (or at your table) to advance to the next round. Most of the prize money is typically awarded to those who do the best in the final round.

# Getting an Edge

Why does a smart experienced tournament player have an edge? Basically, because he or she uses strategies that are specifically pointed toward doing what is necessary to win the tournament or advance to the next round. Occasionally this strategy may seem outlandish. For example, suppose it is the last hand of a blackjack tournament. You have a small lead over an opponent, and the two of you are contending for a big prize. You each bet the maximum. The dealer's upcard is a six. You are dealt a total of 19. Your opponent has been dealt a blackjack. His 3-to-2 payoff will give him first place (and the big prize) even if your 19 beats the dealer. You now have only one choice and that is to double down. As unbelievable as it sounds this becomes the right play if the difference between first and second place is large. Of course, in a regular blackjack game only a crazy person would make such a play. We will give some other examples shortly. For now this should give you an idea of how tournaments can differ from normal play.

# Some General Principles

Probably the most important general point to keep in mind is that you should not play in a tournament if you cannot afford to lose all of your buy-in. Since the prize money for a tournament is almost always far greater than the amount of money you are betting, it is very unlikely that you should be concerned with the money involved in your bet. In general, you have to bet your money as if it was play money. You simply make the best possible tournament play under the circumstances without regard to the specific casino edge on that bet. In other words, the proper play is the one that gives you the best chance of beating your opponents. It is not at all necessarily the play that would be the best gambling play if you were not in a tournament.

The next general principle you should remember is that when you need to get a certain amount to win or to advance to the next round it *does you little good to get more than that.* If you finish the tournament with significantly more than what you needed, you have probably done something wrong. Good players will usually end up any round with just enough to advance or nothing at all. If by the last hand or the last roll you have not reached your goal, you almost always should be betting everything you have. You should not be afraid of going broke. In fact, you will go broke in most of the tournaments that you play.

The above concept can come into play well before the last hand. As an example, suppose in a particular tournament it appears that you need to end the round with $780 to advance, (or to win, or to beat somebody for second place, or whatever.) Let's say that you have $700 and there are still three hands or three betting opportunities to go. (This example works best in blackjack tournaments, but it applies to other tournaments as well.)

If you have three hands left and you need to finish with $780, you certainly shouldn't wait until the last hand to try to do it. But you shouldn't bet too big right away either. Rather, what you should do is bet $100, and then if you win cut down to $5. If you lose, go to $200, and if you win cut down to $5. If you lose again, bet your remaining $400. By betting in this manner, the only way you don't achieve your goal is if you lose three hands in a row. This is just one of a myriad of examples.

This example also shows that you need to be well aware when the last few rounds are at hand, and have a well-thought-out strategy for them. This typically includes betting a large percentage of your bankroll in an attempt to catch up and surpass the chip leader(s). If this bet fails, it may be necessary to bet everything that's left (sometimes on a big longshot) and hope you get lucky.

But your betting should be influenced by how you are doing in relation to your competition. If you are in the lead your bets should usually be small or should be similar to how everyone else is betting. You must always remember that you are not trying to beat the dealer, you are just trying to finish ahead of your competition. Therefore, as the leader, try to bet in such a way that no matter what the outcome of your hand is, you will still maintain your lead. (See Example No. 1)

But the opposite is true if you need to do some catching up. For instance, if you are in a craps tournament and the leader bets the "pass line," you probably want to bet the "don't." This way, if you win your opponent will simultaneously lose, and you will have made a large gain on him. Likewise, in a baccarat tournament you would bet "bank" if the leader was betting "player."

Finally, it may be necessary to make bets that have a large house percentage. The previoulsy mentioned doubling down on a total of 19 is an example. Another example would be in a craps tournament where your only shot on the last roll would be to win a bet on "double 6s." If so, then you should bet it even though this is normally one of the worst bets on the craps layout.

**Special Note:** At this point, we should say that we can only give you a small fraction of all the information that you ought to have if you want to be a professional casino tournament player. It would take a whole book to tell you everything. Fortunately, there is such a book. It is Stanford Wong's *Casino Tournament Strategy,* and if you plan to pursue this area, it is a book that you will have to read over and over again.

# Examples

To help you get a feel for how casino tournaments can differ from normal play we are supplying a few examples. For more examples of strategy changes see *Casino Tournament Strategy* by Stanford Wong.

**Example No. 1: Blackjack tournament.** Last hand of the round. You must win your table to advance to the next round. You are the chip leader. The one player who can catch you bets the maximum of $500. You also bet $500. (If you have a small lead this will usually insure it stays that way, unless you lose your bet *and* he wins his.) The dealer shows an eight. Your opponent stands on 14. You have 12.

This is a perfect example of how a normally bad play becomes the clearly right play in a tournament. Of course you should stand on 12. Now you can't lose. You will do the same as your opponent and thus maintain your lead. Had you hit, you might bust, and then go on to watch the dealer cost you the tournament by busting also.

**Example No. 2: Blackjack tournament.** Last hand of the round. One winner. You have a small lead on one player and an insurmountable lead on the others. You must bet first.

Now you must bet small and hope he loses his expected big bet. Had you bet big *he* would have bet smaller hoping *you* lose. Since a player wins well under half his blackjack hands this gives you the best chance to stay on top. However, you should not bet the minimum. Rather you should bet an amount that gives you some flexibility to double down or split to retake the lead if it appears that your opponent will almost certainly win his hand. (Precise examples are covered in Wong's book.)

**Example No. 3: Blackjack tournament.** Last hand. One winner. You have $1,000. Leader has $1,250. Everyone else is out of it. Leader is first and bets $500 (stupidly).

Your best play is to bet $245. This insures a win if he loses. A $5 bet would do the same thing. However by betting $245, you improve your chances just a bit more. That is mainly because a $245 bet, unlike a $5, bet will give you a win in those rare cases where he pushes and you get a blackjack. (Your $1,367.50 will beat his $1,250.)

**Example No. 4: Horse Racing tournament.** The player with the biggest bankroll at the end of the week wins the money.

The idea here is to estimate the amount you need to win and to bet in a way that gives you the best chance to hit almost precisely that amount. Here's a simplified example. Suppose you need to multiply your bankroll by 10. If there is no restriction on the size of your bets you should bet everything on one 10-to-1 shot. This should give you about a 7 percent chance to win the tournament. If instead you had made two bets, half your bankroll on each, on two 5-to-1 shots you only win the tournament if they both win. That's about a 3 percent shot.

Most tournaments are not this simple. However, they almost all have rules that can be taken advantage of with similar logic rather than handicapping ability.

**Example No. 5: Video Poker tournament.** Best results advance to the next round.

Again, the idea is to try to find out what you need to advance and to go for almost precisely that. For example, you would *not* draw two cards to a royal flush if you also had a one-card flush draw unless you needed a big boost to your bankroll. Most likely your strategy would change as the round wears on and you have a better idea whether you need to take chances or not.

**Example No. 6: Slot tournament.** Best results advance to the next round.

Rest your arm the day before. Play fast. Pray.

**Example No. 7: Baccarat tournament.** Last bet. One winner advances to last round.

You are in the lead and your only competition bets $200 on the bank and $100 on the tie. You bet $200 on the bank and $100 on the tie also. If you didn't see this, you need to get some sleep.

**Example No. 8: Craps tournament.** Last bet. One winner. The guy in front has a $700 lead on you and bets $500 on the pass line.

If you are in second place, a big bet on the don't pass gives you the best chance to catch him. But if someone who has more than you is also betting big on "don't," you have to switch to another bet that can pass both of them if it hits.

**Example No. 9: Keno tournament.** Biggest ticket wins.

If you can bet everything you have on a one spot, and hitting it ought to be just enough to win the tournament, then that is clearly what you should do. Otherwise see Wong's book.

# In Closing

There is no question that casino tournaments can be a lot of fun and the last couple of hands can be very exciting. But they are also profitable providing that you know the proper strategies and, as we have shown, these strategies are frequently very different from what would be considered to be normally correct.

In a typical tournament there will be some "tourists" who are there for the fun of it. They "know" how to play. You won't see them betting the "double 6s," doubling down on a total of 13, betting on a horse that's a longshot, or betting their money opposite to the tournament leader. They know better than that, and that's why you'll have an edge.

# Part Eight

# Poker and Poker Tournaments

# Poker and Poker Tournaments

# Introduction

When people think of professional gamblers they typically think of poker players. They are right to do that. Professional horse players may be more numerous, and more money may have been won by the great sports bettors, but for a day-in, day-out good living, it is hard to beat poker.

For those of you who become good enough, poker is the surest way to earn a living gambling. We say this not only because we are poker players ourselves, but for several obvious and objective reasons. Though much money has been won on sports, horses, blackjack, or slot machines, there is always going to be some risk that something will go terribly wrong with these games in the future. That is, there is no guarantee that they will stay in their profitable form forever.

In the case of blackjack, you may not be able to get much playing time. Casino conditions and rules may change and/or you may get "barred." (There is almost no doubt that you will get barred at some places. This is just a fact of life if you choose to play a lot of blackjack.)

In the case of horses and sports, there is always the possibility that the bookie or the public will smarten up to some degree and/or that the principles mentioned in this book and elsewhere might not hold as strongly as they once did. And in the case of slots, there may not always be machines worth playing.

This is not to say that you shouldn't vigorously pursue those games if that is where your talents or inclinations lie. But if there is a choice, we will always choose poker. So should many of you. When you play poker you are using principles that are, for the most part, irrefutable. You are not usually dealing with opinions. You are dealing with cold logic — and mathematics. Even the psychological factors are pretty clearcut. Furthermore, when you play poker in a casino you are in an environment that welcomes your business. You are not normally in danger of being barred since you're not playing against the house.[103] The casino is not losing while you are winning. You are instead playing against other players and the house will either take a small percentage of the pot as its payment or charge a rental fee for your seat.[104] In fact, since good players start games and keep the games going, you will discover that you are a welcomed and valued customer. Therefore, unlike other games, if you get real good at poker, there is still little doubt that it will always be there for you (with lots of places to choose from).

As far as the kind of money that can be won playing poker, there should be no problem in winning that $100,000 a year if you get good enough. Of course, you won't become an expert overnight. It takes a combination of study, experience, and much thinking about the game.

Notice that we said $100,000. Numbers well in excess of that are only obtained by a small number of players who become incredibly good. These are the true champions. But that $100,000 a year or close to it is a virtual certainty if you play poker as well as

---

[103] There have been cases — very rare cases — where a player is winning consistently and is barred because the other players complain. However, almost invariably when this happens the player not only is winning, but is also obnoxious. We don't know of any poker players who have been barred purely for poker skills.

[104] Rental fees or "time charges" as they are commonly called are generally in force in the bigger games. Most smaller games are subject to the house "rake." These fees are the only disadvantage that you have when playing poker. If you are a good player you ought not to worry about it too much. But there are exceptions, especially in Europe, where even big games, at this point in time, are charging quite a bit relative to the size of the bets.

the typical professional and select the best games to play in. (You can, of course, make far more than this if you get lucky in a few poker tournaments. We discuss tournaments later in this section.)

In this chapter we will tell you what it means to be an excellent poker player. (We assume that you have some experience at the game. For those with less experience we include an excerpt from the *Fundamentals of Poker* by Mason Malmuth and Lynne Loomis at the end of this chapter. For complete beginners we recommend that you obtain and read that booklet first.) But before we do that, we will talk about some general ideas. First, you need to know what is entailed in being a professional poker player, or, if you rather, a professional gambler who is is deriving most of his gambling income from poker.

# Reading Books

There are numerous talents you should possess or develop if you are planning to make your living from poker. But talent will do you little good if you do not first learn the games well. After you finish reading this chapter, if you are willing to work hard, and get some experience, you ought to become as good as most professionals. However, there is no way we can tell you everything in just one chapter. There is just too much to cover.[105] If you really desire to become a professional, not only do you have to get experience, but you *must* read more than just this book. You have to read other *good* books on poker that go into more detail. And that means that you have to read *our* books. These include *Hold 'em Poker* by David Sklansky, *Hold 'em Poker for Advanced Players* by David Sklansky and Mason Malmuth, *Seven-Card Stud for Advanced Players* by David Sklansky, Mason Malmuth, and Ray Zee, and *High-Low-Split Poker for Advanced Players* by Ray Zee. Which of these books should you start with? That depends on what you want your specialty to be, which poker game you think you might enjoy playing the most, or which poker game is widely played in your area.[106] You will also need to read, no matter what your game, *The Theory of Poker* by David Sklansky. This last text is an absolute necessity. It does not cover any particular game, but goes into the underlying theories of poker in general using examples from

---

[105] This statement is not as true for the other chapters as it is for poker. The subject is too vast. However, we will give you enough information in this chapter to make it easy for you to make an informed decision about whether to pursue "Poker for a Living."

[106] At the time of this writing and for the past few years, more new players are entering the hold 'em arena than the other games. However, seven-card stud and Omaha eight-or-better are also widely played.

all games. Many pros will tell you that this is the book that made the big difference in their games. By the way, one quick reading of these books won't do the trick. They require much study and we know many people who have literally worn the covers off their copies. In addition, any serious dedicated person will eventually read all the worthwhile poker books even if it is not on the game that they are playing everyday.[107] (If you are a complete novice or have had virtually no experience with "casino" poker you should read the *Fundamentals of Poker* by Mason Malmuth and Lynne Loomis. See the appendix at the end of *Gambling for a Living* for other recommended reading.)

---

[107] There are poker books not written by or published by Two Plus Two, that have some good thoughts in them. We are hesitant in recommending them however, because they invariably contain the occasional error that could be your undoing. The fact is virtually all poker pros who got good via books, did it via *our* books.

# Picking Good Games

No matter how well you play poker, the fact of the matter is that your profits will come not from just your own skill, but also from the lack of skill of your opponents. *There is simply no getting around this fact.* It is not like golf where a pro will beat an 80 shooter virtually as often as he will beat a 90 shooter. In poker you do a lot better if you can find 90 shooters to play against.

Your edge (and profits) stem from the difference between you and your opponents. If you are a great player who is forced to play against only good opponents your profits won't be as high as a somewhat lessor player playing the same stakes against bad players. Bad players are a rarity in the very biggest games. But they are not at all rare in the medium-size games. This means that if you are interested in being a professional poker player and have not reached the absolute upper level of championship skills, the most important thing that you should be aware of is *game selection*. The idea is that you pick the most profitable game, the game that is easiest to beat. That is, you pick the game that has the weak or terrible players in it.

This is something we don't really mention in our other poker books because those books were simply intended to make you into a good player. This book is intended to turn you into a professional gambler. And the sad, but true fact is, that the biggest factor in your success as a professional poker player is the *difference* between your skill and your opponents' skill rather than simply how good you play. This principle cannot be emphasized enough.

What follows from this is that if you are going to seriously try to make a living playing poker and if you are in a place where you can choose your games (because there is more than one), then that is what you must do if you want to maximize your success. Do not just walk into a casino or cardroom as many players do and play the game you think you are the best at. It may be right to play in a different type poker game (or different stakes) where you are not quite as adept because it is "softer."[108]

For example, if you consider yourself better at seven-card stud, it still may be right for you to choose a hold 'em game if that game looks very "juicy." Notice that this means that one of your biggest goals should be to learn to play all games well, particularly hold 'em and stud. The exception to this, of course, would be if you are playing in a casino or in a state or town that does not offer a large selection of games, and you are not willing to travel to those places that do. However, the fact is that there are many legalized casinos and cardrooms that do offer poker in more than one of its variations at the middle limits and higher. You will typically find seven-card stud, hold 'em, and sometimes Omaha eight-or-better high-low-split, and lowball draw. There are other variations as well.

Picking good games may also mean that you play stakes other than what you normally play. You should have no qualms about playing somewhat smaller than your normal size game if the smaller game is much easier to beat. Your only concern is your average hourly win. You must think of poker as a job where your average hourly win is what you are "earning." So keep in mind that sometimes a $15-$30 game is worth more to you than a $30-$60, game even though you might be able to easily afford (and beat) the $30-$60 game as well.

On the other hand, there may be times you will want to play in a game somewhat bigger than the one you normally play in. If you usually avoid that game because it tends to be tougher, you should still be ready to jump into it those times it happens to get good — as long as you can afford the increased fluctuations. Even if bankroll

---

[108] The only exception is for those truly world-class players who are so good at their specialty that if they stick to the very highest games they are almost certainly going to make more than if they are selective. Because they are playing so high and they are so much better than almost anybody they can just go to the game they like to play. But we are only talking about approximately twenty people in the entire world.

is a problem, you still might try to get into a super juicy bigger game by selling a piece of your action and/or play extra tightly. Either strategy should result in a higher hourly rate than your regular game.

(Of course, you don't usually win in a short period of time exactly what you expect to. In poker, as in almost all other forms of gambling there is a great deal of short-term luck. Some hours you will do much better than expected and some hours you will do much worse and perhaps even lose. In fact, you will have many losing hours [and losing days for that matter]. You will also have hours where you win ten or twenty or thirty times your average hourly win. That's the nature of gambling. But in the long run your total win will be the sum of your hourly expected wins so you need to be honest with yourself about what your expected hourly win is.)

Game selection can involve more than picking the best game in the room. It can also mean picking the best city, the best casino, and/or the best time of day. Of course, you may choose not to. You may decide that certain sacrifices are not worth it. You may be willing to take a lesser hourly rate in order to be able to live where you want or play during the times that you want. We know many professional poker players who try to carry on a relatively normal life and play fairly normal hours — perhaps from ten in the morning to five in the afternoon. But there is no doubt that they are costing themselves money by following this schedule. They realize it themselves. They have simply decided that for the sake of a normal family life they would rather give up income to do things in this fashion. We have no problem with this. It is a decision that you can make also. However, we must tell you that you will only have the luxury of this option if you are good enough to beat the type of games you have settled on — namely those that you tend to find during the day. If you play a notch worse than this, and you still want to be a professional poker player, then game selection will be crucial. It will be the difference between being a significant winner and barely surviving.

(For instance, in Las Vegas the games during the day are filled with many tough players and are usually much harder to beat than the ones during the middle of the night. When it is late, there are usually a lot more tourists, tired players, and even drunk players at the tables.)

Again, the bottom line is that you can make much more money if you choose games wisely. This is particularly true if you have gone to the trouble of learning to play various games. Now you are able to choose from a greater menu of possibilities.

If for some reason you're not playing in a place where games are plentiful — and thus, there is not a choice — that doesn't mean that it is not possible to win. In fact, in some of the smaller places like those in Seattle, Mississippi, and Phoenix, where there are fewer games to choose from, the players tend to be not quite as good. Thus, these games are usually easier games. Still, even at these smaller places game selection can be important. (You should even sometimes choose to not play at all if the game is only marginally beatable.)

When you do make it to the higher games you will invariably run into people who play very well. However, many of them will have two weaknesses. One is that they don't pick games, and the other is that they are only good at one game. Very often these "specialists" have no choice of where to play because they have never learned the general theory underlying poker. They have just fallen into the proper strategy for their particular game.

One of the authors (Sklansky) likes to consider them as his unpaid shills. He is sometimes berated for not playing in the toughest games because he won't play when it is just these experts sitting at the table. Why should he (or you, for that matter)? There is probably a better game elsewhere in the room, and the fact is that the only reason the "experts" are playing against each other is because they don't know how to play the other games. Don't feel inferior to them because they might be able to play that one particular game a hair better than you. Actually, they are doing you a favor. They are also your unpaid shills, keeping the game going for you until a bad player sits down. In fact, we thought we would like to take this opportunity to thank them for being nice enough to keep the game going while we are playing in other, better games, waiting for their game to get good.

# Defining a Good Game

What do we mean when we say a good game? A good game simply means a poker game where your opponents are playing incorrectly. By incorrectly we mean *differently* from the way we will show you. (But it could mean playing the way *other* authors say.)

To find a good game you usually need to find one of two possibilities. You must either find a game where most of the players are mediocre, or a game where at least one of them is terrible. It would be nice if you could find both, but either one of these options should suffice. Mediocre players are people who make a lot of the mistakes we are going to be warning you about. Terrible players are typically players that play far too many hands, play them in a meek fashion, and generally go too far with the hands they play.

That's basically what we mean by a soft game or a good game. Again, your profits come from the difference between your level of play and theirs, not just your level of play itself.

# Game Size

How big do you have to play to make a good living? Is $10-$20 large enough? What about the huge games that you sometimes see in the major cardrooms? Obviously, you can play as small as you want when you are first learning how to play. In fact, we recommend that you start out small and then move up as your skill level increases. But if you are seriously planning to be a professional gambler, there is a minimum size game, *and that is almost certainly $10-$20.*

Anything smaller won't produce enough income if you are seriously trying to make a good living from playing poker. This is because the rake is proportionally higher, the game is slower (because the players are a little worse), and most importantly the pots have less money in them. Besides, most $10-$20 games are still pretty soft.

However, $10-$20 games won't make you the $100,000 a year we promised. $20-$40 games might if you become an excellent player and have found a good spot. (As of this writing, that includes places like Seattle, New Jersey, and California.It does not include Las Vegas where the best $20-$40 players usually play. Things are constantly changing, however, so you have to check it out for yourself.)

Making $100,000 per year means about $50 per hour. Thus, to reach that figure you would normally need to be at least a $30-$60 player. In all, there are probably about two hundred people across the United States who play somewhere between $20-$40 and $75-$150 and make $100,000 per year, and you can too if you study and have the talent.

It is true that you can make reasonable money (if you play very well) at the small limits. We believe, for instance, that a top player could average $20 an hour in a typical $6-$12 game. However, we are sure there is no one winning at this rate in a $6-$12 game. That's because in order to make $20 an hour (at this limit) you have to be so good that you would be playing and winning more in a bigger game instead.

If you cannot make as much in a $10-$20 game as you can in a $6-$12, game then we can tell you that you cannot make very much in the $6-$12 game either. If this is the case, your game still needs a lot of work. However, this principle doesn't hold for the bigger games. There are people who can make good money playing $15-$30 who would make less if they tried to play $30-$60. That's because, as we have already mentioned, the better players move up and by the time you hit the $30-$60 limit there will be many good players at the table.

For sure, the higher you play the less you can win in proportion to the size of the game. This is true even for champion players. Typically a champion player who can make $30 an hour in $10-$20 cannot make $60 an hour in $20-$40. He might clear $50 an hour at this limit and perhaps $65 an hour at $30-$60.

If you are not a top player the gain from playing bigger games is even less. In fact you might find that you can make $20 an hour in $10-$20 and only $15 an hour in $20-$40. But that is on a day-in and day-out basis. If you are astute you might select $10-$20 or $20-$40 as your base game, but you will constantly be on the lookout for those times when a bigger game figures to be more profitable.

Later on in this chapter we present a chart where we give our opinion of the hourly rate that very good, excellent, and super players can win in various games depending on the stakes and how selective they are. You will need to study this chart. But for now, suffice it to say that only great players can make more in very big games than they can in medium-size games.

It would be nice if you became a truly great player, but to be realistic, most of you won't. However, you almost certainly can become a very good player, and very good players are capable of winning between $30 and $50 an hour in medium-size games. Thus, $100,000 a year is an obtainable figure.

# Bankroll Requirements

The previous discussion concerning choosing your stakes assumed that you have enough money to withstand the natural fluctuations of the game. It won't do you any good to become the best player in the world if you play in a game too large for your bankroll and then go broke because of your short-term bad luck . So how much money do you need to play safely at some particular level?

This topic is covered in detail in Mason Malmuth's book *Gambling Theory and Other Topics.* But if you just want a rule of thumb, it is that you ought to have about three hundred big bets (unless you are a very good player, where you might be able to get by on less).[109, 110] In other words, you need about $6,000 for $10-$20, $9,000 for $15-$30, and at least $30,000 for $50-$100. (You need slightly less if you are willing to go to a lower limit if you start depleting your bankroll and there is no shame in going to lower stakes. Sometimes it is the smartest thing you can do.)

This suggested bankroll does not take into account your expenses. We recommend that you have enough additional money to cover your expenses for about a year when you first start out gambling. *And that money should not be part of your gambling bankroll.*

Though a good player may occasionally go through three hundred bets, you should not let this fact delude you into thinking

---

[109] On the other hand, if your championship play leads you to the biggest games where your opponents are tougher, your hourly rate will be less than a big bet per hour, and your bankroll requirement will actually *increase.*

[110] For a simplified discussion of bankroll requirements, see the essay "Is Your Wallet Fat Enough" in *Poker, Gaming, and Life* by David Sklansky.

that you are a winning player when you are not. The amount of money that you ought to win as a professional poker player should be fairly close to one big bet an hour if not more. Anything less than that is not worth doing (unless you are playing in very big games). And, if you go through three hundred bets it is highly doubtful that you are a bet-an-hour long-run winner. This is explained once again in more detail in *Gambling Theory and Other Topics*.

Still, the fact remains that the short-term luck factor in poker (and other forms of gambling) is relatively large. While this means that you will have many losing days, it also means that the bad players will have many winning days. This is the "hook" that will keep them playing, and it is the main reason why many poker games stay good.

# Play Your Best

One important concept that should go without saying, is that it is absolutely necessary to play your best at all times. The fact is, however, that many poker players don't do this. Blackjack players have little choice but to stick to the rules and play exactly as their counting system tells them. But in poker, it is much easier to stray. Poker players call this "steaming."

Steaming is common in poker because there are so many marginal hands that you can talk yourself into playing when you are losing. Even professional players will frequently find themselves losing a lot more during a particular session than they can reasonably expect to get back quickly. A professional $20-$40 player, for instance, is trying to average winning about $300 a day. But it is not uncommon for him to find himself down $1,000 or more. At $300 a day he can expect to get this back in a little over three days. He should not try to get it back all at once.

It is absolutely imperative that you do not try to get back big losses quickly. If you do, you will play hands that you shouldn't. You must only play to win your average hourly rate rather than recover big losses. If you get back all of it, as will occasionally happen, that's fine, but don't count on it.

Even though we consider the concept of always playing your best to be self-evident, it is one major downfall of many poker players. (It can also be the downfall of sports and horse bettors, where one of their major advantages *should* come from the fact that they can refrain from betting when the game or the odds aren't right.) If you are intent on winning every day you are going to be drawn into making bad bets if you're losing. Please don't. You must think of your earn in an average sense.[111]

---

[111] If you are interested in more discussion when we talk about "average expectation" see *The Theory of Poker* as well as some of our other books.

If you are having trouble accepting the fact that you probably won't get a bad loss back quickly, one way to stop yourself from trying so hard to get even is to keep in mind that there will always be another game tomorrow. When you are playing in a weekly home game, it's a bit more understandable if you try too hard to win for that day. You won't get another chance for a while. In the case of a casino or a cardroom poker game, however, it is really ridiculous to start playing badly just to try to make that day a winning day.[112]

(It is also ridiculous, by the way, to quit when you are ahead simply because you are winning. If the game merits continued play and you are not tired, you should keep playing. You cannot look at each individual day. This is not like a baseball game where you simply count your wins versus your losses. In poker, what counts is your total runs versus your opponent's total runs over a long period of time.)

---

[112] We need to make one point about players who steam: Most of them would still be losing players even if they didn't steam. In fact, we suspect that many mediocre players steam in order to give themselves an excuse for their poor results. The truth is, they would lose anyway, and their steaming simply assures their results. Although it is important that you don't steam, the discipline to avoid steaming is *not* one of the main attributes of great players. (In fact, some champions do steam occasionally.) Rather, the main attribute is that they *play well.* Lots of players don't steam. Few play well.

# Patience

Related to the idea of always playing your best is, of course, the attribute of patience. The fact is, a large part of winning in poker comes simply from not playing bad hands. If you happen to be dealt many bad hands in a row you have to throw away many hands in a row. This is boring, but it had better not matter to you. If you are playing for the excitement of the game you are in trouble. You must look at it like a business. If you need to have constant action you are better off as a backgammon or gin rummy player, where the action is nonstop. If you want to be a professional poker player, patience and the ability to refrain from playing an unprofitable hand is a must.

# Strategic Concepts

We are now going to talk more specifically about how to win at poker. There are many general concepts of strategy that apply to virtually all games. Although we will not go into minute details, we will give a serious overview of the things that the top players think about.

If you are new to poker it will seem like an awful lot. But with experience these ideas and concepts will eventually come easily to you. This is where study and thinking about the game will really make a difference. For some people, poker is a twenty-four-hour-a-day preoccupation as well as an occupation. These are usually the best players. (Again, we remind you of the excerpt from the *Fundamentals of Poker* to be found at the end of this chapter for those of you who are new to the game.)

## Tight Play

A moment ago we talked about patience. There is no place where this is more important than in starting hand selection. The fact is, with few exceptions, professional poker players play fewer hands than nonprofessionals. They play *far* fewer hands than bad players. We concede that there is a lot more to winning at poker, especially in the medium or bigger games, than just playing good starting hands. However, this is usually a fairly big part of where your profit comes from. In some games, just playing "tight" can account for as much as half your profits.

Exactly how tight you should play depends on what kind of game it is, the structure of the game, and most importantly the size of the ante.[113] The more you have to put into the pot before you get your cards the more money it will cost you in the long run to

---

[113] In proportion to the other bets, especially the opening bet.

immediately throw your hand away. So it follows that the larger the ante the more hands you ought to play.

Now this is an over-simplification. Other factors include your position, how much you can bet in the later rounds, whether you have the type of hand that prefers many players or few players, how aggressive or passive your opponents are, as well as how good they play. In general, the better your opponents play — the ones, that is who have entered the pot — the less hands you should play. If unskillful players have entered the pot you should be more apt to enter the pot yourself with a marginal hand. But the fact remains that except for short-handed games or games that have giant antes, you must throw away a large percentage of your starting hands.

As for those times where this rule doesn't apply, (the giant ante games and the short-handed games), these games are so tricky that only a very small percentage of pros ever get to the point where they feel comfortable in them. And you do not need to get to that point in order to become a very successful poker player.

# The Size of the Pot

Professional poker players always consider the size of the pot before making any decisions. This is something that cannot be emphasized enough. Almost all other authors when describing how to play a hand ignore pot size. They do not consider how many bets are in the pot and what it will cost you. This is totally wrong. The size of the pot is the single most important factor in many of your strategy decisions. (When we say the size of the pot we of course mean in proportion to the size of the bet.)

For instance, professionals know that as the pot gets big, hands should be played much differently than when the pot is small. Obviously they know that the bigger the pot, the less likely it is that they should throw their hand away. But they know other things as well. For instance, in a large pot they know that you should try to win the pot instantly or at least cut down the field with both fair and good hands (except for absolute locks). In smaller pots you should be more likely to throw away your mediocre hands, and slow play

— "suck in" other players — with your good hands. But as the pot gets bigger you should be less likely to throw away your mediocre hands and be reluctant to slow play your better hands.

In fact, while it might be correct to fold a particular hand in a small pot, if the pot is large not only would you now not fold that exact same hand but it might be correct to raise with it!

The concept of pot size is closely related to the concept of ante size. At the beginning of a hand the only money in the pot is the ante, and thus it determines the pot size. Good players are taking into account how big the ante is because they realize that the smaller the ante the fewer hands in general they need to play. (Taking this to the extreme, if there is no ante at all and you are playing draw poker, you could wait until you were dealt a royal flush and you couldn't lose.)

Poker is a game where you are constantly balancing your risk versus reward. This is true whether you are considering checking, betting, raising, bluffing, calling, or folding. Since your "reward" is the pot, no decision should ever be made without carefully considering the size of that reward.

# Pot Odds

A similar concept to the size of the pot is, of course, pot odds. The idea of pot odds is something that many poker players know, but usually only in one context — when they are drawing to a hand such as a straight or a flush and they are trying to decide whether there is enough money in the pot to profitably call a bet. This is a straightforward pot odds problem. However, many other situations where pot odds matter are not nearly as straightforward. Even drawing to a straight or a flush is not such a simple question if there is more than one round of betting to come. It also is not that simple if there is a chance that the straight or the flush is already beaten or will be beaten.

Pot odds also matter when bluffing or when deciding to call somebody else's possible bluff. For example, if you think that there is only a 10 percent chance that your opponent is bluffing you, but the pot is offering you 15-to-1 odds, you should call. Even though you will probably lose, this call will show a profit in the long run. This, of course, is a simple example of using the aforementioned risk versus reward ratio.[114]

# Aggression

Another general strategic concept that all professionals know is that you should almost always be aggressive whenever you have a reasonable hand. In limit poker, if you are not aggressive most of those times when you have something of value, you are letting people play cheaply or even giving them what is known as a "free card." This gives them a chance to "draw out" on you for free, or for a small price, which might cost you the pot. You cannot worry about the possibility of losing a bet if the reward for betting or raising might be to get somebody who might have otherwise outdrawn you to throw his hand away. You are risking a bet in order to save a pot. So even if your aggression costs you a bet more than half the time, it doesn't mean that it's not the right play. When someone who would have outdrawn you folds, it makes you many bets. (There is, of course, another reason to bet fair hands even when that bet doesn't save you the pot by keeping others from out drawing you. When they don't fold and *don't* outdraw you, your bet just makes you more money.)

Constantly calling other people's bets is not a winning strategy. In most games, the better players are finding themselves either betting or folding much of the time. This is not to say that there are not situations where calling is the right thing to do. But as a general principle, the better players are usually betting or folding. There are

---

[114] There are actually a few different types of odds. David Sklansky coined the terms implied odds, effective odds, and reverse effective odds to describe these different type of pot odds situations. We will not go into detail here, but they are all found in *The Theory of Poker*.

logical reasons for this. One is that if you are betting there is always a chance that you're going to win the pot without a fight. Another reason is that since you are playing "tight," you usually have the best hand, and it is important that you make people pay to stay in with you.

Besides betting or folding, the better players also do a lot of raising. In fact, they raise a lot more than bad players except for those maniacal type players who raise indiscriminately. Of course, they are not in the pot as often as weaker players but when they are in they are usually the aggressor.

We discuss this subject in detail in some of our books. The general principle is that when your hand can be outdrawn, failing to bet or raise with it, though dangerous on a one-time basis, is clearly the better strategic play in the long run. Those of you who play meekly, that is, only check and call with your decent hands, have no chance of winning against skilled opponents. (There are, of course, specific exceptions where you may want to slowplay or deceive or where you are extremely wary that you are beaten. But in general, in limit poker you must be aggressive.[115])

The bottom line is, if you are a professional player you are usually going to be betting unless you intend to fold. If someone else bets, you frequently are going to be raising unless you intend to fold. This is true for both theoretical and common sense reasons.

# Position

The next concept that only professionals understand well is position. They know it is very advantageous to act last in a poker game, and conversely, it is disadvantageous to act first. If you can see what your opponent does before you have to do anything, this

---

[115] In no-limit games this concept is not nearly as true because your bet in relation to the size of the pot is much bigger. However, no-limit is very rarely played, and there are very few no-limit professionals.

will help you in a variety of ways. It will tend to save you money when your hand is beaten, and it will tend to make you extra money when you have the best hand.

Suppose you have a great hand and your opponent is first to act. He will often bet and you can then raise. But if you are first, you have to bet yourself unless you want to risk making nothing by trying to check raise. This is just one example of why it is better to be in last position. It is true for weaker hands as well as better ones. Thus, professionals know they have to play much more carefully when they are first — and, in fact, play far fewer hands because of the inherent disadvantage of their position. Conversely, their starting hand requirements loosen up quite a bit when they know they will be last.

The game of Caribbean Stud is really a simplified poker game based partially on this concept. The casino is basically a poker player in last position. Thus, in spite of its simple rote rules of play, it has an edge over even expert players who are in essence playing in first position.

Again, this is a subject that can be explored in greater detail. Those who are interested, please consult our books (especially *The Theory of Poker* and both hold 'em books).

# Deception

Deception also plays a role in successful poker strategy. This means playing your hand differently than the obvious way your hand would seem to require. An example of deception is, of course, bluffing, but there are many other examples as well: For instance, not raising with a great hand in order to suck people in, betting with only a mediocre hand when there are more cards to come, and betting with a flush draw when there are more cards to come. Deception means representing a hand other than the one you really have.

However, professionals know something about deception that many players don't. It is that deception is not really as important as most people think. It should only be used occasionally (very occasionally against weak opponents), and it is usually profitable only *when the pot is small.*

By playing a hand differently from what the logic or mathematics would tell you, you are costing yourself money unless you have fooled your opponents so much that you can gain it back on a later round (or possibly a later hand). This will not be the case in most situations. It is especially not the case when the pot gets bigger or *when your opponents are not strong enough to read your hand anyway.*

So what about bluffing? Non-poker players think that bluffing is a major part of the game. But a pure bluff is rarely the right thing to do because it simply almost never works.[116] Novice players usually lose their money quickly partially because they bluff too much. They frequently learn the hard way that bluffing is only rarely correct in a limit game.

There are, of course, exceptions where a pure bluff will show a profit, but, in general, bluffing is not one of the major arsenals of the professional poker player, especially in the medium-size games of Las Vegas or the other cardrooms around the country.

# Psychology

That brings us to the next strategic concept, which is *psychology.* Just because your pure bluff should be a rarity it does not mean that psychology is irrelevant. It is still fairly important because if you can catch somebody bluffing, or if you yourself can get away with a bluff, it is highly profitable since a whole pot is involved. Doing either one of those two things makes you a lot of money, even if you are only occasionally successful.

---

[116] On the other hand a *semi-bluff,* (where with more cards to come you bet a weak hand that has chances of improvement) can be a profitable play for mathematical as well as psychological reasons. The semi-bluff is analyzed in detail in *The Theory of Poker.*

What you have to do is put yourself in the mind of the other person. This is the key idea — to put yourself in the other person's head. That doesn't mean just figuring out what he has. It also means figuring out what he is *thinking*. Only then are you using psychology to its utmost in poker.

Besides trying to read *his* hand you must figure out what he thinks *you* have. If you can discern that he is thinking that you have something other than what you really have, then you can take advantage of that. By the same token, if you think that he is putting you on what you really do have, you must be more cautious. Many examples of this are given in the *Theory of Poker* and some of our other books.

# The Last Round

A very important concept that you absolutely must understand is the fact that the last round of betting is quite different from all other betting rounds. When there are no more cards to come, you often should play your hand differently than when there are more cards to come. You have to take more chances when there are more cards to come. If you don't, as we said earlier, you are risking giving someone else a free card (if you don't bet). Similarly, if there are more cards to come and someone else bets, you may be forced to play even if you know you're beaten because you may be getting the right price to try to "draw out." *But these ideas don't apply when the cards are all out.*

How to play "on the end" is actually an extremely complex subject, although it was never really covered at all until David Sklansky first brought it up in *Hold 'em Poker* and then later expounded on it in much more detail in *The Theory of Poker*. There is really no way of getting around the necessity to read the chapter called "Head-Up on the End" in that book so that you can fully understand the complexities of how you must change your strategy on the last round as opposed to the earlier rounds.

Here is one simple example that we have used before. Suppose you are playing seven-card stud and you have

that is, four jacks showing, on the sixth card. Your opponent is showing a pair of queens. Even though your four jacks are showing, it is imperative that you bet your hand. If your opponent does have three queens you should not allow him to draw to that fourth queen for free. If he does not have four queens already he will probably fold, but that's better than giving him a free chance with three queens. Of course, if he doesn't fold the three queens he is making a terrible mistake by trying to catch the one case queen.

However, suppose he does call and it is now the seventh card. *Those same four jacks would now be a ridiculous hand to bet.* Yet many beginners bet in this spot. Since there are no more cards to come the other player will only continue to play if he has you beaten. If you *are* foolish enough to bet, your opponent will almost certainly either fold (when he can't win) or raise when he can beat four jacks.

This is a trivial example of how strategies change from the earlier rounds to the last round. It is absolutely necessary that you have a full understanding of last round play before you can hope to be a highly successful player.

# Upcards

There is one general principle we need to mention that applies only to some types of poker games. It is the idea of changing your play based on the "liveness" of your cards in those games where you can see "upcards." Thus, we are talking about stud games. This usually means seven-card stud, although it could also be high-low-split or razz.[117] The principle does not apply to games like Omaha or hold 'em, where there are community cards. To someone new to poker, it may appear that stud and hold 'em are very similar games. In fact, many unknowledgeable people will refer to hold 'em as a form of stud. But the games play strategically very differently, and one of the differences is the impact that upcards have on stud strategy.

When playing seven-card stud, professional players are very aware of how the upcards that are showing change the proper strategy.[118] They understand that certain borderline hands can go from highly playable to absolutely unplayable depending on what upcards they see. The opposite is also true.

Look at this simple example: You start with

In one case there are no jacks or fives showing — your hand is "live." In another case one jack and two fives are showing — your hand is "dead." Even though you are holding what appears to be the same hand in both cases, namely a pair of jacks with a five kicker,

---

[117] Razz is seven-card stud played for low. The definitive discussion of razz strategy is contained in the book *Sklansky on Poker* by David Sklansky.

[118] Actually, upcards influence strategy in a few ways. Obviously the mere strength of your opponent's upcards has a lot to do with how you play your hand. So does the *order* in which he received them. This section, however, only addresses strategy changes based on the *denomination* of the upcards (including those in hands that are folded) as they pertain to your hand and its chances for improvement.

the live hand is usually going to be good enough to play, whereas the dead hand should usually be thrown away.

Another example would be a hand like

where the absence of sixes, sevens, eights, nines, tens, or jacks showing makes the hand almost certainly worth playing and maybe even worth a raise. On the other hand, if some of these cards were showing the 10♣9♦7♥ becomes junk that you should usually throw away. This is another subject that is gone into in some detail not only in *The Theory of Poker* but also in our book *Seven-Card Stud for Advanced Players,* as well as in *Sklansky The Video.*

# Head Up Versus Multi-way

Up to this point we have been telling you about strategic concepts that professional players know and that the average player doesn't know. Here's one that even most professionals don't know. It has to do with how hands behave depending on whether they are in a multi-way pot, as compared to a short-handed or head-up pot. This particular concept was first discussed in *Getting the Best of It* by David Sklansky in the chapter called "Another Gambling Paradox."

If you have a good but not great hand that appears to have little chance of improvement, the more players who are drawing to beat it the worse it is for you. *This is true in spite of the extra pot odds that you are getting.* For instance, suppose you have a straight on the fifth card in seven-card stud against one other person who is drawing to a flush. Assume this person has a 45 percent chance to beat you. Since you are the favorite you should of course get more money in the pot. Now suppose there are two such draws out against you. The chances that you will win that three-way contest are 55 percent times 55 percent, which is only 30.25 percent.[119] This means that the addition of one other player has reduced your chances to the point where you actually have the worst of the three hands, even though against either one of them you have the best hand.

The foregoing type of situation will occur often during most poker games, so knowing this concept is extremely important. The general idea is that if you do have such a hand (good but not likely to improve) you try to "thin out the field" as much as possible. However, if you feel that you cannot thin out the field you instead totally stop gambling with the hand. It might even be correct to throw it away.

As we said this particular concept is fairly unknown to many pros, even the top ones. They get away without knowing it because they are usually in tough games where there is very rarely a multi-way pot. However it is one of the reasons why many otherwise good players have trouble in wild, loose games where almost all pots are multi-way.

The bottom line is that in multi-way pots there are two basic conclusions that you must keep in mind. One is that you need to be careful when you have a hand that has little chance of improvement and there are many players drawing at it, and the other is that you yourself should be much more apt to play those drawing hands when you can expect a multi-way pot. An example from hold 'em is a hand such as

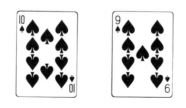

---

[119] See the appendix on probability.

which can become highly profitable when there are many opponents. However, this same hand in a head-up pot is possibly not even worth playing.

# Game Theory

Another concept that most pros don't know about is something called "game theory." Game theory is nice to know although frankly it probably won't add that much to your profits unless you are playing in very tough games. But when it comes time to consider bluffing or when it comes time to try to figure out whether someone else is bluffing, there is a mathematical method originally developed by John Von Neuman which does not require judgment.The jist of it is that you make your decisions based on a random process. For instance, you would randomly bluff a certain percentage of the time. One way to do this might be by looking at your watch and firing away depending on the position of the second hand.

The same is true when you are trying to decide to call somebody who might be bluffing. In this case you would usually call him because of the size of the pot, but you would occasionally fold again depending on a random event. The actual frequency of your calls and your bluffs can be precisely calculated.[120]

Here's an example. Suppose you are drawing to a flush in seven-card stud and you need a heart "down the river." You could decide to just look at the top of the card that you receive and if it is a red ace, king, or queen you might bet without ever checking to see whether it was a heart or a diamond. When you do something like that you thwart those people who might be able to read your hand by any "tells" that you might throw off.

This is, as we said, another concept that many pros don't know and it's nice to have this knowledge in your arsenal, especially when you are in a tough game.

---

[120] The method is explained in more detail in *Getting the Best of It* and *The Theory of Poker*, both by David Sklansky.

# Reading Hands

A strategic concept that can be very important is what is known as *reading hands*. All the top pros excel in this area, and you should make an effort to do the same. This is especially true once you get above $10-$20 where players are playing reasonably well. In fact, one of the major marks of the champion poker player is that he is able to figure out what his opponents have to a much larger degree than the merely good player. Usually they do this not by picking up "tells," — body language that might give a clue about the hand that someone is holding — although that could be helpful.[121] Rather the better players read hands via *deduction* by rethinking the earlier rounds of play, (as well as the earlier hands that the opponent played). When an expert is up against a reasonably good player he can frequently tell you exactly what his opponent's cards are. (This is obviously harder to do against terrible players who don't play rationally and is also somewhat more difficult to do against great players who will trick you just enough that you can't be sure what they have.) The ability to read hands well takes talent. But even without this talent you can get pretty good at it by studying and thinking about the game as well as getting experience.

We have pointed out that you would like to play as much as possible against terrible players, but if you are going to be a professional you obviously can't restrict yourself to games where there are only "fish." Rather, you will find yourself in games where many of your opponents do play quite well. One of your biggest edges should come from the fact that you can figure out these

---

[121] The problem we have with the idea of using tells in the bigger games is that it is a catastrophe when your opponent realizes that you are trying to pick up his tells and then he turns around and doublecrosses you. This could mean that you throw away the best hand when you would have normally called, simply because you thought you picked up a tell that he had a better hand.

opponents' hands and then make superior playing decisions based on this information.

Again, the idea is to think about what hands a player would play in the way he did on earlier rounds, and by the time a hand is over you should have a good idea what he has. Examples of this technique can be found in *Hold 'em Poker* as well as some of our other books.

# Thinking Ahead

One last talent and strategic concept that professionals use is similar to reading hands. It is also similar to chess-type thinking. It is the idea of visualizing the future possibilities, the future moves. For instance, in hold 'em, the expert will use this technique to get a better idea of whether or not to just call on the flop with a good hand, hoping to check raise on the next card. He can see in his mind all the various possibilities and how the other players will react on the next round depending on what card comes off. He can thus see which future scenarios will work out to a successful check raise, and which ones won't.

The same technique can be used in seven-card stud. The expert player will be able to see the various prospective futures depending on what cards come out. He will know how to play, for instance, on fourth street because he will have a good idea of what will happen depending on what cards come out on fifth street. He is able to evaluate the various alternatives and give the proper weight to the different possibilities.

This is similar to what chess players do. (But chess players don't have to take probability into account.) They visualize the future and make decisions based on that. This is not so easy to teach. It may be one of those talents that separates the great player from the merely very good player. If you have that talent, all the better. But even if you don't, you can still make plenty of money playing poker, if that's what you want to do.

# Your Hourly Rate

We now present a chart on this page and the next showing what we believe your hourly win expectation should be depending on how well you play and on how selective you are. These are realistic numbers based upon our experience, observations, and calculations.

| Limit | Expectations (per hour) | | |
|---|---|---|---|
| | Very Good Player | Selective Very Good Player | Excellent Player |
| $10-$20 | $20 | $30 | $25 |
| $15-$30 | $25 | $40 | $35 |
| $20-$40 | $25 | $45 | $40 |
| $30-$60 | $20 | $45 | $45 |
| $50-$100 | $0 | $30 | $50 |
| $75-$150 | -$50 | $0 | $50 |
| $100-$200 | -$100 | -$50 | $50 |
| $150-$300 | -$300 | -$100 | $0 |
| $300-$600 | -$1,000 | -$300 | -$300 |

(Continued on following page.)

| Limit | Expectations (per hour) | | |
|---|---|---|---|
| | **Selective Excellent Player** | **World Class Player** | **Selective World Class Player** |
| $10-$20 | $35 | $30 | $40 |
| $15-$30 | $50 | $40 | $55 |
| $20-$40 | $60 | $50 | $65 |
| $30-$60 | $80 | $60 | $85 |
| $50-$100 | $100 | $80 | $110 |
| $75-$150 | $125 | $100 | $140 |
| $100-$200 | $125 | $125 | $160 |
| $150-$300 | $125 | $150 | $200 |
| $300-$600 | $0 | $100 | $250 |

The first thing you should understand is that your results depend on your skill level. If you are going to make money in a casino poker room, you have no hope unless you are *at least* a very good player. Secondly, you should understand that you can't expect to make anything of consequence if you are playing below $10-$20. So assuming that you meet these criteria, what limit should you be playing?

First, notice that even if you are an excellent or possibly even a world-class player it doesn't automatically mean that you should be playing in the biggest game in the room. It should come as no surprise that, for the most part, the higher you play the tougher the games are. This is only slightly tempered by the fact that the higher you play the lower the rake or time charge. So don't expect to win twice as much if you play twice as high.

Of course, you would gladly accept one-and-a-half times as much money playing twice as high if you thought you could make it.[122] Unfortunately, as the stakes go up, there is the possibility that you won't make that much. You may not even make as much. Whether you do or not depends on how well you play and on how selective you are in choosing your games. Remember, your win rate is not so much determined by how well you play but by the difference between how well you play and how well your opponents play.

When you examine the above chart you will notice that we give win rates for three skill levels. We have also separated them into selective players and not-so-selective players. When we say a selective player we mean a player who will only play the better situations. To be more precise, we are going to call a selective player somebody who only plays about twenty hours a week, even though he may spend many additional hours finding those twenty hours worth of better games.

A not-so-selective player isn't nearly as picky. Although he doesn't just sit in the first game he finds, and does at least try to find the best game in the room, once he does find that game he will almost always play.

This chart gives our opinion of what you ought to make per hour in various stakes games in typical cardrooms under the various criteria we have set. If you look closely at this chart a few things should stand out. For instance, notice that the higher games are basically out of reach except for the very best players. If you are merely a very good player you should recognize this and stay away from games above $30-$60. Any game above $15-$30 is probably best avoided except on a selective basis.

Another thing to notice is how being selective helps you. For instance, a selective excellent player can beat a $20-$40 game for more than a nonselective world-class player. In fact, he can beat any

---

[122] That is, if you can afford it. To play twice as high with only 1½ times the hourly rate you can easily need three (not two) times as much money. See *Gambling Theory and Other Topics* by Mason Malmuth for a further explanation.

game except for the very highest if he is selective for more than a world-class player could beat it if he's not selective.

Another thing that you might notice is that being selective is not as important if you are a world-class player. A good player ought to be able to approximately double his win rate by choosing his games wisely. An excellent player is only going to double his win rate by being selective if he is playing in the higher games. Thus, an excellent player ought to be not very selective when he is playing in the smaller games. And the small number of world-class players do not need to be that selective at all.

Furthermore, if being this discriminating does in fact restrict you to twenty hours of play, your weekly "earn" won't really go up very much although your fluctuations will go down.[123] So to be selective may not be as important as it seems, especially if poker is your only method of making money. However, if you have become an all-around professional gambler who is also possibly playing blackjack, slots, betting horses, or finding promotions, you certainly ought to be very selective in your poker since you can make more money much of the time doing other things.

Thus, one of the things that should determine whether or not you should be discriminating in the games you play is whether or not you are a full-time poker player. If that is the only way you are going to make your money (and you are very good at it), you should concentrate more on getting your time in than on being extremely selective. If, on the other hand, you have other ways of making money (including outside the gambling field), you should probably only play in the better games.

---

[123] If you are on a small bankroll the fact that your fluctuations will be reduced is reason enough to be selective.

# How to Play a Tournament

So far, when we have discussed poker we are referring to what are known as side games. These are simply the normal poker games that you see in a casino or cardroom. There is, however, another way to make money at poker, especially if you are willing to travel. We are talking about poker tournaments.

To have the best of it playing poker tournaments, you must first be an excellent player. You also need a large bankroll to withstand the inevitable swings.[124] You also need to make some changes in strategy.

So, assuming you play poker well, what changes, if any, should you make when playing a poker tournament? The answer is, you follow your standard strategy most of the time, but occasionally you change it, sometimes dramatically. It is a mistake to think that there should be drastic changes that constantly dominate your play just because you are in a tournament. However, the changes that you do make are based on a few factors that distinguish tournaments from regular poker games. They are discussed below.

**Factor No. 1: The other players are probably playing differently than usual.** Whereas the fact that you are playing a tournament should technically not change your strategy very much, the truth of the matter is that *most* players *do* change their strategy a great deal. This, in turn, must affect your strategy. In general, you will find that most of your opponents are playing much tighter than they usually do. This means you must also tighten up, especially tightening up on your calls and value bets. However, you should be more inclined to bluff as your opponent will be more inclined to fold than usual, and you may want to enter the pot (with a raise)

---

[124] See the essay entitled "Is Your Wallet Fat Enough for Tournaments" in *Poker, Gaming, and Life* by David Sklansky.

with slightly weaker hands than you normally would, providing that no one else is in yet.

**Factor No. 2: You can win all the way up to second with only a few chips.** Most tournaments pay prizes for second and third place (many pay down to ninth place and more). A typical prize structure for a small tournament is 60 percent of the total prize pool for first place, 30 percent for second, and 10 percent for third. A typical large tournament, where many places are paid, will offer 40 percent for first place, 20 percent for second, and down from there. Because of this, your strategy should change during the late stages of a tournament when there are only a few players left. This is especially true if you have very few chips. If you have, for instance, a very short stack and there are four players left, you should play extremely tightly in the hopes that one of the other players will get knocked out. Now you sneak into third place.[125] (This strategy does not apply to those tournaments in which you only keep the value of the chips you have in front of you when the tournament ends.)

Conversely, if you find yourself with a lot of chips against two or three short stacks, you can rob them blind as they keep folding, hoping that some other player will go broke.

**Factor No. 3: If you lose your chips, you must quit the game.** If you are the best player at your table you should try to avoid risking all your chips on any one hand unless you are a substantial favorite. In a normal game, you can buy more chips if you go broke with the expectation of getting even. In a tournament, however, as the best player, you are better off not pushing small edges if this risks your going broke. Rather, make sure you have chips to play another hand. (This principle does not apply if you are allowed an additional buy-in if you go broke.)

---

[125] However, if you notice that the other players are anteing off their money waiting for you to go broke, then you must switch strategies and gamble.

**Factor No. 4: You can't choose your opponents but you can usually count on eventually going to a different table as players get knocked out and tables combine.** If you are at a very tough table that figures to be broken up soon, play very conservatively so that you can be sure you will have chips when you go to an easier table. If, however, there are only tough tables left, go ahead and play your normal game since things don't figure to get better.

**Factor No. 5: Understand that the chips change value.** In regular play, your chips are worth exactly the value that is printed on them. But this isn't the case in poker tournaments. To quickly see this, suppose you win a large tournament. You now have all the chips but you only get 40 percent of the prize money. That is your chips are now only worth 40 percent of the amount printed on them.

What this means is that when playing a tournament the more chips you have the less each individual chip is worth, and the less chips you have the more each individual chip is worth. This idea becomes stronger as the tournament progresses and can dramatically impact correct tournament strategy, especially very late in the tournament. Here are a few strategy tips along those lines:

1. When you are playing in a tournament that offers rebuys it is usually correct to do so if you go broke.
2. If you are offered a chance to "add-on" at the end of the rebuy period you should do so only if you are low on chips. If you are in a good chip position you should pass on this option.
3. Attack the short stacks since their chips are worth more than yours. (To put this in another way, their risk versus reward criteria are different than yours so you take advantage of that.)
4. If you are in a good chip position, especially late in a tournament, try to avoid confrontations with other large stacks unless you are holding a very strong hand.
5. Don't give up and throw off your last few chips. If you are low on chips keep in mind that these chips are probably worth much more than their face value. This means that if you can conserve a few chips so that you can play another hand, it is usually correct to do so. We have seen many a tournament won

by a player who had gotten down to almost nothing but kept his cool.

*The following sections on seven-card stud and Texas hold 'em are excerpts from the* Fundamentals of Poker *by Mason Malmuth and Lynne Loomis. Keep in mind that this booklet is intended mainly for beginners and thus omits many advanced concepts that you will eventually need to learn if you want to play poker for a living.*

# Seven-Card Stud Primer

## How to Play

In seven-card stud, each player generally posts an ante prior to the cards being dealt. To begin the hand, all players are dealt two downcards and one upcard. The player with the lowest upcard is required to start the action on the first betting round with a small bet, which is called the bring-in. If more than one player has the same rank of low card, then suit in alphabetical order — clubs, diamonds, hearts, spades — determines who must start the action.

The first player to the left of the bring-in has three options: He may throw away his hand, call the bring-in, or raise to a full bet. If he folds or calls the bring-in, the person to his left has the same options; however, if the first player raises to a full bet, the next person now has the options of folding, calling the full bet, or raising again. The action proceeds clockwise in this manner until all players have exercised their options and all bets have been called.

All players remaining in the hand then receive three more upcards and a final card face down, with a betting round after each card is dealt. In these subsequent four betting rounds, the player with the high hand on board acts first. If two hands are of equal high value, the player to the left of the dealer initiates the betting action. At the showdown, the player who makes the best five-card poker hand from the seven cards he possesses, wins the pot.

Most limit seven-card stud games have a double limit, with the lower limit used in the early betting rounds and the higher limit (which is usually twice the lower limit) used in the later rounds. Thus the lower bet is allowed on the first and second betting rounds — referred to as third street and fourth street, which correspond to the first three cards and the fourth card — and a double-sized bet is required on the third, fourth, and fifth betting rounds. These later rounds correspond to the fifth, sixth, and seventh cards, and are called, respectively, fifth street, sixth street, and seventh street, or "the river." There is one exception: If a player has an open pair on fourth street, either a single or a double-sized bet may be made.

Here's an example. Suppose you are playing $15-$30 seven-card stud. Everyone will ante $2, the player with the low card will bring it in for $5, and the first player to his left will have the options of folding, calling the $5 bring-in, or completing to $15. Once the bet has been raised to $15, all subsequent bets and raises on both third and fourth streets will be in $15 increments, unless a player makes an open pair on fourth street. In this case, any active player has the options of betting or raising either $15 or $30. All bets and raises on the last three betting rounds will be in $30 increments. Typically, cardrooms allow three or four raises. But "head up" the number of raises is unlimited.

# Strategy Tips

As we have stated, seven-card stud is an intricate game, and determining the best possible play in a given situation involves numerous factors. So before we get into specifics on what hands to play and how you should play them, here are a few more general tips that will help you make the correct decisions.

**Tip No. 1: Play live hands.** Seven-card stud, as its name implies, is a seven-card game. Consequently, you should play hands that have a good chance to improve. For example, if you start with three cards of the same suit — called a three flush — and several other cards of this suit are out on board, your hand is said to be *dead* and therefore should be thrown away. By the same token, if only one or two of your suited cards are showing, you have a *live* hand of value that should be played in most situations.

**Tip No. 2: Big pairs play better against only one or two opponents, while drawing hands prefer lots of company.** A hand like

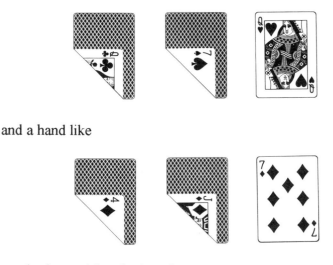

and a hand like

are both good hands, but they play much differently. Big pairs usually do best when played in short-handed pots, because against only a few opponents, a big pair has a reasonable chance of winning with little or no improvement.

The opposite is true of the drawing hands, such as a three flush or a three straight. Although these are good starting hands, they have no immediate value. Moreover, you will not complete your flush or straight very often. You therefore prefer to have many opponents, so that when you do make your hand there will be lots of money in the pot.

**Tip No. 3: Small and medium pairs are much worse than big pairs.** A hand like

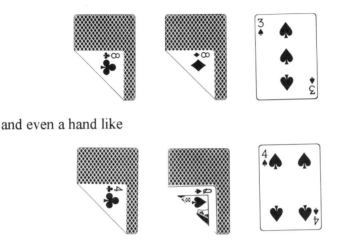

and even a hand like

are occasionally good hands. But, in general, there is a big difference in strength between these hands and the big pairs. For example, when you play a small or medium pair, one of your opponents easily can catch a card higher than your pair, which might give him a bigger pair that will beat you.

**Tip No. 4: Having one or more high cards adds value to your hand.** We have just touched on this. Holding a high card allows you to catch another card of the same rank, which might be enough to win the pot. Having more than one high card is even better.

**Tip No. 5: Be aware — and beware — of scare cards.** A scare card is a card that either improves your hand or allows you to catch another card that will improve your hand. For example, catching a suited jack on fourth street to go along with a king adds enormous value to your hand. Your opponent now has to worry about a possible straight or flush, as well as a possible big pair.

Likewise, you need to be concerned when your opponent catches a scare card.

**Tip No. 6: It is often correct to "chase."** Even though you should be selective of the hands you play, once you enter a pot, it is often correct to go all the way. This is sometimes true even when you are sure you don't have the best hand. Of course, if your hand becomes hopeless, you should discard it. But in many situations, you will have enough ways to win that chasing is worthwhile.

# Starting Hands

There are four main categories of starting hands in seven-card stud: three of a kind, also referred to as rolled-up trips; big pairs; small and medium pairs; and the drawing hands. There are also some other hands that you occasionally should play, but a discussion of them is beyond the scope of this section.

**Category No. 1: Three of a kind.** This is the best starting hand in seven-card stud, but you won't get it very often — in fact, you get it on the average of only once in every 425 times you are dealt in.

Because rolled-up trips are so strong, it usually doesn't matter how you play them. Still, you don't want to be dealt three queens and win only the antes. So if you are in an early position and think a raise will drive out the other players, you should just call. On the other hand, if several players are already in the pot before the action gets to you, your raise is unlikely to make them fold. But remember, although three of a kind is a powerful hand, it is not invincible and occasionally does get beat.

**Category No. 2: Big pairs.** The big pairs are almost always playable and should be played aggressively. The exception is if you are likely to be up against someone who holds a larger pair. In this case, you should consider throwing your hand away, unless your kicker — the side card to your pair — is higher than your opponent's probable pair.

When you play a big pair, you generally go all the way to the river. However, if your opponent pairs his third-street card (known as the door card) or makes something else threatening — such as a four flush on board — you should usually fold.

**Category No. 3: Small and medium pairs.** Determining whether to play a small or medium pair can be fairly complicated. The two most important considerations are the availability of the cards you need — that is, whether your hand is live — and the size of your kicker. As already noted, a high card can add value to your hand. Nevertheless, playing a pair of fours when you can see a four across the table is usually a mistake — even if your kicker is an ace.

**Category No. 4: The drawing hands.** Hands such as three flushes and three straights are often playable. Again, the cards you need must be available, and having a high card is helpful in determining whether to play head up. Unlike the pairs, drawing hands have no present value; you play them because they have the potential to become very strong.

# Play on the Later Streets

Even though the most important decision you will make in seven-card stud is on third street, you don't want to neglect the later streets. Winning depends on correctly assessing an almost infinite number of situations, and errors in judgment can spell disaster. The tips that follow will help you to recognize and take advantage of profitable opportunities, as well as to dodge the perils, often encountered on fourth street and beyond.

**Tip No. 1: It is very dangerous when an opponent pairs his door card.** When this happens, you should exercise caution, as there is a good chance that your opponent now has three of a kind. And even if he doesn't have trips, he's still likely to hold a quality hand. So unless your hand is also of high value or the pot is very large, you should throw your cards away.

**Tip No. 2: If you make what appears to be the best hand on a later street, you should bet out.** In seven-card stud, it is generally a mistake to check a hand that you think is the best, especially if it is somewhat exposed. For example, suppose you make a flush on sixth street. Since some of your suited cards are exposed, your opponent will suspect a flush, and if you check, he will check behind you. As a result, you not only might lose a double-sized bet, but the free card you give may cost you the pot as well.

**Tip No. 3: It is sometimes correct to check and call.** Suppose your opponent catches a third suited card and you think he may now have a flush. Although you should be aggressive in many situations, this is not one of them. The correct play here is usually to check and call. If your opponent does have a flush, you save money, since you don't have to call a raise; if he doesn't have a flush, he often will bet to represent one, so the money goes into the pot anyway.

**Tip No. 4: You usually should call on fifth street when you have a small pair and a high overcard to an opponent's probable pair.** In seven-card stud, it is often correct to chase, particularly when your hand has a strong potential of beating the hand you are up against. This means that you should call a fifth-street bet from a probable high pair when you have a smaller pair and an overcard kicker — especially if your kicker is an ace — as long as your hand is live and you have no reason to believe your opponent has two pair.

**Tip No. 5: If you get to sixth street, almost always go to the river.** In general, if you have called the fifth-street bet, it is correct to also call the bet on sixth street and look at the last card. The reason for this is that the pot typically has grown large enough and you usually have enough ways to win — even with a weak holding — that it is profitable to call. However, if your opponent makes something extremely threatening on sixth street and your hand is weak, it obviously is correct to fold.

**Tip No. 6: If you can beat a bluff, you usually should call on seventh street.** Unless your hand is completely hopeless, folding on the river can be a costly mistake. You have to catch a bluff only once in a while for your calls to be correct. This is because the typical seven-card stud pot is large, relative to the last bet.

# Texas Hold 'em Primer

Texas hold 'em is a fast and exciting form of poker. The game is also surprisingly complex and requires a great deal of skill to play at the expert level. To the uneducated eye, hold 'em appears to be very similar to seven-card stud. But in fact, there are several critical differences between the two games. To begin with, the starting hand decision in hold 'em, though very important, is not the dominating factor that it is in stud. If you do not also play reasonably well on the later streets, the best you can hope for in hold 'em is to break even in the long run.

Hold 'em is also more of a positional game than seven-card stud, because the order of betting does not change from round to round. In addition, a hold 'em starting hand consists of just two cards instead of three cards. This means that you have less of an idea in the beginning of how strong your hand ultimately will be after all seven cards have been dealt.

But perhaps the most important difference between the two games is that Texas hold 'em uses community cards, which are dealt face up in the center of the table and are part of each active player's hand. This makes it much more difficult to draw out on an opponent. For example, if you start with two kings, your opponent starts with two aces, and a pair appears on board, you both have two pair. When you make two pair in seven-card stud, you frequently will beat a lone higher (starting) pair. This does not occur as often in Texas hold 'em.

## How to Play

In hold 'em, a small flat disk, called a "button," is used to indicate the dealer position. Prior to the cards being dealt, the first player to the left of the dealer position posts a small blind, and the second player to the dealer's left puts up a big blind, which usually is equal to the first-round bet. Blinds are "live" bets, which signifies two things. First, a blind is a "real" bet, and to enter the pot, a player in a blind position needs only to make up the difference, if any, between his blind and the current bet. Second, players in the blinds have the option of raising when the action gets back to them, even if there has been no prior raise. When each hand is completed, the dealer button is moved one position to the left, and the procedure of posting blinds is repeated, so everyone pays their fair share.

To start the hand, each player, beginning with the small blind, receives two cards dealt face down, one at a time. Action is initiated on the first betting round by the player to the immediate left of the big blind, who has the options of discarding his hand, calling the big blind, or raising an equivalent amount. The action moves clockwise in this manner until all players have exercised their options and all bets have been called. On all subsequent betting rounds, the first active player to the left of the dealer button starts the action.

After the first round of betting is completed, three cards — referred to as "the flop" — are turned face up simultaneously in the center of the table, and another round of betting occurs. The next two board cards — specified as either "fourth street" and "fifth street" or the "turn card" and the "river card" — are then dealt face up one at a time in the center of the table, with a betting round after each card. As noted previously, these board cards are community cards and are shared by all active players in the hand.

At the showdown, the player who makes the best five-card poker hand, using any combination of the five cards on board and the two cards in his hand, wins the pot. In hold 'em, more than one player often will have the best hand. When this happens, the pot is split.

Limit hold 'em games generally have a two-tiered betting structure, with the lower limit used in the first two betting rounds and the higher limit (which is usually double the lower limit) used in the final two rounds of betting. As an example, suppose you are playing in a $10-$20 hold 'em game. The first player to the left of the dealer position will put in a $5 small blind, and the second player to the dealer's left will post a $10 big blind. On the first round of betting, the player to the immediate left of the big blind will have the options of discarding his hand, calling the $10 big blind, or raising $10, for a total bet of $20. Subsequent bets and raises both before the flop and on the flop will be in $10 increments. All bets and raises on fourth and fifth streets must be in $20 increments.

# Strategy Tips

Texas hold 'em is deceptive. It appears easy to play, yet beneath that simple facade lies a game of extraordinary complexity. Many variables must be considered when making decisions, and figuring out the correct play is often difficult. So before we discuss specific hands and how they usually should be played, here are some general tips that will help you determine the best course of action.

**Tip No. 1: Know what the best possible hand is and how likely it is to be out.** With certain upcards, the potential for many different strong hands increases. With other upcards, however, the number of combinations is dramatically reduced. For example, if the board is

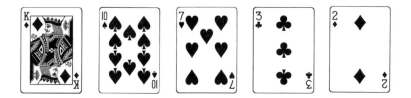

no one can have a straight, a flush, or a full house. The best possible hand is three kings.

Whether someone is holding the best possible hand — which in the poker vernacular is referred to as "the nuts" — frequently can be determined by the number of players in the pot and the previous action. The more players there are and the more betting and raising that have taken place, the more likely it is that one of your opponents has the nuts.

**Tip No. 2: Recognize when you hold the best possible hand.** Although this tip is actually a continuation of the one just given, its importance is such that it rates a separate listing. If you have the nuts and fail to recognize it, you will miss betting and raising opportunities, which in turn will cost you money. And thinking you have the best possible hand when you don't can be even more expensive. However, by paying close attention to the board, you will avoid making these costly errors. As an example, if the board is

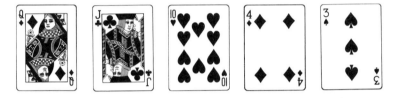

and you hold ace-king, you can't be beat. You therefore should get as much money as possible into the pot. But if the board shows the 3♦ instead of the 3♠, you can lose to a flush and should proceed with caution.

**Tip No. 3: Position is significant.** Texas hold 'em is known as a fixed-position game as opposed to a random-position game. In other words, the order in which the players act each round is predetermined, rather than determined by the strength of the exposed cards as it is in stud. We have already noted the advantage of acting last in poker. This means (among other things), that you should be more selective of the hands you play in early position than of those you play in late position.

**Tip No. 4: Don't overrate suited hands.** Having two cards of the same suit definitely makes your hand better, but many beginning players tend to overrate the value of suited cards. In short, a hand like 10-6 should almost always be thrown away, whether it is suited or not.

**Tip No. 5: High cards are much better than low cards.** It's just as easy to make a pair when you have high cards as it is when you have low cards. If you hold

your opponent has

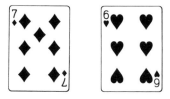

and both of you flop a pair, you have the better hand. Consequently, you would prefer to have your hand made up of big cards.

# Starting Hands

There are five categories of hold 'em starting hands that we will discuss: big pairs, small and medium pairs, two high cards, suited connectors, and big-little suited. Most other hands should be thrown away, unless you have the big blind and the pot has not been raised.

**Category No. 1: Big pairs.** A pair of tens and higher is an excellent starting hand. With a high pair, you not only can make an even bigger hand, but also can completely miss the board — that is, your hand does not improve — and still have a reasonable opportunity to win the pot. Obviously, the chances of winning with two aces are better than the chances of winning with two tens. In general, however, all high pairs have immediate value and should be played aggressively.

**Category No. 2: Small and medium pairs.** In hold 'em, as in seven-card stud, there is a big difference in strength between big pairs and smaller pairs. A hand like

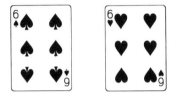

seldom wins the pot without improvement. Moreover, the odds against this hand improving to three of a kind on the flop are almost 8-to-1 (although you can also flop a straight draw).

Since small and medium pairs rarely win without improving, they have little immediate value and therefore can be classified as drawing hands. And to profitably play these hands, you need several opponents in the pot.

**Category No. 3: Two high cards.** Two unsuited high cards is usually a playable hand but not a great hand. Even though ace-king almost always should be played, a hand like

often should be folded, especially if someone has raised. In addition, this hand must hit the flop to win in a multi-way pot.

If your hand is suited, you should be more inclined to play. But remember the warning given earlier: Don't overrate the value of two suited cards.

**Category No. 4: Suited connectors.** Hands like

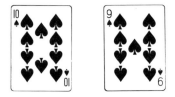

are only fair at best. And if your hand contains a gap, (e.g. 75s or Q9s), you cannot play it as often since your straight possibilities have decreased. This type of hand usually should be thrown away in early position, and you should not call a raise even from a late position unless many players are already in the pot.

**Category No. 5: Big-little suited.** An ace or a king with a small card of the same suit is similar in value to the suited connectors and should be played as such. Of course, ace-little suited is better than king-little suited.

# Play after the Flop

As we mentioned earlier, your starting hand decision in Texas hold 'em, though very important, is not the dominating factor that it is in seven-card stud. To be a winner at hold 'em, you must play well not only before the flop, but also on the flop and beyond. If your play on the later streets is poor, the best you can hope for is to break even. Following are a few tips that will help you make the correct decisions for play after the flop, which in turn will largely determine your overall success in this complex game.

**Tip No. 1: Bet most of your draws.** Suppose you have two suited cards and two more of your suit flop, giving you a flush draw. You usually should bet this hand. (If you don't bet, you almost always should call.) Even though your flush draw currently has no value, betting gives you two ways to win the pot. First, everyone might fold immediately, and second, the flush card might come and you will win anyway.

**Tip No. 2: If you don't improve on the flop, be willing to abandon your hand.** Suppose you are dealt

Even though this is a good starting hand, there is no guarantee it will be worth very much once the flop comes. If that is the case, you should frequently abandon it immediately. Failure to do so can prove quite costly.

**Tip No. 3: It is sometimes necessary to throw away a big pair.** When you hold a big pair, you often don't need to improve your hand to win. But sometimes the flop will be so detrimental that you should fold. For example, suppose you hold

in a seven-handed pot, the flop comes

and there is a bet, a raise, and three callers. Under these circumstances, you should throw your hand away, as there are too many ways that you could be or will be beat.

**Tip No. 4: In multi-way pots, be aware that you might be drawing dead.** Suppose the flop is

and you hold

Even though you are trying to make a straight — which is often a very strong hand — you may already be beat by a player who has either jack-seven or queen-jack for a higher straight. In addition, if a jack hits the board, anyone holding a queen will beat you. Clearly, you should throw your hand away in this spot if you are against several opponents.

**Tip No. 5: Discard small pairs when they miss the flop.** Remember, when you play a small pair, you generally must improve to three of a kind. If you don't improve, your hand has little value and usually should be mucked. (The usual exeception is when you flop a straight draw.) As emphasized earlier, the odds against making trips on the flop are almost 8-to-1.

**Tip No. 6: If you flop a flush draw you usually should continue to play even if a pair shows.** When a pair flops, there is an increased chance that you will run into a full house if you make your flush. Even so, the odds against making your flush with two cards to come are only 2-to-1, and a typical pot offers much more than this.

# In Closing

Besides money, there's another reason why you should consider poker as your game of choice. It's a great game and it is a lot of fun to play. But you need to be careful that poker doesn't become *too* much fun. If it does you may find yourself playing too many hands and making too many fancy plays. And there go your profits.

We also don't want to mislead anyone into thinking that poker is a game where you quickly master it and start leaving your favorite cardroom with wheelbarrels full of money. It doesn't work that way. As we have already said, to become an excellent poker player you will need to study, get experience, and do a great deal of thinking about the game. This is why we recommend that you start small and work your way up to the bigger limits. If you can't win much at the $10-$20 limit, don't expect to win anything at all at $30-$60. Remember, the players generally get better as you move up. However, if you are willing to put in the time and the effort it can be well worth it. We know because we've done it. (And still do.)

# Part Nine

# Putting It All Together

# Putting It All Together

# Introduction

In this text we have given you a great deal of information on how to become a professional gambler. But you don't just go down to the nearest casino and start raking in the money. You need to have a plan — a well-thought out plan.

You will also need to do your share of homework. This includes studying *Gambling for a Living* as well as some of the other books we've recommended.[126] Then you have to decide where your talents lie and what you are willing to do. You will need to think about whether you have the patience for poker, are willing to do the amount of travel that many top blackjack players do, or if playing video machines will become too monotonous for your liking.

You also need to think about whether gambling is right for you in the first place. Will you be able to handle the bankroll swings, the sometimes lonely life, the unusual hours? In addition, what sacrifices are you willing to make? Are you willing to lose some sleep, move to a new location, or pass on your favorite game when an unusually good opportunity comes along elsewhere?

And finally, are you able to leave the game a loser? Over the years we have seen many talented people who had a good chance of being very successful fail simply because they could not leave a loser when they no longer had the best of it. You must keep in mind that most profitable gambling activities are also highly fluctuating. If a bad night will cause you to "steam" and blow off your profits

---

[126] Many of the books we recommend are written by and published by Two Plus Two publishing. We do this simply because we know that they are the best in the specific areas of gambling we are discussing.

from the previous week, then you should think again about undertaking this profession.

# Where Should You Live?

Now that gambling is available in many places throughout the country you must think about where you will live. If you are living in Las Vegas like we do, your decision may be simple. Probably you should stay put. But suppose you're living somewhere else where there is little or no gambling. Then you have to decide whether or not it's worth it to move. We can't answer that question for you. Obviously your personal situation will have a lot to do with your decision. Certainly you shouldn't make any major or irrefutable decisions that you can't go back on, especially if you aren't sure you can win.

For some people, moving may not be worth the effort — not only because their personal life is too disrupted but because their talents lie specifically in a game that is available in their current location. Here are a few examples.

If you are almost sure that it is poker that will make up most or all of your "salary," there is no reason to seek out places that have casinos or sports books. All you need is a cardroom. Furthermore, if your talent as a poker player is less than world class you don't need to go to where the biggest games are. This doesn't mean that you can't make $100,000 a year if you are an excellent player. There are poker games as large as $30-$60 in Washington, Mississippi, Phoenix, Chicago, Northern California, and San Diego, as well as a few other places. In these games the best player is going to make this "salary" if he is willing to put in the time. (These size games are also available in Los Angeles, Las Vegas, Atlantic City, and Connecticut where much bigger games are also offered.)

If you think that horse racing is going to be your main source of support you might be able to get by living near a track. However, it would be much more profitable if that track also offered races from other places. And frankly if horse racing is in fact your game, you almost certainly would be better off in Nevada where you have race books that offer races from a multitude of tracks. Las Vegas is

274

probably preferable to Reno since Las Vegas books will, in general, take bigger bets on a nonparimutuel basis.

If you are a sports bettor, once again Nevada is the place to be, especially if you don't want to run into trouble with the law. Also you will have many sports books to choose from, and as we pointed out, getting the best line can make a big difference.

If blackjack is your game, you have a lot of options. Nevada is probably once again your best bet. But Atlantic City, Mississippi, and possibly some other places, including locations near some Indian casinos, are also viable options. Our experience is that the large Las Vegas casinos are in general the most tolerant when it comes to card counters. But wherever you live, be prepared to do your share of traveling.

And finally if you are mainly going to be looking for either slots or casino promotions it's hard to beat Nevada. Although, in this situation Reno might actually be better than Las Vegas. That would be something you would have to check out.

If you are really serious and want "to take the bull by the horns," you won't have any steady residence. You will be on the road often. It will be a possibly lonely existence but also a rather interesting and exciting one. You will simply go where the best games are. You won't stay in any one place that long.[127] You may keep a small apartment as a base of operations — and again we would recommend Las Vegas, but you will be wherever the most profitable games are. That is pretty much what we used to do — spending some time in Southern California, playing all games in Las Vegas, making frequent trips to Reno and Lake Tahoe, and hitting some of the other cardrooms and casinos around the country.

When we heard of a good game, that's where we would be. If you do that, if you know what you are doing, and if you put your

---

[127] By the way, the best games, particularly poker, are frequently in new locations that have just opened. For instance, at the time of this writing the voters in Michigan have approved casino gambling. If poker comes in, Michigan could be a great place to play for the next few years.

time in, $100,000 a year is a very reasonable figure. And if you work very diligently on your games, you can do even better.

# How Much Do You Need?

In many occupations you need a set of tools to be successful. The same is true if you are a professional gambler. In this case your tools are your knowledge (or skill) and your bankroll. As we have mentioned before, most forms of gambling have a large short-term luck factor. This is actually good (especially in the case of poker) because it is the "hook" that keeps the games going. It means that losing players will have some winning nights and thus will return to play again. But it also means that you, the professional gambler, can have some significant losing streaks and you will need to make sure that you have enough money to survive when these inevitable streaks occur.

We point this out because one of the things that has been known to be the downfall of many professional gamblers is that they are underbankrolled. Again, the fact is, no matter how well you play, that occasional bad streak will occur. But we will not be responsible for those of you who will use the above statement as an excuse to keep on going through more money when you do not in fact really have an edge. So please don't fool yourself. If you have not become an expert player then having a $50,000 bankroll will simply mean that you will lose $50,000. But if you *are* an expert player having that $50,000 could very easily make the difference between success and failure.

In the case of blackjack, the calculation is fairly clear cut. If you play well enough to make a top bet an hour, you need approximately a two-hundred-bet bankroll, not including your expenses. That is a two-hundred-bet gambling bankroll. To make $100,000 a year at blackjack playing twenty hours a week, you would have to make $100 an hour. Therefore, you would need

$20,000. That's the absolute minimum.[128] To be safe you would be wise to have twice that amount.

As far as poker is concerned, there is an excellent essay in *Gambling Theory and Other Topics* by Mason Malmuth that explains what kind of a bankroll you need for various hourly rates. For instance, for an excellent player to make $100,000 a year playing $50-$100, he needs a bankroll in the range of $50,000. Of course it can vary some depending on the style of your opponents and whether you are playing mostly seven-card stud, hold 'em, or some other form of poker.[129] One thing is for sure, there are many good poker players who don't realize that they are in danger because they are playing in games that are too large for their cash reserves.

As far as other games are concerned calculations cannot be as precise.[130] If you are lucky enough to find a casino promotion like

---

[128] If you are playing the shoe games and using a large bet spread you will be making less than your top bet per hour even though you can still make $100 an hour. In this case you will need substantially more than $20,000.

[129] Also see *Poker Essays* by Mason Malmuth for estimated bankroll requirements for different games at different limits.

[130] We do however have a rule of thumb that works quite well in both sports and horse racing. We suggest that each of your individual bets be of the size such that if you win, you have increased your bankroll by about 3 percent. (We assume of course that your bets have an edge.)

For example, if your bankroll is $50,000 you should bet about $1,500 if you are getting even money, and $300 if you are getting 5-to-1, and $15 if it's a 100-to-1 exacta or parlay card. Each of these bets will result in a profit of $1,500 which is 3 percent of $50,000. You might even bet more than $1,500 if you are betting a horse to place or show, and your bet isn't dropping the odds.

If you follow this scheme and truly have an edge on your bets the big six promotion or the parlay card promotion mentioned earlier in the text you don't need very much to guarantee a win. On the other hand, if you are playing quarter video poker progressives, depending on the point at which you start shooting for the royal flush jackpot, you could go through quite a bit of money in your quest for about a $20 an hour profit. An estimate would be about a $20,000 bankroll.

The bottom line is this: If you are, in fact, an excellent player (although not world class) who knows how to take advantage of all the things that we talk about in this book, you really do need to have $30,000 to $50,000 if you want to play at a level that will make you $100,000 a year. This doesn't mean that you need to have that much in your bankroll to start your gambling career. With $10,000 to gamble with, and perhaps another $5,000 to live on, you ought to be able to win at a faster rate than your living expenses. Eventually you will bring your bankroll up to the $30,000 to $50,000 that is necessary to feel comfortable. Of course, if you work hard and do all that we talk about, within a year or two that $30,000 or $40,000 ought to be $100,000 or $200,000. Then bankroll will not be a problem at all except that it might entice you to play bigger than you should. Don't make that mistake either.

---

you should have no trouble getting rich while taking no real chance of going broke.

We also want to discuss the subject of when you should quit playing for the day. Very often many "pseudo" gambling authorities stress this topic. They call it "money management." In reality money management is a very silly concept[131] that doesn't have any place in *Gambling for a Living*.[132] Yet we are constantly asked, "When is it correct to quit?"

Recently in *Card Player* magazine, an article by Arnold Snyder addressed this topic,[133] answering a question that a reader had sent in. It is so good we are repeating it here. Though it addresses blackjack, the ideas that Snyder presents actually pertain to all beatable gambling games:

# When to Quit
## by Arnold Snyder

*Question:* I have never seen a serious discussion on the topic of when to quit playing. Could you provide me with some guidance on this from both perspectives — that is, when do you quit when

---

[131] We are not *speaking* of *bankroll management* which is an important concept.

[132] See *Gambling Theory and Other Topics* by Mason Malmuth for a discussion of "The Extremely Silly Subject of Money Management."

[133] Arnold Snyder is also the publisher of an outstanding quarterly magazine called *Blackjack Forum,* which we highly recommend. For those of you who want more information on *Blackjack Forum*, you can contact RGE Publishing, 414 Santa Clara Ave., Oakland, CA 94610. In addition, Snyder has also written several books on blackjack including one of our favorites, *Blackbelt in Blackjack.*

you're winning, and when do you quit when you're losing? It seems to me that I tend to play too long sometimes, but I also wonder at other times if I quit too soon. I really hate it when I'm ahead for a trip, then lose it all back in the last few hours of play. So, sometimes when I'm up, I quit even if I've got time to play more. Then I wonder if I quit too soon, because maybe I would have kept winning. I'm using the Hi-Opt I counting system from the *World's Greatest Blackjack Book* by Humble and Cooper.[134] I play single-deck blackjack mostly in the Lake Tahoe area casinos. I play at the $2 and $3 minimum tables, and my biggest bets are $20.

*Answer:* If you ask a professional player, "What do you do when you're winning?" he'll answer, "I keep playing. "If you ask him, "What do you do when you're losing?" he'll answer again, "I keep playing."

A professional does not base his decisions to quit or continue playing on win/loss results. If the game is good, regardless of his personal results, he will continue playing. If the playing conditions deteriorate — that is, the shuffle point worsens, he feels tired, he feels heat because of the betting spread that he's using, or whatever — it's time to quit, whether he's winning or losing.

What you are trying to do is predict whether you will win or lose in subsequent sessions based on the win/loss results of your most recent sessions. This is not possible. Assuming that you are using a good card-counting system and that you are using it accurately in beatable games, you may expect to win more money than you will lose if you keep playing. The more you play, the more you will win in the long run. It's that simple.

I must assume, naturally, that you also have a sufficient bankroll to play at the betting level that you are playing, as well as to continue playing when you are losing. A professional player does not quit playing when negative fluctuations take a chunk out of his playing bank; he simply reduces his bet size accordingly.

---

[134] The Hi-Opt I count is very similar to the High-Low count that we presented in the blackjack chapter.

I also will assume that you are playing in honest games — which I would assume to be so if you are playing in major Nevada casinos. Don't make the mistake that many neophyte card counters make of assuming that if they're losing, it's time to quit because the game must be crooked.

One way to counteract the futile practice of trying to predict quitting points is to think of all your card-counting sessions as one long session — which, from the statistician's perspective, they are. There is a simple mathematical formula for calculating your expected dollar profit from card counting. You multiply your long-run advantage, times your average bet, times the number of hands you've played.

If you're using the same system in similar games with the same betting spread, your advantage and your average bet always stay essentially the same. The only way to increase your expected profit is to increase the number of hands that you play. This is one factor in this formula over which you have total control.

There are, to be sure, many players who would share your feelings of frustration at being ahead for a trip, then losing all of your winnings back in the last few hours of play. You can be sure that anyone who has played a lot of blackjack has done this many times, and it's always depressing. At the level that you're playing (pretty small stakes), I must assume that any income that you make from your blackjack playing is not critical to your lifestyle. I would assume that even if you are a talented card counter, you primarily are playing for enjoyment. So, if it makes you feel better to quit when you're ahead, just do it. In the long run, this tactic will not make more money for you, but if it makes you feel better on any given trip, do it.

My guidance is this:
- If you're winning, keep playing. If you're losing keep playing.
- If you're breaking even, keep playing.
- If you're tired quit.
- If you're making strategy mistakes, quit.
- If they start shuffling up on you, quit.

- If the third-base player is a terrible player, keep playing.
- If the dealer gets four blackjacks in a row, keep playing.
- If the player to your right doubles down on hard 16 versus a dealer's ace, keep playing.
- If you keep losing your count, quit.
- If you're playing with your rent money, quit.
- If you're really not a card counter, but just some guy who read a book about it and likes bragging to your friends and family, and even when you lose, you tell them that you won, quit playing and get a life.

# In Closing

We would again like to stress how important your bankroll is and how dangerous it is to play in games that your bankroll cannot support. Obviously, if you play in games that are too small for your bankroll you won't make what you should. (This assumes you play well enough to attack a higher limit.) But what is interesting is that if you consistently play in games that are too large for your bankroll you also won't make what you should. This can be proven mathematically. But even without mathematics, common sense should tell you that "constant adventuring will eventually lead to a disaster, thus leaving you with less money than someone who always plays in the optimum game."[135]

For those of you who are still concerned about when it is right to quit we recommend that you reread Arnold Snyder's essay. For those of you who can't quit when you are tired and stuck, making errors, and are playing in a poor game, we again recommend that you reread Snyder's essay.

Finally, to those of you who have read this book carefully and have decided to embark on a gambling career using the principles herein, we wish you "average luck." That's all you will need if you have been paying attention.

---

[135] See *Gambling Theory and Other Topics* by Mason Malmuth for more discussion.

# Appendix A
# Probability

This appendix is for those of you who are not conversant with basic probability. For a more in-depth treatment we recommend the first five chapters in *Getting the Best of It* by David Sklansky and *The Mathematics of Games and Gambling* by Edward Packel as well as a basic statistics text. If you are interested in more sophisticated gambling math we also recommend *Gambling Theory and Other Topics* by Mason Malmuth.

Basically, probability is the measure of how frequently something will occur if you give it enough time. This is known as getting into the long run.[136] For instance, if you were to take one card out of a deck and you did this over and over again, you should have selected a diamond one-fourth of the time. If you were to flip a coin, you ought to get a head one-half of the time as long as the coin is fair. If you throw one die you ought to get a four one-sixth of the time.

This of course should be plain common sense to all of us, but let's get a little more precise. First, understand that the probability of an event is always measured by a number between zero and one. Let's look at our card-picking experiment again. We expected to get a diamond one-fourth of the time. One-fourth is a fraction — a number between 0 and 1. In fact, all probabilities will be fractions except when they represent events that are impossible, which have the probability of zero, or when they represent events that are certain to occur, which have the probability of one.

Of course, probability doesn't have to be put into fraction form. It could also be stated as a decimal or a percentage. In the

---

[136] In some forms of gambling getting into the long run can take an extremely long time. See *Gambling Theory and Other Topics* by Mason Malmuth for more discussion.

card-picking example it would be .25 or 25 percent. It could also be stated as 1 out of 4. Finally, it could be put into odds form where the odds against picking a heart would be 3-to-1 against. We will come back to that shortly.

Notice that when we said that the probability of a diamond is one-fourth we were really doing a little bit of arithmetic in our head since there are 13 diamonds in a 52-card deck and thus the precise probability of picking a diamond is 13 out of 52, or 13/52. But just like in normal fractions, probabilities can be reduced to lowest terms. We could say the probability of picking a diamond is "thirteen fifty-seconds." For simplicity sake we reduce that fraction to ¼.

$$\frac{13}{52} = \frac{1}{4}$$

Again, it doesn't have to be stated as a fraction. It can be a percentage, a decimal number, and so forth.

Probability can also be stated in terms of odds. It is sometimes useful to change probabilities to odds, and experienced gamblers will often discuss their gambling probabilities in these terms. (The vast majority of probability problems, however, require that you keep the calculations in the form of a fraction. You cannot easily calculate probabilities if you use the odds method of expressing them.) The way odds work is that they separate the losers from the winners and make a ratio. If you win one out of four then that means you lose three out of four. Odds therefore say that the ratio of your losses to your wins is 3-to-1. If you won 3 out of 8 the probability of your winning would be ⅜. The odds would be 5-to-3 against. The general formula would be (n-w)-to-w where n is the total of all possibilities, w is the number of possible winners, and n-w is the number of possible losers.

So far we have discussed the probability of a single event occuring. What if we need to know the probability that two events both happen? The answer can frequently be found by simply multiplying the probabilities of each event. For instance, the probability of throwing two dice and getting two fours is just

$$\left(\frac{1}{6}\right)\left(\frac{1}{6}\right) \ or \ \frac{1}{36}$$

However, there is one caveat. Sometimes the two events are related to each other. If the first event occurs it will have an impact on the chances of the second event. In that case you have to change the probability of the second event to take into account that the first event happened. For instance, what is the probability of being dealt two aces in hold 'em? The probability that the first card is an ace is 4 out of 52 or 1 out of 13. But the probability that the second card will be an ace if in fact the first card was an ace is now 3 out of 51 or 1 out of 17. Since we are asking for the probability that two things *both* happen that would be

$$\left(\frac{1}{13}\right)\left(\frac{1}{17}\right) = \frac{1}{221}$$

If we wanted to know the probability of three things all happening we would have to multiply the probability of each one of them, again with adjustments as needed. For instance the chances of starting with three hearts in seven-card stud would be

$$\left(\frac{1}{4}\right)\left(\frac{12}{51}\right)\left(\frac{11}{50}\right) = \left(\frac{11}{850}\right)$$

Adjustments are not always needed. For example, if we wanted to know the probability that the Dodgers and the Yankees will play in the World Series we need merely to multiply the probability that the Yankees win the pennant times the probability that the Dodgers win the pennant. This is because the Dodgers are in the National League and the Yankees are in the American League. One doesn't affect the other.[137]

On the other hand, being in different leagues (or conferences) doesn't always mean that adjustments aren't necessary. For instance, if we want to know the probability that the Miami Dolphins play the San Francisco Forty-Niners in the Super Bowl there would be a slight adjustment from strict multiplication if they played each other during the season. That is because the probability that the Miami Dolphins would reach the Super Bowl would be slightly affected (downward) by the fact that the San Francisco Forty-Niners reached it.

Now suppose we are interested in the probability that *at least one* of two events happens. This can involve adding probabilities. Suppose we ask what is the probability that either the Yankees or the Orioles win the pennant and we know that there is a 10 percent chance that the Yankees will win and a 5 percent chance that the Orioles will win. Then there is simply a 15 percent chance that one or the other of them will be the American League Champions.

$$15 = 10 + 5$$

It gets slightly more complicated, however, if two teams both could win. If we wanted to know the probability that the Yankees *or* the Dodgers win the pennant we must take the possibility of their *both* winning into account since these two teams are in different

---

[137] This is no longer true at the time of the writing of this second edition as there is now interleague play. But assume the old way for the purposes of the examples we give.

leagues. Let's suppose the Yankees have a 20 percent chance and the Dodgers have a 30 percent chance. You cannot just add them up and say that there is a 50 percent chance that one or the other will win. To do this problem you must recognize that sometimes they will both be league champions. This will happen 20 percent times 30 percent, or 6 percent of the time. And we must subtract this figure from 50 percent to get the right answer which is 44 percent. Do you see why?

There is another way of doing this problem that is used frequently by those who regularly do these type of probability calculations. Instead of calculating the probability that either the Yankees or the Dodgers win the pennant, the approach is to calculate the probability that they *both fail.* That is 80 percent times 70 percent or 56 percent. Since they both do fail 56 percent of the time, then at least one of them will have succeeded 44 percent of the time.

$$44\% = 100\% - 56\%$$

This is, of course, the same answer, and it serves to show that these problems can sometimes be approached in more than one way.

The last idea that we want to discuss is what is known as permutations and combinations. First, notice that if something can be done 5 ways, and something else can be done 8 ways, then the compound event can be done in 40 different ways. For example, suppose you have 5 different pairs of pants and 8 different shirts. This means that you have 40 different combinations. Each one of the different shirts can be worn with any one of the 5 different pair of pants. Thus, we have 5 times 8 or 40 outfits. If we added a third category such as shoes you would multiply that number in there too. This is called the multiplication principle.

The multiplication principle can be used in a more complex way in combination problems. Combination problems are simply counting the number of ways of choosing a committee, so to speak, out of a larger population. (The next few pages are taken verbatim from *Getting the Best of It* by David Sklansky.)

As an example, suppose I have three extra season tickets to the Yankee home games. I can therefore, take three guests to every one of them. I have nine friends who I think will make good companions, and I need to pick three of them to invite. I do this every time the Yanks play at home. So as not to insult anybody and to add variety for myself, I decide to invite a different group of three (from these nine) every night. It is important to realize that I can form a different group by substituting just one person for another. Thus, Mark, Ted, and George are counted as a different group from Mark, Ted, and Peter.

The question is, how many games can I attend before I have to go with a group of friends that I have already gone with? In other words, how many different combinations of three friends out of nine can be made? The answer is 84 (enough for the whole season), and I'll explain how I got this figure in a moment.

For the time being, it's important for you to understand that the foregoing problem is simply a special case of taking 9 things 3 at a time. Obviously, it is not necessary that we be speaking of people here. As a second example, some bookies offer what they call a Trinella bet. To win, you must pick the first 3 horses to finish a race (the order doesn't matter). In a 9-horse race, how many different Trinellas do you have to choose from? Once again the answer is 84. It is simply another case of 9 things taken 3 at a time. You would have to bet 84 different Trinellas in a 9-horse race in order to assure yourself a winner.

The mathematical symbol for combinations is either a capital "C" or tall parenthesis ( ). Thus, 9 things taken 3 at a time is written

$$_9C_3$$

or, more frequently,

$$\binom{9}{3}$$

And 12 things taken 5 at a time would be written

$$_{12}C_5 \quad or \quad \binom{12}{5}$$

From here on we will use only the more commonly used parenthesis symbol. "N" things taken "r" at a time, which is the way mathematicians like to describe a general combination problem, is thus written as

$$\binom{n}{r}$$

To evaluate any individual combination, it is necessary to form a large fraction. To show you how to do this, let us take

$$\binom{10}{4}$$

as an example. The bottom of the fraction, or denominator, is simply the numbers 1 through 4 multiplied together

$$\overline{(1)(2)(3)(4)}$$

This is because four is the bottom number in the combination symbol. If it had been, for instance, a six, the denominator of the fraction would be

$$(1)(2)(3)(4)(5)(6)$$

To obtain the numerator of the fraction, you start with the number on top of the combination symbol and start multiplying each successive lower number until there are as many numbers in the numerator as there are in the denominator. Thus,

$$\binom{10}{4}$$

would be

$$\frac{(10)(9)(8)(7)}{(1)(2)(3)(4)}$$

or

$$\frac{5{,}040}{24}$$

For those of you who may have forgotten that a fraction is really just a division sign,

$$\frac{5,040}{24}$$

simply means

$$24\overline{)5,040}$$

The answer in this case is 210.

A very important combination is the number of poker hands. This is 52 choose 5, which is 2,598,960.

$$\binom{52}{5} = \frac{(52)(51)(50)(49)(48)}{(1)(2)(3)(4)(5)} = 2,598,960$$

Many poker problems can be done using this particular figure. Suppose you are interested in the probability of being dealt a straight flush. Notice that there are 36 different straight flushes (not counting royal flushes). Thus, the probability of being dealt a straight flush is 36 out of 2,598,000 or about 1 in 7,219.

We have just given the barest introduction to probability. Hopefully it will be enough so that you do not feel totally uncomfortable with some of the more technical comments we make in this book. However, it is very likely that most of you will have to read further, and we hope that you do.

# Appendix B
# Recommended Reading

Even though there are many books written on gambling, only a small number of them are really worth reading, and some of these are only worth reading for their entertainment or historical value. What follows are the books that we recommend (in alphabetical order), and some comments about them. We have also included the name of the publisher and the date of the latest printing.

## Gambling Theory

**1. *Can You Win* by Mike Orkin (1994: W. H. Freeman and Company).** This is a highly readable probability book for the novice or somewhat less-experienced player interested in casino games, sports betting, and lotteries.

**2. *The Casino Gambler's Guide* by Allan Wilson (Currently out of print).** One of the first "legitimate" (in other words non-fallacious) books on gambling. The blackjack system is somewhat out-of-date, but the discussions on systems and biased roulette wheels are still terrific. Most serious gamblers will want to look at this book, especially if they are just starting out.

**3. *Gambling Theory and Other Topics* by Mason Malmuth (1994: Two Plus Two Publishing).** The text attempts to answer the question of why a small number of people are very successful at gambling. It covers a wide spectrum of topics. The reader will be introduced to the dynamic concept of "non-self-weighting" strategies and shown how they apply not only at the gaming tables but also in real life as well. In addition, risk and fluctuations are discussed in terms of the statistical standard deviation, and it is explained how these relate to each other as well as to your bankroll.

Other topics include bankroll requirements, win-rate accuracy, free bets, which blackjack count is best, lottery fallacies, dangerous ideas, poker tournament strategies (including when it is correct to rebuy), settling up in tournaments, and much more.

**4. *Getting the Best of It* by David Sklansky (1997: Two Plus Two Publishing).** The text is divided into six sections: Mathematics of Gambling, General Gambling Concepts, Sports and Horse Betting, Poker, Blackjack, and Other Casino Games. It covers some of the most sophisticated gambling concepts ever put in print, plus includes a comprehensive discussion of the basic mathematics of gambling, yet is written in such a way that even the most nonmathematical of readers can understand it. Topics include mathematical expectation, combinations, Bayes' Theorem, the eight mistakes in poker, checking in the dark, playing tight, the key card concept, casinos and their mistakes, betting sports, hedging and middling, knowing what's important, the Law of Averages and other fallacies, and much more.

**5. *The Mathematics of Gambling* by Edward O. Thorp (1984: Gambling Times, Inc.).** A well-written book that discusses many interesting gambling topics including an analysis of mathematical systems, optimal betting (which includes "bet sizing"), a comparison of different blackjack systems, and an explanation of why baccarat is not susceptible to card-counting techniques.

**6. *The Mathematics of Games and Gambling* by Edward Packel (1981: Mathematical Association of America).** An excellent discussion of mathematics and probability that is important to gambling. The book is enjoyable to read and is filled with many helpful examples. Highly recommended for those who are weak in this area.

**7. *Poker, Gaming, & Life* by David Sklansky (1997: Two Plus Two Publishing).** This volume is a collection of recent articles written by David Sklansky that have appeared in various publications including *Card Player* and *Poker World* magazines. A few have never appeared in print.

Most of the articles are about poker and gambling. However, David has recently branched out into other areas that lend themselves to his unique style of analysis and some of these essays are contained in this book.

**8. *Theory of Gambling and Statistical Logic* by Richard Epstein (1977: Academic Press).** This is one of the most amazing books in the gambling field. It is a graduate-level text for those with a sophisticated background in math and statistics and is filled with a wealth of information.

# Blackjack

**1. *Basic Blackjack* by Stanford Wong (1995: Pi Yee Press).** The text covers every blackjack rule imaginable and how it affects the house edge as well as the proper basic strategy. If you ever have a question about the value of an unusual rule, then this is the book to look at. It also contains much material that originally appeared in Wong's book *Winning Without Counting,* which is now out of print.

**2. *Beat the Dealer* by Edward O. Thorp (1966: Vintage Books).** This is the book that started it all. Even though the strategies are slightly out-of-date by today's standards, this book is still absolutely must reading for anyone interested in playing blackjack.

**3. *Beat the One- (Two-, Four-, Six-, Eight-) Deck Game* by Arnold Snyder (1987: RGE Publishing).** This is really a series of five books that gives detailed information on how to play against a specific number of decks. This material is extremely valuable for very serious players since it can help you determine exactly what your betting scheme should be for any particular game you go after.

298 Appendix B: Recommended Reading

**4.** *Blackbelt in Blackjack* **by Arnold Snyder (1983: RGE Publishing).** An excellent book on the game. Includes Snyder's Zen count, which is one of the best modern-day counts, and much practical advice for current casino play. Absolutely must reading for any serious player. It is particularly good if you are new to blackjack.

**5.** *Blackjack Essays* **by Mason Malmuth (1996: Two plus Two Publishing).** This manual is designed to help today's blackjack player succeed in today's modern casino environment. Unlike most blackjack books, the text assumes that the reader already knows how to count cards and introduces techniques and concepts that should be useful to the successful player well into the 1990s and beyond. Topics covered include card domination (also know as shuffle tracking), theoretical concepts, blackjack biases, current blackjack, mistaken ideas, supplemental strategies, playing in a casino, obsolete techniques, and front loading.

**6.** *Blackjack Forum* **by Arnold Snyder (Quarterly: RGE Publishing).** This is a quarterly magazine that is not only very informative, but often humorous as well. Many of the back issues are still available.

**7.** *Blackjack Secrets* **by Stanford Wong (1993: Pi Yee Press).** This is an introduction to card counting and explains "how to get away with playing a winning game of blackjack in casinos." It contains much of Wong's best material and should be must reading for all serious players. Topics include dealer "tokes," comps, playing blackjack full time, getting barred, and double exposure blackjack.

**8.** *Current Blackjack News* **by Stanford Wong (Monthly: Pi Yee Press).** This newsletter offers the most current blackjack information available and informs the reader of various casino "specials."

**9.** *Fundamentals of Blackjack* **by Carlson R. Chambliss and Thomas C. Roginski (1990: Gambler's Book Club Press).** A concise, yet thorough survey of many of the ideas present in the blackjack literature. This text contains good discussions of rule variations, appropriate basic strategy, different counts, bet sizing, and other topics.

**10.** *Fundamentals of "21"* **by Mason Malmuth and Lynne Loomis (1995: Two Plus Two Publishing).** If you are new to blackjack or have only played a small amount in a casino environment, then this is where you should start. You will be shown how the game is played, learn basic strategy, and be introduced to simple card-counting techniques.

**11.** *Million Dollar Blackjack* **by Ken Uston (1995: Carol Publishing Group).** One of the best books ever written on the game, by one of the game's premier players. The book contains excellent count systems, advice on how to play the multiple decks, blackjack team methods, as well as a great deal of practical advice. However, the advice recommending the more complex counts is not accurate.

**12.** *Professional Blackjack* **by Stanford Wong (1994: Pi Yee Press).** One of the premier books on card counting. It contains the most thorough discussion of the High-Low Count System in print as well as much more practical advice.

**13.** *Read the Dealer* **by Steve Forte (1986: RGE Publishing).** A book for the very serious blackjack player who is trying to get every extra edge. The book is well written and very well thought out. However, many players will probably get into trouble using these powerful techniques since they will see tells because they want to and not because they are there. However, if applied correctly, this information can sometimes substantially increase your expectation.

**14.** *The Theory of Blackjack* **by Peter Griffin (1996: Huntington Press).** A mathematical text that analyzes the game of blackjack at a very sophisticated level of detail. It contains much valuable information that is not found anywhere else. Most of the extremely complex math is separated from the main material.

**15.** *Turning the Tables on Las Vegas* **by Ian Andersen (1978: Vintage Books).** A good study that delves into using some of the psychological factors available to the skilled player to ensure a win. It contains a good discussion on how to survive in a casino environment. Well-written and definitely one of the better books on casino blackjack.

# Poker

**1.** *Big Deal* **by Anthony Holden (1995: Bantam Press).** If you are interested in what it might be like to be a professional poker player, especially one playing the tournaments, then this is the book to read. It won't help you play any better, but it does a great job of describing the "ups and downs" that all professional players go through.

**2.** *The Biggest Game in Town* **by A. Alvarez (Currently out of print).** This entertaining text is about the World Series of Poker and some of the more famous players who regularly participate in that event. The book won't help you play any better, but it will give you a feel of what "big time" poker can be like for those small number of people who get this good.

**3.** *The Body Language of Poker* **by Mike Caro (1996: Carol Publishing).** This text is the definitive work on tell play — that is, on how to interpret the body language of poker — and should be read by all serious poker players. The book contains more than 250 photographs, as well as detailed descriptions of what is happening and the motivation behind each tell.

Even though we recommend this text, we need to warn you that expert players, if they realize that you have read this work, are capable of reversing the tells Caro describes. However, against unsophisticated players, particularly those who populate the lower limits, there is value in many of these ideas.

**4. *Fundamentals of Poker* by Mason Malmuth and Lynne Loomis (1992: Two Plus Two Publishing).** This is a beginners book that provides general poker guidelines and contains sections on Texas hold 'em and seven-card stud, as well as a section on six other forms of poker. If you are new to poker and are looking for something to get you started, this book should be ideal.

**5. *High-Low-Split Poker, Seven-Card Stud and Omaha Eight-or-Better for Advanced Players* by Ray Zee (1994: Two Plus Two Publishing).** This is the third book in the "for Advanced Players" series but in reality it is really two books in one. Many of the concepts applicable to seven-card stud eight-or-better are similar to those for Omaha eight-or-better. Some of the ideas discussed in the seven-card stud eight-or-better section include; starting hands, disguising your hand on third street, when an ace raises, fourth street, fifth street, sixth street, seventh street, position, bluffing, staying to the end, scare cards, and much more. Some of the ideas discussed in the Omaha eight-or-better section include; general concepts, position, low hands, high hands, your starting hand, how to play your hand, play on the flop, multi-way versus short-handed play, scare cards, getting counterfeited, your playing style, and much more

**6. *Hold 'em Poker* by David Sklansky (1996: Two Plus Two Publishing).** The first definitive work on the game of hold 'em poker. This book is absolutely must reading for anyone planning to play anywhere hold 'em is offered. It is designed for someone relatively new to the game. It is probably best known for the Sklansky Hand Rankings, which made the game much simpler to quantify and understand. Some of the topics include; how Texas hold 'em is played, the importance of position, the first two cards, the key "flops," strategy before the flop, semi-bluffing, the free card, slowplaying, check raising, head-up on fifth street, and how to read hands. The "1997" edition was updated to account for today's modern "double-blind" structure.

**7. *Hold 'em Poker for Advanced Players* by David Sklansky and Mason Malmuth (1994: Two Plus Two Publishing).** Texas hold 'em has become the most popular form of poker played in the casinos and cardrooms of America, particularly in the West. This book is written for today's modern game (with the double-blind structure) and for playing against today's typical tougher player. It offers the strongest strategy ever put into print. Anyone who studies this text, is well-disciplined, and gets the proper experience should become a significant winner.

**8. *Omaha Hold 'em Poker (The Action Game)* by Bob Ciaffone (1992: Self published).** This is an excellent book, written by a professional player, which offers accurate advice for the relatively new game of Omaha and includes a short section on Omaha high-low split, eight-or-better. Anyone who studies this text, is well-disciplined, and does not play too high should be on the right path toward success. Topics include reading the board properly, betting small sets, the importance of being suited, and proper evaluation of starting hands.

**9. *Poker Essays* by Mason Malmuth (1996: Two Plus Two Publishing).** This text is a collection of essays that the author wrote for various publications from 1988 to 1991. It contains many of the author's current ideas on poker and related subjects. Topics covered include; general concepts, technical ideas, structure, strategic ideas, image, tournaments, cardroom procedures, and four poker quizzes. The book is designed to make the reader do a great deal of thinking about the game.

**10.** *Poker Essays, Volume II* **by Mason Malmuth (1996: Two Plus Two Publishing).** This text contains those essays that the author wrote from 1991 through early 1996. Topics covered include: general concepts, technical ideas, structure, strategic ideas, cardroom procedures, quizzes, and erroneous concepts. As with the original *Poker Essays,* this book is designed to make the reader do a great deal of thinking about the game.

**11.** *Poker Strategy, Winning with Game Theory* **by Nasmith Ankeny (Currently out of print).** This is an excellent book on draw poker and is based on a game-theory approach. Many strategic concepts are also discussed, and most serious players would probably want to look at it even though these ideas won't help much if you are playing seven-card stud or Texas hold 'em.

**12.** *Seven-Card Stud for Advanced Players* **by David Sklansky, Mason Malmuth, and Ray Zee (1994: Two Plus Two Publishing).** Seven-card stud is the other dominant form of poker that is played in virtually all cardrooms across America. It is an extremely complex game and deciding exactly what the right strategy should be in any particular situation can be very difficult. Because of this very few authors attempted to analyze it.

When this book was written, a major gap in the poker literature was closed. Anyone who studies this text, is well disciplined, and gets the proper experience should become a significant winner at the game.

**13.** *Sklansky on Poker* **by David Sklansky (1994: Two Plus Two Publishing).** This text is a combination of *Sklansky on Razz* and *Essays on Poker,* with much new material added. Many of the ideas in the essays section are not as sophisticated as some of the others that Sklansky has put in print, but they are still absolutely essential to winning play. Topics include having a plan, choosing your game, playing according to your bankroll, and the three levels of expert poker. There are also four important chapters on tournament play.

The razz section of the book will show you how the experts play this form of poker. Not only are the rules and structure of the game discussed, but advice is also given on how to play the first three cards, as well as all the other streets. Even if you never play razz, you should still read this text if you are serious about poker since many concepts that are important to all forms of poker are most easily illustrated by this game. Anyone who reads and studies this book not only will improve his overall play, but should be able to play razz virtually perfectly.

**14.** *Super System — A Course in Power Poker* **by Doyle Brunson (1994: B&G Publishing).** This text is considered a classic source of information on most major limit games played, as well as on no-limit hold 'em. The book was written by two-time World Champion Doyle Brunson in collaboration with some of the best players in the world, including Bobby Baldwin, Mike Caro, Chip Reese, and David Sklansky. Unfortunately, as the years have gone by some of the information it contains has become outdated. For instance, most high-low split games are played today with a qualifier for low, and the excellent high-low split section does not discuss this concept. The structure of limit hold 'em has changed, and this dramatically affects some of your strategy decisions. And jacks-or-better draw poker is hardly spread anymore. However, the section on seven-card stud is still excellent and the book contains much general overall poker wisdom.

**15.** *The Theory of Poker* **by David Sklansky (1994: Two Plus Two Publishing).** In many ways, this is the best book ever written on poker. Unlike some of the books listed above it is not a "how-to" book, but a book on theory that discusses in-depth strategy and many sophisticated concepts. If you are new to poker you should probably start with books like *Hold 'em Poker, Hold 'em Poker for Advanced Players,* and *Seven-Card Stud for Advanced Players.* However, once you begin to get the hang of it and you decide that you want to become a top player, this is the book that you will have to spend a lot of time with. Many top pros read their copy over and over again.

**16. *Total Poker* by David Spanier (1995: Oldcastle Books).** This is a delightful look at what playing poker is like. It features some of the personalities who have made a name for themselves in the poker world. It won't help you win any money, but it will give you a flavor for the excitement of the game.

**17. *Winning Concepts in Draw and Lowball* by Mason Malmuth (1993: Two Plus Two Publishing).** This book is written for both the amateur and the professional player. It is partitioned into sections designed to help players improve their skills and it teaches one how to think like a top player, which is absolutely essential to winning play.

**18. *Winning Poker Systems* by Norman Zadeh (1974: Wilshire Book Company).** This is another book that is now somewhat out of date due to the changed conditions in the California cardrooms, but it is still an excellent source for certain aspects of poker theory, and it discusses some strategic concepts that are not covered well in most other books.

# Poker Videos

**1. *Sklansky the Video* by David Sklansky and Ben Tracy (1994: A Ben Tracy/Joe Marks Production).** Filmed in part during the 1994 World Series of Poker at Binion's Horseshoe Hotel and Casino in Las Vegas, this 90-minute video concentrates on both general concepts as well as Texas hold 'em, seven-card stud, and Omaha high-low-split.

**2. *Sklansky: The Seminar* by David Sklansky and Ben Tracy (1994: A Ben Tracy/Joe Marks Production).** This is a "companion" tape to Sklansky the Video. It is the complete seminar which was filmed during the 1994 World Series of Poker at

Binion's Horseshoe Hotel and Casino in Las Vegas. Sklansky focuses on tournament strategy and how to apply probability to poker.

# Video Poker

**1. *Expert Video Poker for Las Vegas* by Lenny Frome (1994: Compu-Flyers).** This was one of the first books that correctly tackled the video poker machines of Las Vegas.

**2. *Deuces Wild Video Poker* by Bob Dancer (1996: self published).** One of the three Dancer reports on video poker. This is the guide that most serious players use today. It contains a "quick and dirty"strategy, an intermediate strategy, and a professional strategy.

**3. *Fundamentals of Video Poker* by Mason Malmuth and Lynne Loomis (1995: Two Plus Two Publishing).** This is another book in the *Fundamentals* series. If you are new to video poker, this book provides excellent instructions for the basic game.

**4. *9-6 Jacks of Better Video Poker* by Bob Dancer (1996: self published).** One of the three Dancer repo*rts on video* poker. This is the guide that most serious players use today. It contains a "quick and dirty" strategy, an intermediate strategy, and a complete strategy.

**5. *Professional Video Poker* by Stanford Wong (1993: Pi Yee Press).** Wong shows you how to play jacks-or-better video poker virtually perfectly. He provides professional-level strategies that are relatively easy to master.

**6. *10-7 Double Bonus Video Poker* by Bob Dancer (1996: self published).** One of the three Dancer repo*rts on video* poker. This is the guide that most serious players use today. It contains a "quick and dirty" strategy, an intermediate strategy, and a professional strategy. Note that while this game is difficult to master and only returns slightly above 100 percent, it is also the most popular game among serious video poker pros who play the higher denomination machines.

**7. *Winning Strategies for Video Poker* by Lenny Frome (1996: Compu-Flyers).** If you want to learn how to correctly play almost any form of video poker then this is the book for you. It is actually a collection of tables that show you the perfect strategy for a wide variety of games.

# Horse Racing

(Note: The following books have been recommended to us by knowledgeable people who we respect. However, we can not personally vouch for their accuracy. Thus, we list them without comment.)

**1. *Dr. Z's Beat the Racetrack* by William Ziemba and Donald Hausch (Currently out of Print).**

**2. *Horse Racing Logic* by Glendon Jones (1989: Liberty Publishing Company).**

**3. *Science of Winning* by Burton P. Fabricand (1995: Oldcastle Books).**

**4. *Winning at the Races* by William L. Quirin (1975: William Morrow & Company).**

# Other Topics

**1. *Comp City: A Guide to Free Las Vegas Vacations* by Max Rubin (1994: Huntington Press).** The author tells you almost everything you will ever need to know about how to squeeze the maximum in comps out of the casinos, what it will cost to do so, and how much risk you will be taking. He does not discuss these ideas in conjunction with beating the casinos. However, many of his ideas can be used in conjunction with what we tell you about beating the games. We do want to warn you not to go overboard on trying for comps. Doing this will frequently bring you more scrutiny (from the casino), which may shorten your playing career.

**2. *Fundamentals of Craps* by Mason Malmuth and Lynne Loomis (1995: Two Plus Two Publishing).** This booklet will tell you virtually everything you will need to know concerning how to play craps. It covers the basic game and tells you which bets are the "least bad."

**3. *The New Gambler's Bible* by Arthur Reber (1996: Crown Trade Paperbacks).** This is an excellent text for those of you just starting out. The author covers all the games and explains which ones can be beat and which can't. He also supplies decent strategies. If you are new to gambling, this text is an excellent place to start.

**4. *Optimal Strategy for Pai Gow Poker* by Stanford Wong (1993: Pi Yee Press).** This is clearly the best work on pai gow poker and should allow you to get an edge in the games at most "California casinos."

**5. *Welcome to the Pleasure Dome* by David Spanier (1997: University of Nevada Press).** An enjoyable and fascinating "inside look" at the City of Las Vegas, both its past and its future.

# Index

house quinella 109-111, 120
house quinellas 109-111, 136
insurance 16, 17, 25, 27, 39, 45, 56, 57
jacks-or-better 143, 147, 156, 304, 306
jockey biases 133
Jones, Glendon 307
Kelly Criterion 40
kicker 147, 238, 257, 258,
Las Vegas 1, vii, ix, 2, 41-43, 48, 82, 90, 106, 113, 142, 154, 157, 164, 168, 184, 186, 189, 191, 192, 194-196, 219, 222, 235, 274, 275, 300, 305-308
last round 208, 236, 237
Let It Ride 4, 160, 176
line 63-71, 74-78, 80, 82, 83, 85, 88, 90, 91, 94, 96, 100, 112, 116, 117, 121, 126, 167, 168, 184, 186-189, 191, 198, 204, 208, 220, 233, 240, 275, 279
live hand 239, 254
live 4, 8, 138, 219, 239, 253, 254, 257, 258, 274, 275, 279
live hands 253
Loomis, Lynne x, 5, 9, 169, 214, 216, 252, 299, 301, 306, 308
lowball draw 218
Malmuth, Mason vii-x, 5, 9, 40, 58, 169, 181, 187, 214-216, 246, 252, 278, 280, 284, 285, 295, 298, 299, 301-303, 305, 306, 308
Mason Malmuth's 224
matchup 70, 72, 90, 91
matchups 72, 85, 91, 100
medium pairs 255-257, 264, 265
Megabucks 139, 140
middle 30, 53, 82, 83, 86, 87, 218, 219,
middles 83, 85
money management 280
multi-way 239, 240, 265, 268, 301
multiplication principle 289
negative deck 26
negative decks 26